The Most Holy Eucharist

Fr. Thomas J. McGovern

The Most Holy Eucharist

Our Passover and Our Living Bread

SOPHIA INSTITUTE PRESS

Manchester, New Hampshire

Sophia Institute Press
Box 5284, Manchester, NH 03108
1-800-888-9344

www.SophiaInstitute.com

Sophia Institute Press® is a registered trademark of Sophia Institute

Library of Congress Cataloging-in-Publication Data
McGovern, Thomas J.
   The Most Holy Eucharist : our passover and our living bread / Thomas J. McGovern.
      pages cm
   Includes bibliographical references (pages   ).
   ISBN 978-1-933184-90-6 (pbk. : alk. paper) 1. Lord's Supper—Catholic Church. I. Title.
   BX2215.3.M34 2013
   234'.163—dc23
                                                                    2013003182

First printing

*In grateful memory of those generations
of Irish men and women who,
despite a bitter persecution over a period of 250 years,
fought valiantly and successfully to maintain their devotion
to the Holy Sacrifice of the Mass and the Blessed Eucharist,
in which endeavor many generously gave their lives,
laypeople as well as priests.*

Contents

Introduction

The Eucharist is one of the great mysteries of our Catholic Faith. Down through the centuries it has been a constant source of spiritual nourishment for generations of Catholics and has filled their hearts with the joy of knowing that, in their Communions, they have received the very Body and Blood of Christ.

In his first encyclical, *Redemptor hominis*, Bl. John Paul II reflected on the unfathomable dimensions of this great truth:

> The Church lives by the Eucharist, by the fullness of this Sacrament, the stupendous content and meaning of which have often been expressed in the Church's Magisterium from the most distant times down to our own days. However, we can say with certainty that, although this teaching is sustained by the acuteness of theologians, by men of deep faith and prayer, and by ascetics and mystics, in complete fidelity to the Eucharistic mystery, it still reaches no more than the threshold, since it is incapable of grasping and translating into words what

the Eucharist is in all its fullness, what is expressed by it and what is actuated by it. Indeed the Eucharist is the ineffable Sacrament![1]

John Paul II is telling us that there is still much to learn about the Eucharist, that our knowledge "still reaches no more than the threshold"; yet we can say that the Church, in her living tradition, treasures a great deal of eucharistic wisdom and has a well-developed eucharistic liturgy.

As John Paul II prepared for the Jubilee Year, he wrote in the Bull of Indiction convoking this event for the year 2000:

> For two thousand years, the Eucharist has been the cradle in which Mary has placed Jesus, entrusting him to the adoration and contemplation of all peoples, that, through the humility of the Spouse of Christ, the glory and the power of the Eucharist may gleam all the more—that Eucharist that the Church celebrates and preserves at its heart. Under the sign of the consecrated bread and wine, Christ Jesus, risen and glorified, the light of nations (Lk 2:32), reveals the continuation of his Incarnation. He is still risen and alive in our midst, to nourish believers with his Body and Blood.[2]

Love reaches its ideal in the eucharistic sacrament. It is a unity that assimilates us more and more to Christ, and through total identification with the suffering Christ, it leads to real holiness. As well as identifying us with Christ, Holy Communion

---

[1]   Bl. John Paul II, Encyclical Letter *Redemptor hominis* (March 25, 1979), no. 20.

[2]   Bl. John Paul II, Bull of Indiction of the Great Jubilee of the Year 2000 (November 29, 1998), no. 11.

Introduction

is food and "does for the spiritual life all that material food and drink do for the bodily life, namely to sustain, increase, restore, and delight."[3]

I have not tried in these pages to write a textbook on the Eucharist or to cover every aspect of it. My primary objective is to provide a book that will help people grow in love for the Mass and for the Blessed Sacrament. To deepen Eucharistic devotion, however, requires a solid theological basis. Hence the first five chapters cover the basic doctrinal aspects of this mystery. The next two chapters focus on devotion to the Blessed Eucharist, during Mass and outside of it.

Blessed John Paul II made an outstanding contribution to eucharistic theology during his long pontificate. In chapter 8, I have summarized the main points of this contribution, basing my study mainly on John Paul II's principal documents on the Eucharist. In chapter 9, I have reviewed the Eucharist in the teaching of Pope Benedict XVI, who made a significant contribution to the Church's teaching on the Eucharist.

Chapter 10 is a study of the main liturgical elements involved in the celebration of the Mass. Finally, chapter 11 is an examination of the commitment to the Mass in Ireland during times of severe religious persecution. It has much to say about the nature of this sacrifice and about Christian loyalty to it.

I would like to thank Fr. Charly Connolly and Fr. Tom O'Toole, who read through previous versions of this text and offered many helpful suggestions and ideas.

Fr. Thomas J. McGovern

---

[3] St. Thomas Aquinas, *Summa Theologica*, III, Q. 79, art. 1; cf. *Catechism of the Catholic Church* (CCC), nos. 1391–1401.

The Most Holy Eucharist

Chapter 1

The Scriptural Foundations of the Eucharist

The Eucharist Rooted in the Old Testament

We begin our study of the Eucharist by examining the different texts in Sacred Scripture about this great sacrament, because Scripture is the primary source of the Church's teaching about the Eucharist as sacrament and sacrifice. We will consider the scriptural sources in some detail because in them we listen to the words of Christ himself.

The meaning of the Eucharist is rooted in the faith of the people of the Old Testament, especially in the doctrine of the covenant. The covenant was a treaty to describe the relationship God established with the Chosen People. God's new relationship with the Israelites was sealed with the pouring of blood (sacrifice) and the eating together of some of the sacrificial food (communion) (cf. Exod. 24:1–11). The blood was sprinkled on both the altar (symbolizing God) and the people: "I will be their God and they shall be my people" (Jer. 31:33).

Our Faith tells us that Jesus is the mediator of the New Covenant (cf. Heb. 12:24). At the Last Supper he echoed the words of Moses: "This is my blood of the covenant" (Matt. 26:28), or "This is the new covenant in my blood which will be poured out for you" (Luke 22:20). By sharing the cup of the New Covenant we enter into this new relationship established by Christ, who poured out his Blood on the Cross. Jesus' death is that of the Passover Lamb, the suffering servant of God, led like a lamb to the slaughter (cf. Isa. 53:7).

The paschal lamb of the Jewish feast was a promise and a figure of the true Lamb, Jesus Christ, immolated in the sacrifice of Calvary on behalf of the whole human race. He is the true Lamb who took away the sin of the world. By dying he destroyed our death; by rising he restored our life.[4] He is the Lamb who by his voluntary sacrifice really obtains what the sacrifices of the Old Law merely symbolized, namely, satisfaction to God for the sins of mankind.[5]

He is the Lamb of God, the one whose life, given for us and poured out for us, brings healing and peace. By our communion in the Body and Blood of Christ, we are drawn deeper into the community of the New Covenant. By partaking of the Eucharist we are united with the living Christ in his work of reconciliation (cf. 2 Cor. 5:18–20).[6] This Old Testament reference is summarized in the *Catechism of the Catholic Church* as follows:

In the Old Covenant bread and wine were offered in sacrifice among the first fruits of the earth, as a sign of grateful acknowledgement to the Creator. But they also

---

[4] *Roman Missal*, Easter Preface I.
[5] Cf. Francis Fernandez, *In Conversation with God*, vol. 4 (London: Scepter, 1991), 161.
[6] Cf. Catholic Bishops' Conferences of England and Wales, Ireland, and Scotland, *One Bread, One Body* (Dublin, 1998), no. 24.

received a new significance in the context of the Exodus: the unleavened bread that Israel eats every year at Passover commemorates the haste of the departure that liberated them from Egypt; the remembrance of the manna in the desert will always recall to Israel that it lives by the bread of the Word of God; their daily bread is the fruit of the promised land, the pledge of God's faithfulness to his promises. The "cup of blessing" at the end of the Jewish Passover meal adds to the festive joy of wine an eschatological dimension: the messianic expectation of the rebuilding of Jerusalem. When Jesus instituted the Eucharist, he gave a new and definitive meaning to the blessing of the bread and the cup.[7]

By celebrating the Last Supper with his apostles in the course of the Passover meal, Jesus gave the Jewish Passover its definitive meaning. Jesus' passing over to his Father by his death and Resurrection, the new Passover, is anticipated in the Supper and celebrated in the Eucharist, which fulfills the Jewish Passover and anticipates the final Passover of the Church in the glory of the kingdom.[8]

St. John's Gospel[9]

In considering the institution of the Blessed Eucharist in Scripture, let us first turn to St. John's Gospel, which records Jesus' extensive discourse in Capernaum, in which he promised the Eucharist. In St. John, the Word is made flesh so that he

---

[7] CCC, no. 1334.
[8] Ibid., no. 1340.
[9] This chapter draws extensively on the commentary in *The Navarre Bible* on the different eucharistic texts: Matt. 26:26–29; Mark 14:22–25; Luke 22:17–19; 1 Cor. 10:16; 11:23–26.

may give us that same flesh to eat, to nurture and develop our supernatural life. The Word comes to unite God to humanity by mutual indwelling in eucharistic Communion.[10]

It was around the time of the Passover when Jesus gave his discourse on the Eucharist. On the previous day, he had taken the initiative in satisfying the hunger of the multitude that had been following him; with five barley loaves and two fish he fed five thousand people (cf. John 6:5–14)—a spectacular miracle that prepared the hearts and minds of his hearers for the great revelation he would make to them about the bread of life the following day.

The profusion of detail about this miracle—the *names* of the Apostles who address our Lord, the fact that the loaves are made of *barley*, the *young* boy who provides the wherewithal, and Jesus' telling the Apostles to gather up the leftovers—shows how accurate this narrative is. This miracle shows Jesus' divine power over creation, and his largesse recalls the abundance of messianic benefits. The miracle is a symbol of the Eucharist, of how Christ wants to feed all humanity with his own Flesh and Blood.

Later that night Jesus comes to the disciples, walking on the waters of the Sea of Galilee. They have been rowing against the wind for about five kilometers, and the Lord appears to them to strengthen their faith and to show once more his power over the forces of nature.

Jesus' discussion about the Eucharist in Capernaum opens with a dialogue between him and the Jews (vv. 26–37), in which our Lord reveals himself as the bringer of messianic gifts. Then comes the first part of the discourse (vv. 35–47), in which

[10] Cf. Aidan Nichols, *The Holy Eucharist* (Dublin: Veritas, 1991), 19.

Jesus presents himself as the bread of life, meaning that faith in him is food for eternal life. In the second part (vv. 48–59) Christ reveals the mystery of the Eucharist: *he* is the Bread of Life who gives himself sacramentally as real food. This food, which only God can give us, consists mainly of the gift of faith and sanctifying grace. Through God's infinite love we are given, in the Blessed Eucharist, the very author of these gifts, Jesus Christ, as nourishment for our souls.

The Jews ask Jesus for a sign like the manna that had been given to their fathers in the desert. But little do they suspect that the manna was a figure of the great supernatural messianic gift that Christ would bring to mankind—the Blessed Eucharist. Jesus tries to bring the Jews to make an act of faith in *him* so that he can openly reveal to *them* the mystery of the Blessed Eucharist—that he is the bread "which comes down from heaven, and gives life to the world" (v. 33).

It was precisely to elicit this act of faith that Jesus had worked the two miracles the day before—the multiplication of the loaves and his walking on the water. However, the Jews' disbelief prevents them from accepting what he revealed. When they murmur against him for saying, "I am the bread of life which has come down from heaven" (v. 41), Jesus makes this solemn declaration: "I am the bread of life. Your fathers ate the manna, and they died. This is the bread which comes down from heaven that a man may eat of it and not die. I am the living bread which has come down from heaven; if anyone eats of this bread he will live forever; and the bread which I shall give for the life of the world is my flesh" (John 6:48–51).

With this assertion, which he repeats because of his audience's doubts (cf. John 6:35, 41, 48), Jesus begins the second part of his discourse, in which he explicitly reveals the great mystery of the Blessed Eucharist. Christ's words have such a tremendous realism about them that they cannot be interpreted in a figurative way: if Christ were not really present under the species of bread and wine, this discourse would make absolutely no sense. This is so great a mystery that it has always acted as a touchstone for Catholic Faith. It is proclaimed "the mystery of faith" immediately after the Consecration at Mass.

The manna during the Exodus was a figure of this Bread—Jesus Christ himself—which nourishes Catholics on their pilgrimage through this world. Communion is the wonderful banquet at which Christ gives himself to us: "the bread which I shall give for the life of the world is my flesh" (v. 51). These words direct our minds toward the Last Supper, at which the Eucharist became a reality. The words "for the life of the world" refer to the redemptive value of the sacrifice of Christ on the Cross.

"The Jews then disputed among themselves, saying, 'How can this man give us his flesh to eat'" (v. 52). Christ's hearers understand perfectly well that he meant exactly what he said, but they cannot bring themselves to believe what he says. Had they understood him in a metaphorical, figurative, or symbolic sense, there would have been no reason for them to be so surprised and no cause for an argument.

This critical, even hostile attitude, recalls the approach of the Jews in the desert who protested over and over against Moses. At the beginning, when they see the miracles of Jesus, they are full of enthusiasm and they want to proclaim him king. But afterward they pass to the opposite extreme and turn their backs on him in their incomprehension.

"So Jesus said to them, 'Truly, truly I say to you, unless you eat the flesh of the Son of Man and drink his blood, you have no life in you'" (v. 53). Once again Jesus stresses very forcefully

that it is necessary to receive the Eucharist in order to share in
the divine life and develop the life of grace received initially in
Baptism. "He who eats my flesh and drinks my blood has eternal
life, and I will raise him up on the last day" (v. 54). Here Jesus
states clearly that his Body and Blood are a pledge of eternal
life and a guarantee of the resurrection of the body. St. Thomas
Aquinas explains this as follows: "The Word gave life to our
souls, but the Word-made-flesh nourishes our bodies. In this
sacrament is contained the Word not only in his divinity but
also in his humanity; therefore, it is the cause not only of the
glorification of our souls but also of that of our bodies."[11]

"For my flesh is food indeed, and my blood is drink indeed"
(v. 55). In the same way as bodily food is necessary for life on
earth, Holy Communion is necessary for maintaining the supernatural life of the soul, which is why the Church exhorts us
to receive this sacrament frequently. St. Francis de Sales makes
the following comments in this context:

> The Savior has instituted the august Sacrament of the
> Eucharist, which truly contains his flesh and blood, so
> that he who eats this bread may live forever; whoso-
> ever, therefore, makes use of it often with devotion so
> strengthens the health and the life of his soul, that it is
> almost impossible for him to be poisoned by any kind
> of evil affection. We cannot be nourished by this flesh
> of life, and live with the affections of death.... Chris-
> tians who are damned will be unable to make any reply
> when the just Judge shows them how much they are to
> blame for dying spiritually, since it was so easy for them
> to maintain themselves in life and in health by eating his

[11] St. Thomas Aquinas, *Commentary on St. John.*

body which he has left them for this purpose. Unhappy souls, he will say, why did you die, seeing that you had at your command the fruit and the food of life?[12]

"He who eats my flesh and drinks my blood abides in me and I in him" (v. 56). The most important effect of the Eucharist is intimate union with Christ. The very word *communion* suggests sharing in the life of our Lord and becoming one with him. As Vatican II points out: "Really sharing in the Body of the Lord in the breaking of the Eucharistic bread, we are taken up into communion with him and with one another. 'Because the bread is one, we, though many, are one body, all of us who partake of the one bread'" (1 Cor. 10:17).[13]

"As the living Father sent me and I live because of the Father, so he who eats me will live because of me" (v. 57). By receiving in this sacrament the Body and Blood of Christ, indissolubly united to his divinity, we share in the divine life of the Second Person of the Blessed Trinity.

For the third time (cf. John 6:31–32, 49, 58) Jesus compares the true bread of life, his own Body, with the manna God used to feed the Israelites every day during their forty years in the wilderness, thereby inviting us to nourish our souls frequently with the food of his Body.

"This Is a Hard Saying"

When many of his listeners find the eucharistic mystery completely incomprehensible (cf. v. 60), Jesus requires them to accept his words because it is he who has spoken them. This is

[12] St. Francis de Sales, *Introduction to the Devout Life*, pt. 2, ch. 20.
[13] Vatican II, *Lumen gentium*, no. 7.

what a supernatural act of faith involves. "This is a hard say-ing," many of disciples said. "Who can listen to it?" This lack of faith in the words of Jesus echoes down the centuries.

Berengarius of Tours, who lived in the eleventh century, took the first serious stand against the traditional doctrine of the Eucharist on the Real Presence and transubstantiation. The most aggressive opponent of the Catholic teaching on the Eucharist, however, was Martin Luther (1483–1546). He de-nied the doctrine of transubstantiation and the teaching that the Mass was a sacrifice. Ulrich Zwingli (1484–1531) and John Calvin (1509–1564), who were contemporaries of Luther, also denied the Catholic doctrine on the Eucharist. Zwingli, like Luther, rejected the sacrificial nature of the Mass; he also re-jected the Real Presence, affirming that Christ's presence in the Eucharist was purely symbolic. Calvin, a Frenchman who became the guiding light of the Reformation in Geneva, tried to bridge the differences between Luther and Zwingli. He too rejected the doctrine of the Mass as a sacrifice and stated that the bread and wine remain after the consecratory words have been said. He denounced adoration of the Blessed Sacrament as something leading to superstition and idolatry.[14]

---

[14] While Henry VIII of England severed links with Rome and set up a national church in England, he still retained his de-votion to the Mass, and no measures were taken against it as long as the king lived. However, his archbishop of Canter-bury, Thomas Cranmer, whom Henry had appointed with-out reference to Rome, was a Lutheran at heart, who had imbibed the doctrines of the Reform during a spell in Ger-many. When Henry departed the scene in 1547, Cranmer was ready to introduce new liturgical arrangements in the fledgling Anglican Church during the reign of Edward VI, the boy king who was the son of Henry. He removed from the

The Most Holy Eucharist

The Promise of the Eucharist

Let us return to St. John's text about the promise of the Eucharist. "After this many of his disciples drew back and no longer went about with him" (v. 66). They gave up following Jesus. He had outlined a wonderful and salvific truth, but those disciples closed themselves to divine grace; they were not ready to accept anything that went beyond their limited horizons.

When Christ asked the Apostles if they too would abandon him, Peter responded with a deep act of faith: "Lord, to whom shall we go? You have the words of eternal life; and we have believed and have come to know that you are the holy One of God" (vv. 68–69). Simon Peter's response is not just an expression of human solidarity but an articulation of genuine supernatural faith, which was due to his deep knowledge of the Master. God does not compel human freedom. We should be eternally grateful to Simon Peter for the magnificence of his reply.

Although John does not give a direct account of the institution of the Eucharist at the Last Supper, his Gospel is shot through with allusions to the rite, which was the center and source of the Christian life of the churches for whom he wrote.

---

missal all reference to the Mass as a sacrifice, and eliminated from the Edwardine ordinal all mention of the priest as a sacrificing priest. In this way he severed the line of apostolic succession and thus the validity of Anglican priestly orders. Cranmer also published the Thirty-Nine Articles of Religion in 1553, which is the core of Anglican doctrine. In article 31 we read that "the sacrifices of the Mass ... are blasphemous imaginings and pernicious deceits." The history of the Reformation in England is a story of brutal state suppression of Catholics over a period of two hundred years.

The Scriptural Foundations of the Eucharist

The Institution of the Eucharist in St. Mark

The institution of the Eucharist takes up just four verses in St. Mark's Gospel: "And as they were eating, he took bread, and blessed and broke it, and gave it to them, and said, 'Take, this is my body.' And he took a cup, and when he had given thanks he gave it to them and they all drank of it. And he said to them, 'This is my blood of the covenant which is poured out for many. Truly, I say to you, I shall not drink again of the fruit of the vine until that day when I drink it in the kingdom of God'" (14:22–25).

The word *this* in the text of the Consecration refers to what Jesus gave to his disciples — that is, something that looked like bread but was no longer bread; rather, it was his own Body. The words of consecration said over the chalice (v. 24) clearly show that the Eucharist is a sacrifice: the Blood of Christ is poured out, sealing the new and definitive covenant of God, in which Jesus is both Priest and Victim. The Church has defined this truth in these words: "If anyone says that in the Mass a true and proper sacrifice is not offered to God, or that to be offered is nothing else but that Christ is given us to eat, let him be anathema."[15]

The words pronounced over the chalice must have been very revealing for the Apostles, because they show that the sacrifices of the Old Covenant were in fact a preparation for and anticipation of Christ's sacrifice. The Apostles were able to grasp that the covenant of Sinai and the various sacrifices of the Temple were merely an imperfect prefiguration of the definitive sacrifice and the definitive covenant that would take place on the Cross and which they were anticipating in this Supper.

---

[15] Council of Trent, *On the Sacrifice of the Mass*, ch. 1, can. 1.

The Most Holy Eucharist

In the Last Supper, then, Christ already offered himself voluntarily to his Father as a Victim to be sacrificed. The Last Supper and holy Mass constitute with the Cross one and the same unique and perfect sacrifice, for in all three cases the Victim offered is the same — Christ — and the priest is the same — Christ. The only difference is that the Supper, which takes place prior to the Cross, anticipates the Lord's death in an unbloody way and offers a Victim soon to be immolated, whereas holy Mass offers, also in an unbloody manner, the Victim already immolated on the Cross, a Victim who exists forever in heaven.

After instituting the Holy Eucharist, our Lord extends the Last Supper in intimate conversation with his disciples, speaking to them once more about his imminent death (cf. John 13–17). His farewell saddens his Apostles, but he promises that the day will come when he will meet with them again, when the Kingdom of God will have come in all its fullness: he is referring to the beatific life in heaven, so often compared to a banquet. Then there will be no need of earthly food or drink; instead there will be a new vine (cf. Isa. 25:6). Definitively, after the Resurrection, the Apostles and all the saints will be able to share the delight of being with Jesus. The fact that St. Mark brings in these words after the institution of the Eucharist ("Truly, I say to you, I shall not drink again of the fruit of the vine until that day when I drink it new in the kingdom of God" [v. 25]), indicates that in some way the Eucharist is an anticipation here on earth of the possession of God in eternal blessedness, where God will be everything to everyone (cf. 1 Cor. 15:28).

At the Last Supper, on the night when He was betrayed, our Saviour instituted the eucharistic sacrifice of His

Body and Blood. He did this in order to perpetuate the sacrifice of the Cross throughout the centuries until He should come again, and so to entrust to His beloved spouse, the Church, a memorial of His death and resurrection: a sacrament of love, a sign of unity, a bond of charity, a paschal banquet in which Christ is eaten, the mind is filled with grace, and a pledge of future glory is given to us.[16]

The gift of the Eucharist is consistent with the plan of the Incarnation. It can be explained only by Christ's infinite love for mankind.

St. Luke's Account

The institution of the Eucharist took place within the context of the Passover meal, which commemorated the wondrous exodus of the Jews from the slavery of Egypt. Every Israelite was familiar with the details of the preparation for the Passover. It involved a rite that Jewish tradition had spelled out in minute detail: the unleavened loaves, the bitter herbs, and the lamb to be sacrificed in the Temple courtyard in the late afternoon. So Jesus sent Peter and John, saying: "Go and prepare the Passover for us, that we may eat it" (Luke 22:8), and he gave them instructions about where to prepare it.

St. John, the beloved disciple, sums up in a single phrase the sentiments welling up in Jesus' soul at the Last Supper: "When Jesus knew that his hour had come to depart out of this world to the Father, having loved his own who are in the world, he loved them to the end" (John 13:1). Our Lord expresses his burning desire to spend the hours prior to his death with those

---

[16] Vatican II, *Sacrosanctum concilium*, no. 47.

whom he loved most on earth, and, as happens when people are taking leave of their nearest and dearest, very affectionate words are exchanged. His love is not confined to the Apostles; he is thinking of all men and women. He knows that his Passover meal marks the beginning of his Passion. He is going to anticipate the sacrifice of the New Testament, which will bring great benefits to mankind. St. Luke's text of the institution is as follows:

> And he took a cup, and when he had given thanks he said, "Take this, and divide it among yourselves; for I tell you that from now on I shall not drink of the fruit of the vine until the kingdom of God comes." And he took bread, and when he had given thanks he broke it and gave it to them, saying, "This is my body, which is given up for you. Do this in remembrance of me." And likewise the cup after supper, saying, "This cup which is poured out for you is the new covenant in my blood." (Luke 22:17–20)

This text contains the three basic truths of faith concerning the great mystery of the Eucharist: 1) the institution of the Eucharist and Jesus Christ's Real Presence in it; 2) the institution of the Christian priesthood; and 3) the Eucharist as the sacrifice of the New Testament. St. Luke's account is substantially the same as that in St. Matthew but is enhanced by his more detailed description of some points.

In contemplating this great mystery, Christian souls have always perceived its grandeur as deriving from the fact of Christ's Real Presence in it. The sacrament of the Eucharist is not only an efficacious sign of Christ's loving presence in an intimate union with the faithful; in it he is present corporally and substantially, as God and man. Certainly, in order to penetrate this mystery one needs to have faith.

After instituting the Eucharist, our Lord instructs the Apostles to perpetuate what he has done: the Church has always taken Christ's words "Do this in remembrance of me" to mean that he thereby made the Apostles and their successors priests of the New Covenant who would renew the sacrifice of Calvary in an unbloody manner in the celebration of holy Mass.

This means that at the center of Christ's entire activity stands the bloody sacrifice he offered on the Cross—the sacrifice of the New Covenant, prefigured in the sacrifices of the Old Law, in the offerings made by Abel (Gen. 4:4), by Abraham (Gen. 15:10; 22:13), and by Melchizedek (Gen. 14:18–19; Heb. 7:1–28).

St. Matthew's Account

St. Matthew describes the institution as follows: "Now as they were eating, Jesus took bread, and blessed, and broke it, and gave it to the disciples and said, 'Take, eat; this is my body.' And he took a cup, and when he had given thanks he gave it to them, saying, 'Drink of it, all of you; for this is my blood of the covenant, which is poured out for many for the forgiveness of sins. I tell you I shall not drink again of this fruit of the vine until that day when I drink it new with you in my Father's kingdom'" (26:26–29). These few verses of St. Matthew's Gospel contain the essential truths of faith about the sublime mystery of the Eucharist: the institution of this sacrament and Jesus' Real Presence in it, and the sacrifice of the New Testament, or the Mass.

In the first place, we can see the institution of the Eucharist by Jesus Christ when he says, "This is my body.... This is my blood." What up to this point was nothing but unleavened bread and wine, now — through the words and by the will of Jesus Christ, true God and true man — becomes the true Body and Blood of the Savior. His words, which have such realism about them, cannot be interpreted as being merely symbolic or explained in a way that obscures the mysterious fact that Christ is really present in the Eucharist: all we can do is humbly subscribe to the faith "which the Catholic Church has always held and which she will hold until the end of the world."[17]

In instituting the Blessed Eucharist our Lord laid down that it should be repeated until the end of time by giving the Apostles the power to perform it. From the accounts in St. Paul and St. Luke (cf. 1 Cor. 11:24–25; Luke 22:19), we can see that Christ also instituted the priesthood, bestowing on the Apostles the power to confect the Eucharist — a power that they in turn passed on to their successors. This making of the Eucharist takes place at Mass when the priest, with the intention of doing what the Church does, says Christ's words of consecration over the bread and wine. At this very moment "a change takes place in which the whole substance of bread is changed into the substance of the Body of Christ our Lord and the whole substance of the wine into the substance of his Blood."[18]

The expression in Matthew's account — "which is poured out for many for the forgiveness of sins" — means the same as "which is poured out for all." Here we have the fulfillment of the prophecies of Isaiah that spoke of the atoning death of Christ for all men (chapter 53). Only Christ's sacrifice is capable of atoning to the Father; the Mass has this same power and effectiveness because it is that very sacrifice.

---

[17] Council of Trent, Decree on the Blessed Eucharist, preface.
[18] Ibid.

The Scriptural Foundations of the Eucharist

St. Paul on Christ's Real Presence in the Eucharist

In the context of informing the Corinthians about food sacrificed to idols, St. Paul says that Christians may not attend banquets that take place at pagan shrines, for that would amount to idolatry.

> The cup of blessing which we bless, is it not a participation in the blood of Christ? The bread which we break, is it not a participation in the body of Christ? Because there is one bread, we who are many are one body for we all partake of the one bread. Consider the practice of Israel; are not those who eat the sacrifices partners in the altar? What do I imply then? That food offered to idols is anything, or that an idol is anything? No, I imply that what pagans sacrifice they offer to demons and not to God. I do not want you to be partners with demons. You cannot drink the cup of the Lord and the cup of demons. You cannot partake of the table of the Lord and the table of demons. (1 Cor. 10:16–21)

By receiving the Body and Blood of the Lord, Christians unite themselves to Christ; similarly those who take part in idolatrous banquets are associating themselves not with false gods, for these do not actually exist, but with demons. So there is a total antagonism between pagan sacrifices and the new rites of Christian sacrifice.

St. Paul's words confirm two basic truths of faith connected with the mystery of the Eucharist: its sacrificial character, adverted to here by drawing a parallel between it and pagan sacrifices, and the Real Presence of Christ in the Eucharist, as can be seen by reference to the Body and Blood of Christ.

The Most Holy Eucharist

The principal effect of the Eucharist is intimate union with Jesus. As a consequence the Eucharist is the sacrament in which the entire Church demonstrates and achieves unity and in which a special kind of solidarity is developed among Catholics. That is why it is called a "symbol of unity" and "a bond of love."[19]

This is summed up as follows in the *St. Pius V Catechism*: "The Body of Christ, which is one, consists of many members (cf. Rom. 12:4–5; 1 Cor. 10:17; 12:12), and of this union nothing is more strikingly illustrative than the elements of bread and wine, for bread is made from many grains and wine is pressed from many clusters of grapes. Thus they signify that we, though many, are most closely bound together by the bond of the divine mystery and made, as it were, one body."[20]

St. Paul on the Institution of the Eucharist

In writing to the Corinthians St. Paul also refers explicitly to the institution of the Eucharist:

> For I received from the Lord what I also delivered to you, that the Lord Jesus on the night when he was betrayed took bread, and when he had given thanks, he broke it, and said, "This is my Body which is for you. Do this in remembrance of me." In the same way also the cup, after supper, saying, "This cup is the new covenant in my Blood. Do this, as often as you drink it, in remembrance of me." For as often as you eat this bread and drink the cup, you proclaim the Lord's death until he comes. (1 Cor. 11:23–26)

[19] Cf. Vatican II, *Lumen gentium*, no. 7.
[20] *Catechism of St. Pius V*, II, 4, 18.

The Scriptural Foundations of the Eucharist

These verses clearly bear witness to the early Christians' faith in the eucharistic mystery. St. Paul is writing about the year A.D. 57, only about twenty years after the institution of the Eucharist, reminding the Corinthians of what they had been taught some years earlier (c. A.D. 51). The words *received* and *delivered* are technical terms used to indicate that a teaching is part of Apostolic Tradition (cf. also 1 Cor. 15:3).

The text contains the three same fundamental elements of Christian faith in the mystery of the Eucharist which we have already seen in the Synoptic Gospels: 1) the institution of this sacrament by Jesus Christ and his Real Presence in it; 2) the institution of the Christian priesthood; 3) the Eucharist as the sacrifice of the New Testament.

"Do this in memory of me": in instituting the Eucharist, our Lord charged that it be reenacted until the end of time (cf. Luke 22:19), thereby instituting the priesthood. The Council of Trent teaches that Jesus, at the Last Supper, "offered his Body and Blood under the species of bread and wine to God the Father, and he gave his Body and Blood under the same species to the apostles to receive, making them priests of the New Testament at that time.... He ordered the apostles and their successors in the priesthood to offer this sacrament when he said, 'Do this is remembrance of me,' as the Catholic Church has always understood and taught."[21] And so, Pope John Paul II teaches that the Eucharist is "the principal and central *raison d'être* of the Sacrament of the priesthood, which effectively came into being at the moment of the institution of the Eucharist, and together with it."[22]

[21] Council of Trent, Decree on the Sacrifice of the Mass, ch. 1.
[22] Bl. John Paul II, *Dominicae Cenae*, no 2.

21

The Most Holy Eucharist

The word *remembrance* is charged with the meaning of a He-brew word that was used to convey the essence of the feast of the Passover—commemoration of the exodus from Egypt. For the Israelites the Passover rite not only reminded them of a bygone event; they were conscious of making that event present, reviv-ing it, in order to participate in it, in some way, generation after generation (cf. Exod. 12:26–27; Deut. 6:20–25).[23] So when our Lord commands his Apostles, "Do this in remembrance of me," it is not a matter of merely recalling his supper but of renewing his own Passover sacrifice on Calvary, which already at the Last Supper was present in an anticipated way.

Unworthy Reception of the Eucharist

The theology of eucharistic Communion too was worked out by St. Paul: "Whoever, therefore, eats the bread or drinks the cup of the Lord in an unworthy manner will be guilty of profaning the Body and Blood of the Lord. Let a man examine himself, and so eat the bread and drink of the cup. For any-one who eats and drinks without discerning the body eats and drinks judgment upon himself. That is why many of you are weak and ill, and some have died" (1 Cor. 11:27–30).

These words are, in the first place, an unambiguous asser-tion of the Real Presence of Jesus in the eucharistic species. It is this Real Presence of our Lord in the Eucharist that explains why one needs to be prepared in body and soul to receive it and why receiving it unworthily has such grave consequences (vv. 27–29). Recalling what St. Paul says in verses 27–28, the Council of Trent teaches that "no one who has a mortal sin on his conscience shall dare to receive the Holy Eucharist before

[23] Cf. CCC, nos. 1362–1367.

making a sacramental confession, regardless of how contrite he may think he is. This holy Council declares that this custom is to be kept forever."[24]

The Letter to the Hebrews

The Letter to the Hebrews emphasizes the superiority of Christ's priesthood over the Levitical priesthood (cf. ch. 7) because it is perfect, permanent, and sealed by God with an oath. In fact Christ is the only true High Priest—his priesthood is unique. Christ's priesthood, which was heralded by that of Melchizedek, is prolonged in the Christian ministerial priesthood. However, Christ continues to be the only true priest, interceding for us with the Father. Catholic priests are only vicars or ministers of Christ, not his successors.

Christ's priesthood is an expression of his love, from which it cannot be separated; since his love is everlasting, so too is his priesthood. His priesthood is everlasting because:

• it is linked to the Incarnation, which is permanent;

• Christ's mission is that of saving all men and women in all periods of history and not simply one of helping them by his teaching and example;

• Christ continues to be present—St. Ephraem says—not in the victims of the sacrifices of the Mosaic worship, but in the prayer of the Church, particularly in the permanent efficacy of the sacrifice of the Cross constantly renewed in the Mass, and in the praying of the Divine Office;[25]

[24] Cf. CCC, no. 1385.
[25] Cf. St. Ephraem, *Commentary on the Epistle to the Hebrews.*

- Christ's sacrifice is perpetuated to the end of time in the Christian ministerial priesthood. Christ not only interceded for us when he was on earth; he continues to make intercession for us in heaven through the glorious signs of his Passion.

The sublimity of Christ's priesthood is a source of encouragement, hope, and holy pride for the priests of the New Testament, given that "every priest in his own way puts on the person of Christ and is endowed with a special grace. By this grace, the priest, through his service of the people committed to his care and all the people of God, is able the better to pursue the perfection of Christ, whose place he takes. The human weakness of his flesh is remedied by the holiness of him who became for us a high priest, 'holy, blameless, unstained, separated from sinners'" (Heb. 7:26).[26]

The celebration of the Sacrifice of the Mass is not at odds with the efficacy and unicity of the sacrifice of Christ, because the Mass is not a new sacrifice involving the shedding of blood, a numerically distinct repetition of the sacrifice of the Cross; it is an unbloody renewal of the sacrifice, to apply its infinite efficacy. The Mass

> is the sacrifice of Christ, offered to the Father with the cooperation of the Holy Spirit—an offering of infinite value, which perpetuates the work of the Redemption in us and surpasses the sacrifices of the Old Law. Holy Mass brings us face to face with one of the central mysteries of our faith, because it is the gift of the Blessed Trinity to the Church. It is because of this that we can consider the

[26] Vatican II, *Presbyterorum ordinis*, no. 12.

Mass as the centre and source of a Christian's spiritual life. It is the final end of all the sacraments.[27]

Christ is a mediator of a New Covenant, ratified by his Blood, which gives an eternal inheritance (Heb. 7:22; 8:6; 9:15). The emphasis is on the sacrificial aspect: Christ is the mediator insofar as he is the atoning priest and at the same time the offered sacrifice; in his sacrifice he is both Priest and Victim.

Christ is priest indeed; but he is priest *for us*, not for himself. It is in the name of the whole human race that he offers prayer and acts of human religious homage to his Eternal Father. He is likewise victim; but victim *for us*, since he substitutes himself for guilty mankind. Now the Apostle's exhortation, "Yours is to be the same mind as Christ Jesus showed" (Phil 2:5), requires all Christians, so far as human power allows, to reproduce in themselves the sentiments that Christ had when he was offering himself in sacrifice—sentiments of humility, of adoration, praise and thanksgiving to the divine Majesty. It requires them also to become victims, as it were, cultivating a spirit of self-denial according to the precepts of the Gospel, willingly doing works of penance, detesting and expiating their sins.[28]

The unique sufficiency of the sacrifice of the Cross compared with that of the Old Law is brought out by Hebrews 10:10: "We have been sanctified through the offering of the body of Jesus

[27] St. Josemaría Escrivá, *Christ Is Passing By* (Dublin: Scepter, 1985), nos. 86–87.
[28] Pius XII, Encyclical *Mediator Dei* (November 20, 1947), no. 22 (italics added).

Christ once for all." This is the point of departure of the Catholic doctrine on the identity of the sacrifice of the Cross and that of the Eucharist, which is a real re-presentation of that sacrifice, with the same Victim and the same High Priest, who offers himself by the ministry of his priests under the same symbols under which he offered himself at the Last Supper.

Christ's sacrifice is not only effective in forgiving our sins; it is a manifestation of our Redeemer's love for us, and it sets an example we should follow. As St. Alphonsus Liguori says:

> And if God forgives us our sins it is so that we might use the time that remains to us in his service and love. And the Apostle concludes, saying, "Therefore he is the mediator of a new covenant." Our Redeemer, captivated by his boundless love for us, chose to rescue us, at the cost of his Blood, from eternal death; and he succeeded in doing so, for if we serve him faithfully until we die we shall obtain from the Lord forgiveness and eternal life. Such were the terms of the testament, mediation or compact between Jesus Christ and God.[29]

Pope Benedict XVI on the Institution of the Eucharist

In volume 2 of his book *Jesus of Nazareth*,[30] Benedict XVI comments on the institution of the Eucharist. While it is beyond the scope of this book to engage with the more recondite technical and exegetical aspects of his commentary, there are a number of points to which we can draw attention. Pope Benedict says that the four accounts of the Eucharist can be grouped

[29] St. Alphonsus Liguori, *Reflections on the Passion*, 9, 2.
[30] Joseph Ratzinger (Pope Benedict XVI), *Jesus of Nazareth, Part Two* (San Francisco: Ignatius Press, 2011).

according to two strands of tradition with differing characteristics. After examining the words of institution given by Matthew and Mark, Paul and Luke, Pope Benedict comments:

> We take it as a given that the tradition of Jesus' words would not exist without reception by the early Church, which was conscious of a strict obligation to faithfulness in essentials but also recognized that the enormous resonance of these words, with their subtle reference to Scripture, permitted a degree of nuanced redaction. The New Testament writers heard echoes of both Exodus 24 and Jeremiah 31 in Jesus' words and could choose to place the accent more on the one or on the other, without thereby being unfaithful to the Lord's words, which in barely audible yet unmistakable ways gathered within themselves the Law and the Prophets....
>
> From her earliest days, the Church has understood the words of consecration not simply as a kind of quasi-magical command, but as part of her praying in and with Jesus; as a central part of the praise and thanksgiving through which God's earthly gift is given to us anew in the form of Jesus' Body and Blood, as God's gift of himself in his Son's self-emptying love.[31]

After Jesus had said the blessing, we note that he "broke the bread." This is something the head of the family used to do, but in the hands of Jesus it acquires a new meaning. It has come to symbolize the whole mystery of the Eucharist: "In the Acts of the Apostles and in early Christianity generally, the 'breaking of bread' designates the Eucharist. In this sacrament we

---

[31] Ibid., 127, 128.

The Most Holy Eucharist

enjoy the hospitality of God, who gives himself to us in Jesus Christ, crucified and risen. Thus breaking bread and distributing it—the act of attending lovingly to those in need—is an intrinsic dimension of the Eucharist."[32]

Here Benedict emphasizes once again an aspect of the Eucharist which he developed in his encyclical *Deus Caritas Est.*[33]

> *"Caritas,"* care for the other, is not an additional sector of Christianity alongside worship; rather, it is rooted in it and forms part of it. The horizontal and the vertical are inseparably linked in the Eucharist, in the "breaking of bread." In this dual action of praise/thanksgiving and breaking/distributing that is recounted at the beginning of the institution narrative, the essence of the new worship established by Christ through the Last Supper, Cross and Resurrection is made manifest: here the old Temple worship is abolished and at the same time brought to its fulfillment.[34]

As Pope Benedict says, the words spoken over the chalice are of extraordinary theological depth. Three Old Testament texts (Exod. 24:8; Jer. 31:31; Isa. 51:12) are woven together in these few words, so that the whole of the earlier salvation history is summarized in them and once more made present.[35]

---

[32] Ratzinger, *Jesus of Nazareth, Part Two*, 129. Cf. the section about the Eucharist and charity.
[33] Benedict XVI, Encyclical Letter *Deus Caritas Est* (December 25, 2005).
[34] Ratzinger, *Jesus of Nazareth, Part Two*, 129–130.
[35] Ibid., 131.

Chapter 2

The Eucharist as Sacrifice

The Sacrifice of the Mass in Sacred Scripture

The Mass is fundamentally the commemoration and the re-presentation of the sacrifice of Calvary. It is the perpetual ful-fillment of the command given by Jesus Christ to his Apostles and, through them, to all his priests until the end of time: "Do this in remembrance of me" (Luke 22:19; cf. 1 Cor. 11:22). So it is with the Last Supper that we begin our discussion of the Eucharist as sacrifice.

Christ's total self-surrender on our behalf, which reaches its culmination on Calvary, is an urgent call to correspond to his great love for each one of us. On the Cross, Jesus consummated his total self-surrender to his Father's will and showed his love for all men, for each and every person. "He ... loved me and gave himself up for me" (Gal. 2:20). Faced with this unfathom-able mystery of love, we have to ask ourselves: *What do I do for him? How do I correspond to his love?*

At every moment of his life on earth Jesus lived a perfect identification with his Father's will, but on Calvary the Son's self-surrender reached its supreme expression.[36] Jesus was not offered up to the Father by Pilate or by Caiaphas or by the crowds on Calvary. Rather, as Priest and Victim, he offered himself to his heavenly Father, shedding his Blood and letting his Body be pierced by the soldier's lance. It was the Father's will that the Redemption be carried out in this way. Jesus accepted it lovingly and with perfect submission. This *internal* offering of himself is the essence of his sacrifice. It is his loving submission, without limits, to his Father's will.

What is striking is the sacrificial nature of the language used in Scripture to describe the Last Supper. Jesus and his Apostles were Jews; hence they were fully cognizant of the circumstances accompanying the solemn institution of the covenant between God and the Hebrew people, and of the words in which it was recorded, which were often read by them or heard in their worship in the synagogue and the Temple. When therefore Jesus, giving his disciples the chalice, said: "This cup is the new covenant in my blood. Do this, as often you drink it, in remembrance of me" (1 Cor. 11:25), no doubt the disciples must have recalled the scene described in Exodus 19 and realized that Jesus was instituting and sealing a New Covenant between God and his people, of which the old had been the type and the promise. And as the Old Covenant had been sealed in the blood of victims offered in sacrifice, so the sealing blood of the New is that of Christ, the Victim who is the sacrifice of the New Covenant.

The sacrificial character of this blood is further emphasized by the added words "which is poured out for many for the

---

[36] Cf. Francis Fernandez, *In Conversation with God*, vol. 2 (London: Scepter, 1989), 185.

forgiveness of sins" (Matt. 26:28), words that proclaim the propitiatory effect of Christ's death. The Last Supper partook of the nature of a sacrifice since Christ's true Body and Blood were there really present and really given and were the immediate subject of his sacrificial words.[37]

Another point to be noted is the connection set up between the Last Supper and the Cross. In a few hours, after the Supper, Jesus was to be delivered to death and was to shed his Blood for men, in forgiveness of their sins. Now in this last solemn meal he wished, by an act of divine anticipation, to give his disciples his Body and Blood and to make them partakers in the sacrifice now so close at hand.

The sacrificial element of the meal at the Last Supper as celebrated by Christ is very evident. It is St. Paul who gives the clearest expression of this aspect of the meal (cf. 1 Cor. 10:16–21).

In summary, then, we can make three points in relation to the Last Supper as celebrated by Jesus Christ:

* It is the establishment of a New Covenant with God's people, expressed in terms that are clearly sacrificial.

* It is the memorial or commemoration of Christ's sacrificial death on the Cross.

* It provides a sacrificial meal in which we participate in the gifts that have been offered in sacrifice.

The conclusion is inevitable: the Last Supper is a real sacrifice, the sacrifice of the Body and Blood of Christ.

---

[37] Cf. B. V. Miller, "The Eucharistic Sacrifice" in *The Teaching of the Catholic Church* (London: Burns and Oates, 1960), 882.

The Most Holy Eucharist

The Prophecy of Malachi

From the earliest Christian times, the prophecy of Malachi has been considered a clear foretelling of the Sacrifice of the Mass. The prophet begins by reproving the priests of Israel for their neglect of God's commands in the matter of divine worship; they were offering unclean and defective gifts on the altar of sacrifice. God, through the prophet's mouth, declares that he will no longer look with favor upon these sacrifices and announces that the time is coming when instead of these defective sacrifices, offered at Jerusalem only, a clean oblation will be offered constantly and in every place in his name: "For from the rising of the sun, even to the going down, my name is great among the Gentiles, and in every place there is sacrifice, and there is offered to my name a clean oblation; for my name is great among the Gentiles, said the Lord of hosts" (Mal. 1:11).

This clean oblation that is to be offered everywhere among the Gentiles is clearly something different from the Jewish sacrifices, which could be offered only in the Temple in Jerusalem and which, since this was destroyed in A.D. 70, have ceased to be. The prophet announces, therefore, the coming abrogation of the old rites and the institution of a new and universal sacrifice. Since the time of the Apostles, ecclesiastical writers have been unanimous in interpreting these words of Malachi as referring to the Sacrifice of the Mass. The Council of Trent authoritatively confirmed this interpretation in its decree on the Sacrifice of the Mass: "And this [the Mass] indeed is that clean oblation that cannot be defiled by any unworthiness or wickedness in those who offer; the clean oblation which the Lord, speaking by Malachi, foretold would be offered in every place to his name, which would be great among the Gentiles."

The Eucharist as Sacrifice

The Sacrifice of the Mass in Catholic Tradition

The language of the Church Fathers about the Eucharist does not have the same precision it has today. This is not surprising, as the full implications of the mystery of the Eucharist took time to crystallize. Belief in the Mass as a sacrifice and in the Real Presence, however, can be traced back to the apostolic Church. This doctrine is also clear from the oldest liturgies of the Mass. It is therefore instructive to review the Fathers' witness to this teaching.

Already in the sub-apostolic age we find St. Ignatius of Antioch (50–117) arguing from the Eucharist to the necessity of unity in the Church. He was a man of sterling qualities who faced up to the persecution of Domitian with great courage, instilling optimism and hope into his flock. He was arrested in Antioch and brought to Rome because he refused to join the pagans in the worship of their gods. The various Christian communities along the route came out to comfort him and offer him the homage of the churches. To each of these communities he addressed letters from Smyrna, exhorting them to obedience and warning them to avoid the contamination of heresy. He also wrote to the Christians of Rome, begging them do nothing to deprive him of the opportunity of martyrdom.

St. Ignatius of Antioch calls the Eucharist "the medicine of immortality, the antidote against death, and everlasting life in Jesus Christ."[38] He admonishes the Philadelphians: "Take care, then, to partake of one Eucharist; for one is the Flesh of our Lord Jesus Christ, and one the cup to unite us with his Blood, and one altar just as there is one bishop assisted by the presby-

---

[38] St. Ignatius of Antioch, Letter to the Ephesians, ch. 20, in Johannes Quasten, *Patrology*, vol. 66.

tery and the deacons, my fellow servants."³⁹ This argument is the same as that of St. Paul in his first letter to the Corinthians (cf. 10:16). What he is saying is that in the Eucharist we all partake of the one Body of Christ and of his Blood; we all assist at one and the same sacrifice; hence we should be one among ourselves. But here, as also in St. Paul, the argument loses all its force unless the Eucharist is really and truly the Body and Blood of Christ. St. Ignatius is very clear: "The Eucharist is the Flesh of our Savior Jesus Christ, which suffered for our sins, and which the Father in his loving-kindness raised from the dead."⁴⁰

St. Justin (100–165), a Christian apologist, was born in Palestine, converted to Christianity about A.D. 130, and taught and defended the Christian religion in Asia Minor and in Rome, where he suffered martyrdom. In coming to the Church he was moved by the moral beauty of Christianity, by its truth. St. Justin's testimony offers an interesting account of the way the early Christians celebrated the liturgy. This is the earliest description we have of the Mass, from about the year 150. It is important because many elements of the liturgy have remained substantially the same from St. Justin's day until now:

---

³⁹ St. Ignatius of Antioch, Letter to the Philadelphians, ch. 4, in Quasten, *Patrology*, vol. 1.

⁴⁰ St. Ignatius of Antioch, Letter to the Smyrnaeans, ch. 7, in Quasten, *Patrology*. The doctrine of the Real Presence is still more clearly implied in the same letter to the Smyrnaeans where, writing of the Docetists who denied the reality of the human nature of Christ, St. Ignatius says: "They abstain from the Eucharist ... because they do not believe that the Eucharist is the Flesh of our Savior Jesus Christ which suffered for our sins and which the Father in his bounty raised up again." (G.D. Smith, "The Sacrament of the Eucharist," in *The Teaching of the Catholic Church*, 851).

The Eucharist as Sacrifice

On the day we call the day of the sun, all who dwell in any city or country gather in the same place.

The memoirs of the Apostles and the writings of the prophets are read, as much as time permits.

When the reader has finished, he who presides over the gathered admonishes and challenges them to imitate those beautiful things.

Then we all rise together and offer prayers for ourselves ... and for all others, wherever they may be, so that we may be found righteous by our life and actions, and faithful to the commandments, so as to obtain eternal salvation.

When the prayers are concluded we exchange the kiss.

Then someone brings bread and a cup of water and wine mixed together to him who presides over the brethren.

He takes them and offers prayers and glory to the Father of the universe, through the name of the Son and the Holy Spirit and for a considerable time he gives thanks that we have been judged worthy of these gifts.

When he has concluded the prayers and thanksgivings, all present give voice to an acclamation by saying "Amen."

When he who presides has given thanks and the people have responded, those whom we call deacons give to those present the "eucharisted" bread, wine and water and take them to those who are absent.

And this food is called by us the Eucharist, of which no one is allowed to partake unless he believes the truth of our doctrines; and unless he has been washed in the laver for the forgiveness of sins, and unto regeneration; and so live as Christ has directed. For we do not receive them as ordinary food, or ordinary drink, but as by the Word of God Jesus our Savior was made Flesh and had both Flesh and Blood for our salvation, so also the food which was blessed by the prayer of the Word which proceeded from him, and from which our Flesh and Blood, by assimilation, receives nourishment, is, we are taught, both the flesh and blood of that Jesus who was made Flesh. For the apostles in the records which they made, and which are called gospels, have declared that Jesus commanded them to do as follows: "he took bread and gave thanks," and said "this do in remembrance of me: this is my body." And in like manner he took the cup, and blessed it, and said, "This is my blood" and gave it to them alone.[41]

This is Justin's account of the celebration of the Eucharist. Apart from describing the Mass, there are two points of dogmatic importance. The first is the evident connection between the Eucharist and the Last Supper, since St. Justin explains one by the other and by Christ's command to his Apostles to repeat what he did. The second point is the witness to the Christian belief in the Real Presence. The eucharistic bread and wine were, for St. Justin and his fellow Christians, not common food and drink, but, quite simply, the Flesh and Blood of Jesus Christ.

The liturgy of the Eucharist unfolds according to a fundamental structure that has been preserved throughout the

[41] St. Justin Martyr, *The First Apology*, 65–67; cf. CCC, no. 1345, and Miller, "The Eucharistic Sacrifice," 890–891.

centuries to the present day. It presents itself in two basic parts, which form an intrinsic unity: the liturgy of the Word with readings, homily, and general intercessions; and the liturgy of the Eucharist, with the presentation of the bread and wine, the consecratory thanksgiving, and Communion.[42]

St. Irenaeus of Lyons (120–190), who witnesses to the tradition of both East and West, proposes the same teaching at the end of the second century.[43] He was born in Asia and heard the gospel preached by St. Polycarp of Smyrna. He became bishop of Lyons, France, about 178 and occupies an exceptional place in Christian literature.

Many pertinent passages could be quoted from the *Adversus Haereses* of St. Irenaeus, in which this great defender of the Faith uses the eucharistic dogma to refute the tenets of the Gnostics, who held that matter was essentially evil. "How could this be so," asked Irenaeus, "if Christ used bread and wine in the Eucharist, elements which 'perceiving the word of God' [that is, through the power of God's word] become the Eucharist, which is the Body and Blood of Christ?"[44]

One other passage in St. Irenaeus is particularly remarkable for its witness to the doctrine of transubstantiation: "The bread that is taken from the earth, perceiving the invitation of God, is no longer ordinary bread, but the Eucharist consisting of two things, an earthly and a heavenly."[45]

Tertullian (160–220), a lawyer by profession, was a pagan until midlife, when he converted about 197 and was ordained

[42] Cf. CCC, no. 1346.
[43] Cf. St. Irenaeus, *Adversus Haereses*, bk. 5, ch. 2, no. 3; cf. Smith, "The Sacrament of the Eucharist," 852.
[44] Cf. Smith, "The Sacrament of the Eucharist," 852.
[45] Ibid.

a priest about 200. By the time he joined the Montanist sect after the year 206, he had already written a number of treatises on Church doctrine. Tertullian advises that great care be taken that no drop of the *sanguis* or fragment of the consecrated bread fall to the ground. What the communicant receives in Church, he says, is the Lord's own Body.[46]

The temptation to idolatry, which was a constant menace to Christians by reason of their close contact with pagans, caused the Fathers of the third century to reiterate the warning given by St. Paul against desecrating the Eucharist (cf. 1 Cor. 8 and 10). So Tertullian had some very strong remarks about those Christians who engaged in the manufacture of idols, "passing from the idols to the church, from the shop of the enemy to the house of God, raising up to God the hands that are mothers of idols, applying to the Lord's Body those hands that give bodies to demons.... What hands deserve more to be cut off than those in which scandal is done to the Body of the Lord!"[47] Tertullian is also the author of that superb expression, "Jesus gives us his Flesh in the Eucharist so that the soul can grow fat on God."[48]

Origen (185–232), a graduate and later head of the school of Alexandria, impresses on the faithful the need to have reverence for the Eucharist: "You who are accustomed to assist at the divine mysteries know how, when you receive the Body of the Lord, you hold it with every precaution and veneration lest any of the consecrated gift should fall. For you believe, and rightly believe, yourselves guilty if through your negligence any of it should be dropped; if you—justly—use such care to

[46] Nichols, *The Holy Eucharist*, 37.
[47] Tertullian, *De Idolatria*, 7, in Quasten, *Patrology*, vol. 2, 336.
[48] Tertullian, *The Eucharist*, in Quasten, *Patrology*, vol. 2, 334.

preserve his Body, do you consider it a lesser sin to neglect his word?"[49]

The writings of St. Cyprian of Carthage (205–258) in the middle of the third century have many references to the sacrifice of the Eucharist. St. Cyprian holds that the Eucharist is a true sacrifice, that it was instituted and first offered by Jesus Christ at the Last Supper, that in it we truly offer to God Christ's Body and Blood under the appearances of bread and wine, and that it is the passion or the commemoration of the Passion of Christ.[50]

In his *Catechetical Instructions* St. Cyril of Jerusalem (315–386) describes how the Eucharist was received in the fourth century:

In approaching, therefore, come not with your wrists extended or your fingers spread, but make your left hand a throne for the right, as for that which is to receive a king. And having hallowed your palm, receive the Body of Christ, saying over it, "Amen." Then having carefully sanctified your eyes with the touch of the holy Body, partake of it, taking heed lest you lose any portion of it; for whatever you lose is evidently a loss to you, as it were, from your own members. For tell me, if anyone gave you grains of gold, would you not hold them with all carefulness, being on your guard against losing any of them and suffering loss? Will you not then much more carefully keep watch that not a crumb fall from your hand of what is more precious than gold and precious stones?

[49] Origen, *De lapsis,* ch. 15, in Smith, "The Sacrament of the Eucharist," 853.
[50] Cf. St. Cyprian of Carthage, in Quasten, *Patrology,* vol. 2, 381–382.

Then after you have partaken of the Body of Christ
draw near also to the chalice of his Blood; not stretching
out your hands, but bending and saying with worship and
reverence, "Amen," hallow yourself by partaking also of
the Blood of Christ. And while the moisture is still on
your lips, touch it with your hands and hallow your eyes
and brow and other organs of sense. Then wait for the
prayer and give thanks to God, who has accounted you
worthy of so great mysteries.[51]

Here St. Cyril is instructing catechumens on the great sacrament they are about to receive for the first time, and so his
teaching is very clear and explicit. He also tells us how the catechumens were taught the doctrine of the Real Presence in the
fourth century: "The bread and wine of the Eucharist were simple bread and wine before the invocation of the holy and ador-
able Trinity, but when the invocation has taken place the bread
becomes the Body of Christ and the wine the blood of Christ."[52]

St. John Chrysostom (350–407) was born in Antioch, was
ordained a priest in 386, and acquired great renown as a preacher
and pastor of souls. In 397 he was appointed archbishop of
Constantinople. In modern times Chrysostom has been called
Doctor of the Eucharist because he is an eminent witness to
the Real Presence of Christ in the Eucharist and its sacrificial
character. He approaches the eucharistic mystery "with fear and
trembling." The Mass is an "awe-inspiring" sacrifice. Pointing
to the altar he says: "Christ lies there slain." "That which is in
the chalice is the same as what flowed from the side of Christ."

---

[51] St. Cyril of Jerusalem, *Catechetical Instruction*, lect. 23, nos.
21, 22; in Smith, "The Sacrament of the Eucharist," 853–854.
[52] Cf. Nichols, *The Holy Eucharist*, 38.

The Eucharist as Sacrifice

"Reflect, O man, what sacrificial flesh you take in your hand! To what table you will approach. Remember that you, though dust and ashes, do receive the Body and Blood of Christ."[53] In his commentary on the Gospel of St. John Chrysostom uses an even stronger expression: "Not only ought we to see the Lord, but we ought to take him in our hands, eat him, set our teeth upon his flesh and most intimately unite ourselves with him."[54]

The sacrificing priest, Chrysostom reminds us, is Christ himself, and the Consecration takes place the moment the words of the institution are pronounced:

> It is not man who causes what is present to become the Body and Blood of Christ, but Christ himself, who was crucified for us. The priest is the representative when he pronounces those words, but the power and the grace are those of the Lord. "This is my Body," he says. This word changes the things that lie before us; and as that sentence "Increase and multiply," once spoken, extends through all time and gives to our nature the power to reproduce itself, even so the saying once uttered, does at every table in the churches from that time to the present day, and even till Christ's coming, make the sacrifice complete.[55]

The Theology of the Sacrifice of the Mass

Christ is present in the Church in many ways:[56] when people pray together, when the faithful perform works of mercy, when

---

[53] St. John Chrysostom, Quasten, *Patrology*, vol. 3, 480–481.
[54] Ibid., *Hom. 46 in Joh.* no. 3; cf. Quasten, *Patrology*, vol. 3, 480.
[55] St. John Chrysostom, *Hom. 1 de prodit. Iudae*, no. 6.
[56] Cf. Vatican II, *Sacrosanctum concilium* (Constitution on the Sacred Liturgy), no. 7.

the Church preaches and governs the people of God. Christ is present in the Church in a more sublime way, however, as she offers in his name the Sacrifice of the Mass. We have St. John Chrysostom's eloquent assurance that the Sacrifice of the Mass and the sacrifice of Calvary are one and the same sacrifice: "I want to go on to an amazing truth.... The oblation which priests now carry out is the same as that which Christ gave to his disciples. It is in no way inferior, for it is not men who are sanctifying the priests' oblation. Even as the words the Lord spoke are the same as those which the priest says, so too the oblation itself is identical."[57]

The *Catechism of the Catholic Church* summarizes this aspect of the eucharistic mystery: "The Mass is at the same time, and inseparably, the sacrificial memorial in which the sacrifice of the Cross is perpetuated, and the sacred banquet of communion with the Lord's Body and Blood."[58] The Mass does not just recall the sacrifice of Calvary; this sacrifice is made present anew. The Eucharist thus applies to the men and women of today the reconciliation won once for all by Christ for mankind of every age.

The Eucharist is the memorial of Christ's Passover, the making present and the sacramental offering of his unique sacrifice, in the liturgy of the Church, which is his Body. In all the Eucharistic prayers, we find after the words of institution a prayer called the *anamnesis*, or memorial.[59] Because it is the memorial of Christ's Passover, the Eucharist is also a sacrifice. "The sacrificial character of the Eucharist is manifested in the very words

---

[57] St. John Chrysostom, *In Epist. 2 ad Timoth. Homil.*, 2, 4; PG 62, 612.
[58] CCC, no. 1382.
[59] Cf. CCC, no. 1362.

of institution: "This is my Body, which is *given* for you" and "This cup which is *poured out* for you is the New Covenant in my Blood" (italics added). In the Eucharist Christ gives us the very Body he gave up for us on the Cross, the very Blood "he poured out for many for the forgiveness of sins."[60]

The sacrificial character of the Mass is shown also in the Eucharistic Prayer:

> *Look, we pray, upon the oblation of your Church*
> *and, recognizing the sacrificial Victim by whose death*
> *you willed to reconcile us to yourself,*
> *grant that we, who are nourished*
> *by the Body and Blood of your Son*
> *and filled with his Holy Spirit,*
> *may become one body, one spirit in Christ.*[61]

John Paul II drew attention to the fact that, despite this vigorous and clear language, the Eucharist is often not seen clearly as a sacrifice.[62] This is perhaps due in some cases to the fact that catechesis on the Mass fails to give adequate attention to its sacrificial dimension.

At the Last Supper Jesus not only gave his Flesh as food and his Blood as drink for the Apostles, but he gave it as *fruit* of the sacrifice to be offered on the morrow. "Every Eucharistic celebration renews this offering sacramentally. The words of consecration cause a mystical renewal of Jesus' sacrifice, that it may benefit humanity more broadly. To be sure, this offering is not made today as it was made in the beginning, with the shedding

---

[60] CCC, no. 1365.
[61] Roman Missal (2011).
[62] Cf. Bl. John Paul II, Encyclical Letter *Ecclesia de Eucharistia* (April 17, 2003), no. 10.

of Christ's Blood. It is made only through a sacramental rite. Still, it remains integral in its spiritual generosity. The entire personal suffering of the Savior, with the totality of his sacrifice, is expressed in the Eucharistic offering."[63]

Those who participate in the Mass are by that very fact engaged in a personal offering joined to that of Christ. In joining the offering of their lives to that of Christ, they should remember that "every eucharistic celebration is a celebration of Christ's great 'yes' to the Father—a 'yes' that victoriously overcomes the 'no's' inspired by sin"[64] (cf. 2 Cor. 1:19–20).

The Body of Christ offered in the Eucharist is not his Body in its earthly state, but a Body that attained its definitive state in the Resurrection. This is why the Mass is celebrated in joy, even though it renews the sorrowful mystery of Christ's Passion. This is why in offering our Mass with Christ, our sorrow is turned into joy; all our concerns take on a new perspective. They are no longer a heavy weight but a reason to be intimately united to Christ.

Since it is essentially identical with the sacrifice of the Cross, the Sacrifice of the Mass has an infinite value. In each Mass there is offered to God the Father an infinite act of adoration, thanksgiving, and reparation, quite independent of the specific dispositions of the people attending or of the celebrant. This is because Christ is at once the principal offerer and the Victim who offers himself. Thus there is no more perfect way of adoring God than by offering the Mass, in which his Son, Jesus Christ, is offered as the Victim and at the same time acts as High Priest.

---

[63] Theological-Historical Commission for the Great Jubilee Year 2000, *The Eucharist: Gift of Divine Life*, 17–18.
[64] Ibid., 18.

Msgr. Ronald Knox offers an interesting insight on this doctrine:

> The Sacrifice of the Mass is a mystery, and perhaps its relation to the sacrifice of the Cross is the most mysterious thing about it. Only this is certain, that the Victim who is there presented to the eternal Father for our sakes is the dying Christ; it is in that posture that he pleaded, and pleads, for our salvation, atoned and atones, for the sins of the world. We herald that death in the Holy Mass not as something which happened long ago, but as something which is mystically renewed whenever the words of consecration are uttered. From the moment of his death on Calvary until the time when he comes in glory, the dying Christ is continually at work, is continually available. It is in this posture of death that he pleads for us, when Mass is offered. And it is in this posture of death that he comes to you and me when he comes to us, the living Christ, in holy Communion.[65]

There is no more perfect way of thanking God for everything that he is and for his continual mercy toward us; there is nothing on earth more pleasing to God than the Sacrifice of the Altar. Each time the holy Mass is celebrated, reparation is made for all the sins of the world, because of the infinite dignity of the Priest and of the Victim. We have here the only perfect and adequate reparation, to which we must unite our own acts of sorrow. It is the only adequate sacrifice that we men and women can offer, and through it our daily occupations, our sorrows, and

---

[65] Ronald Knox, *Window in the Wall* (New York: Sheed and Ward, 1956), 97.

our joys can take on an infinite value. "The Holy Mass is really the heart and the centre of the Christian world."[66]

The Eucharist is also a sacrifice of praise and thanksgiving to the Father for all his benefits, for all that he has accomplished through creation, redemption, and sanctification.[67]

Eucharistic Re-presentation

Christ, who gave his Body and Blood separately to the Apostles at the Last Supper, was himself whole and entire at this ritual meal. The Christ whose Body and Blood is on the altar is whole and entire in heaven. The eucharistic Body and Blood at the Last Supper were the re-presentation of Christ, who would be broken on the Cross the following day, not of the Christ there at the head of the table. Similarly the eucharistic Body and Blood on our altars are the representation not of Christ who is in heaven, but of the Christ who was broken on Calvary.

The eucharistic sacrifice, then, is essentially re-presentation; it puts on the altar the Christ of Calvary, the same body that Mary beheld as she gazed on her dead Son hanging on the Cross. In the eucharistic sacrifice Christ is truly immolated, because the immolation of Christ on Calvary is brought home to us in a realistic manner.[68]

> The Last Supper, which anticipated the death of Jesus; the Eucharistic sacrifice, which re-enacts it; the biblical narratives which describe it; and even the prophecies and events of the Old Testament, which prefigured it, as well as the terrible vision itself on Calvary, are the various

---

[66] Bl. John Paul II, Homily, May 21, 1983.

[67] Cf. CCC, no. 1359–1361.

[68] Cf. Vonier, *A Key to the Doctrine of the Eucharist*, 287.

disclosures or appearances, the views within which the saving action performed by Christ toward the Father is made manifest and glorified. All these appearances are important; all are essential. It is not for us to argue which of these God might have dispensed with. They are all part of the manifestation of the sacrifice of the Cross, and all must be theologically recognized.[69]

By reason of their union with Christ through the Church, the faithful offer the sacrifice with him. They also offer themselves with him. They take part in the Mass, therefore, as those who offer and are offered. On the altar, Jesus Christ presents to God the Father the redeeming, meritorious sufferings he underwent on the Cross, and those of his brothers. If we live the Mass well it can transform our lives. "If we have in our souls the same sentiments and intentions as Christ on the Cross, we will make our whole life an endless act of atonement, an assiduous petition and a permanent sacrifice for the whole of mankind. God will grant you a supernatural instinct to purify all your actions, raising them to the order of grace and converting them into instruments of apostolate."[70]

The Oneness of the Sacrifice

The Lutheran objection to the Catholic doctrine on the eucharistic sacrifice is that the Catholic Church, by teaching the need of a second sacrifice, virtually denies the all-sufficiency of

---

[69] Robert Sokolowski, *Eucharistic Presence: A Study in the Theology of Disclosure* (Washington, DC: Catholic University of America Press, 1994), 62.

[70] St. Josemaría Escrivá, Letter, February 2, 1945, as quoted in Francis Fernandez, *In Conversation with God*, vol. 3, 320.

the sacrifice on Calvary. Catholics have always rejected this accusation and affirm that the Sacrifice of the Altar and the sacrifice of Calvary are one and the same. If the eucharistic sacrifice were in any way a natural sacrifice, it would be simply impossible to avoid the conclusion that there were two different sacrifices, but because the Christian sacrifice is *sacramental*, it may be repeated indefinitely, even though the content is immutable.

We know by faith, however, that the Mass is in fact a true sacrifice; it is "the true and unbloody sacrifice of the Cross."[71] The Last Supper is intimately united to the sacrifice of Calvary. It was at the Last Supper that Jesus instituted the sacrament through which his bloody sacrifice on Calvary would be made present in an unbloody fashion in the Mass.[72]

In his *Credo of the People of God*, Pope Paul VI affirms: "We believe that the Mass, celebrated by the priest representing the person of Christ by virtue of the power received through the Sacrament of Orders, and offered by him in the name of Christ and the members of the mystical body, is the sacrifice of Calvary rendered sacramentally present on our altars."[73]

The Mass refers us backward in time to the sacrifice of the Cross which has already taken place. The sacrifice of the Last Supper refers forward in time to the sacrifice that was about to take place. Furthermore the holy Sacrifice of the Mass was instituted at the Last Supper, not to perpetuate the Last Supper itself, but to perpetuate the sacrifice of Calvary.

In the Mass it is the twofold consecration and the transubstantiation of the bread and wine that alone constitute the essential act of sacrifice. The Council of Trent's decree on the

[71] Council of Trent, Decree on the Sacrifice of the Mass, ch. 1.
[72] Cf. Vatican II, *Sacrosanctum concilium*, no. 47.
[73] Paul VI, *Credo of the People of God*, June 30, 1968.

The Eucharist as Sacrifice

Mass states that in the Mass, "the victim is one and the same, the same person now offering by the ministry of priests, who then offered himself on the cross, the manner alone of offering being different."[74] The priest speaks in the person and in the power of Christ, and through him Christ speaks and offers the sacrifice.

> The deepest reason for the distinctive role of the priest in the Eucharist lies in the fact that only God can offer worthy sacrifice to God: the Christian God is so transcendent to the world, so holy, that no act of human religion is adequate in his presence. Only the incarnate Son of God can make the suitable offering and exchange. The priest must speak and act *in persona Christi*, because only Christ can act in the appropriate way in the presence of the Father; in what other name could the Church speak and act? The offering of the Son of God is not just mentioned or remembered in the Eucharist but expressed and actuated in the Son's own words. The community, in adoration and thanks, joins in this offering, but the offering is first there through the action of Christ, who uses the words and actions of the priest to re-enact his perfect offering sacramentally.[75]

The Entire Church Offers the Mass

The Church also offers it through the ministry of priests. This is a direct consequence of the fact that all the members of Christ's Church form one Body, of which he is the Head. As we

[74] Council of Trent, *Decree on the Sacrifice of the Mass*, ch. 2.
[75] Sokolowski, *Eucharistic Presence*, 18.

have already seen, the sacrament of Baptism leads to a real in-corporation into Christ and in him to a real brotherhood with one another. Since all members of the Church are branches of the one vine, they necessarily share in the life of the Head. Hence when Christ offers the Sacrifice of the Mass through the priest, he does not act alone, but all the members of the Church act with him. We have seen how this becomes a reality through the baptismal priesthood of the faithful.

The liturgical prayers recited during Mass make it quite clear that it is the whole Church that offers the sacrifice. And so we can understand correctly those words of St. Peter: "And like living stones be yourselves built into a spiritual house, to be a holy priesthood, to offer spiritual sacrifices acceptable to God through Jesus Christ.... But you are a chosen race a royal priest-hood, a holy nation, God's own people, that you may declare the wonderful deeds of him who called you out of darkness into his marvelous light" (1 Pet. 2:5, 9).

All the members of the Church form a holy and royal priest-hood because they are a purchased people, purchased with the Blood that the royal Victim shed and the kingly Priest offered and who by Baptism are raised to membership in his body and participation in his priesthood, and therefore taking their part with him in the continual offering of his sacrifice. Accordingly every Mass is pleasing to God because it is offered not only by the spotless High Priest, Jesus Christ, but also by the whole Church.

But although the sacrifice is offered by the whole Church, individual members of the Church do not have the same part in the offering with regard to its fruit. The priest naturally holds the first place, due to the dignity of his office and of his official position. Those who are present at a Mass, following its action

and prayers and uniting their intentions with the priest's, enter into its offering more intimately than those who are not
present.

As an expression of their participation in the Mass, the laity
can place all their intentions on the paten with the priest and
offer them to God so that all the aspects and activities of their
day—work, family life, social relations—become sanctified
through their union with the Sacrifice of the Mass.

Through Baptism we share in the priesthood of Christ and
in its exercise; so likewise we share in Christ's role as victim
in the Mass, as St. Paul outlines: "Now I rejoice in my sufferings for your sake and in my flesh I complete what is lacking in
Christ's sufferings for the sake of his body, that is the Church"
(Col. 1:24). Although Christ's sufferings were superabundant,
the Body must participate in the life of the Head, to share his
sufferings in order to share his glory. So we must bear our share
of sufferings with Christ. To live a fully Christian life necessarily involves some suffering and mortification, putting up generously with the little crosses and contradictions of each day. This
is how we "complete what is lacking" in the sufferings of Christ.

Hanging on the Cross, Christ looked down the ages, and
embracing in his outstretched arms all who were to be his
brethren, he offered them with himself, their sufferings with his
own, in full homage to his Father. If we join all our sufferings
to those of Christ they become true sacrifices, and thus we see
again how the Mass becomes the center of the Christian life.

In summary, holy Mass and the sacrifice of the Cross are
one and the same sacrifice, although they are separated in time.
What is made present once again in the Mass is our Lord's total
loving submission to his Father's will. This internal offering of
Christ is identical both in the Mass and on Calvary. It is the

same Priest, the same Victim, the same oblation and submission to the will of God the Father. The external manifestation of the Passion and death of Jesus goes on in the Mass through the sacramental separation, in an unbloody manner, of the Body and Blood of Christ.

In the Mass the priest is only the instrument of Christ, the eternal High Priest. Christ offers himself in every Mass, in the same way as he died on Calvary, although now he does so through the priest, who acts *in persona Christi*. Christ himself, in each Mass, offers himself up, which is expressed in the separate consecrations of the bread and wine. This is the essence of holy Mass.

Chapter 3

The Real Presence of Christ
in the Eucharist

Union with Christ

The great nineteenth-century German theologian Matthias
Josef Scheeben points out that

> the mystery of the Eucharist is ontologically joined to
> the mystery of the Incarnation, just as the mystery of the
> Incarnation is joined to the Trinity. The Incarnation is
> the presupposition and explanation of the Eucharist, just
> as the eternal generation from the bosom of the Father
> is the presupposition and explanation of the Incarna-
> tion, regarded as the stepping forth of God's Son into
> the world. These mysteries disclose a remarkable analogy
> in their relationships with one another. All three show
> us the same Son of God: the first in the bosom of his
> eternal Father, whence he receives his being; the second
> in the womb of the Virgin, through which he enters the
> world; the third in the heart of the Church where he

sojourns by an enduring, universal presence among men and unites himself to them.[76]

We see in the Eucharist an expression of the ineffable love of God for us, for he desires to unite himself to us in the closest possible manner. It is clear that he wants to treat us not as his servants but as his dearly loved children. The full significance of the mystery of the Eucharist is the real incorporation of men and women in Christ, so that they may partake of his life.

That Christ unites himself to us in the Eucharist in such a way as to form one body with us is the clear teaching of Sacred Scripture and the Fathers of the Church. The Fathers emphasize in the strongest terms that our union with Christ is not simply a moral union, but one that is real and physical. In the Eucharist our body is joined to the Body of the Logos, and so we become flesh of his Flesh. In Communion, Christ takes us to himself and transforms us; he unites us to himself as branches are united to the vine (cf. John 15:1–10). With him, our Head, we grow into one body; he sustains us with his life. So completely do we become one with Christ that we can say with all truth that we belong to the person of Christ and in a sense are Christ himself. As St. Leo the Great says: "Nothing else is aimed at in our partaking of the Body and Blood of Christ, than that we change into what we consume, and even bear in our spirit and flesh him in whom we have died, been buried, and have risen.[77]

We share in the glory the Son has received from the Father (cf. John 17:22); we are deified. Thus the Council of Trullo

---

[76] Matthias Josef Scheeben, *The Mysteries of Christianity* (St. Louis: B. Herder Book Co., 1946), 477–478.

[77] St. Leo the Great, *Sermon* 14, on the Passion of the Lord.

(A.D. 691) says: "God who is offered and distributed for the salvation of souls and bodies, deifies those who receive him."[78]

St. Cyril of Jerusalem is even more explicit: "When you partake of the Body and Blood of Christ you are made one body and one blood with him. Receiving his Flesh and his Blood into our members in this way, we become Christ-bearers. And so according to Blessed Peter, we are made partakers of the divine nature" (2 Pet. 1:4).[79]

In the context of the supernatural grace of divine sonship, the mystery of the Eucharist appears in its full beauty as the seal and crown of our union with God.

In the Eucharist God continues his divine life in us. Scheeben explains:

> On the analogy of natural bread, we tend to regard the Eucharist as a food that is worthy of the children of God and that serves to sustain and strengthen their divine life. But if this food unites us in a special way to Christ, it must do more than sustain the life of the children of God. It must provide a deeper basis for this dignity, and life, and bestow on them an essentially higher beauty than they would otherwise have had.[80]

By means of the Eucharist, then, we become the Body of the only-begotten Son of God, for he has not only taken his Flesh from our flesh, but has returned to us the Flesh he assumed. In the Eucharist we receive the life of God, for eucharistic

---

[78] The statutes of the Council of Trullo were not recognized by Rome, however, because of the anti-Roman bias of some of its canons.

[79] St. Cyril of Jerusalem *Catechetical Instruction*, lect. 4, no. 3.

[80] Scheeben, *The Mysteries of Christianity*, 492–493.

Communion has the function of nourishing the children of God. The idea of man's incorporation in Christ stands out as the distinguishing note in the significance of the Eucharist.[81]

The Real Presence

In promising the Eucharist Jesus said: "He who eats my flesh and drinks my blood has eternal life and I will raise him up on the last day.... For my flesh is food indeed, and my blood is drink indeed" (John 6:54, 55). As the hymn *Ave verum corpus* reminds us, the flesh offered at the Last Supper and immolated on the Cross was the same flesh Jesus received from his Mother, Mary. The word *flesh* suggests the living being in its entirety. To eat the Flesh of Christ is to eat Christ himself, because the gift of his Body involves the gift of his Person. Christ's Person becomes food, and this implies on his part the gift of his *entire* self.

The statement "I am the bread of life" (John 6:35, 48) stresses that Jesus not only gives the bread of eternal life, but that this bread is his very self.[82]

The Real Presence of the Body and Blood of Christ in the Eucharist, clearly enunciated in Jesus' words, has been received in the tradition of the Church as a truth of faith. It has been repeatedly asserted and commented on by the Fathers. This doctrine developed as a result of certain controversies, with the definitive voice being that of the Council of Trent.[83] The council affirmed not only the Real Presence of Christ's Body and Blood, but declared that the *entire* person of Christ — Body, Blood, soul, and divinity — is present from the *moment of*

---

[81] Cf. Scheeben, *The Mysteries of Christianity*, 494–496.

[82] Cf. *The Eucharist: Gift of Divine Life*, 68.

[83] Ibid., 77.

Consecration[84]: "The Eucharistic presence of Christ begins at the moment of the consecration and perdures as long as the Eucharistic species subsist. Christ is present whole and entire in each of the species and whole and entire in each of their parts, in such a way that the breaking of the bread does not divide Christ."[85]

Christ is uniquely present in the eucharistic species.[86] The Council of Trent "openly and sincerely professes that within the holy sacrament of the Eucharist, after the consecration of the bread and wine, our Lord Jesus Christ, true God and true man, is really, truly and substantially contained under these outward appearances."

- He is *really* present independent of the faith of the congregation; that is, it is not our faith that makes him present.

- He is *truly* present: Trent used this word against Zwingli, who taught that Christ was only present symbolically.

- He is *substantially* present: not merely is the power of Christ present (as Calvin taught), but Christ himself is present, God and man, after the Consecration.

In this way the Savior in his humanity is present not only at the right hand of the Father, according to his natural mode of existence, but also in the sacrament of the Eucharist, "by a mode of existence which we cannot express in words, but which, with a mind instructed by faith, we can conceive."[87] This means that Christ's presence in the sacrament will always remain a mystery.

---

[84] Ibid., 76.
[85] Cf. CCC, no. 1377.
[86] Cf. Vatican II, *Sacrosanctum concilium*, no. 47.
[87] Council of Trent, Decree on the Eucharist, ch. 1.

The Most Holy Eucharist

The Nature and Meaning
of Transubstantiation

The fact of the Real Presence in the Eucharist leads us logically to a consideration of the mystery of transubstantiation, through which the Real Presence is effected. Whenever a priest, in the name of Christ, pronounces the words of consecration, with the intention of doing what the Church does, the bread and wine are changed into the substance of Christ's Body and the substance of Christ's Blood. Christ's Body and Blood are produced by an act of divine power through the agency of the priest—as done by Christ himself at the Last Supper.[88]

The decrees of the Council of Trent present transubstantiation and the Real Presence as logically connected with each other:

> But since Christ our Redeemer declared that to be truly his own body which he offered under the form of bread, it has, therefore, always been a firm belief in the Church of God, and this holy council now declares it anew, that by the consecration of the bread and wine a change is brought about of the whole substance of bread into the substance of the Body of Christ our Lord, and of the whole substance of the wine into the substance of his Blood. This change the holy Catholic Church properly and appropriately calls *transubstantiation*.[89]

In other words it is only by such a *total* conversion of the substance of bread and wine into the substance of the Lord's Body and Blood that his words "This is my Body.... This is my

---

[88] Vonier, *A Key to the Doctrine of the Eucharist*, 314.
[89] Council of Trent, Decree on the Eucharist, ch. 4.

Blood" really mean what they say. "The *seeming* bread," says St. Cyril of Jerusalem, "is not bread, though sensible to the taste, but the Body of Christ; and the *seeming* wine is not wine though the taste will have it so, but the Blood of Christ."[90]

The theory of consubstantiation—that both the bread and Christ's Body are present simultaneously—was rejected by Trent. At the moment of consecration, the Body of Christ is not combined with natural bread, nor is it enclosed in the bread as in a container, but it replaces the substance of the bread while the accidents (color, taste, weight, and so forth) remain in existence and untouched. That the accidents of bread and wine continue to exist, even after the substances of bread and wine have been changed, is part of the miracle of transubstantiation.

Concomitance

As the Body and Blood of Christ are one and are not isolated from one other, so too in the sacrament of the Eucharist they are found together—by concomitance. When the priest says, "This is my body," Christ's Body is made present, but his Blood, soul, and divinity are also present. Similarly with the consecration of the wine: the Blood of Christ is made present, but so also are his Body, soul, and divinity.

Through concomitance, then, the whole glorious Christ is in the Eucharist. Referring to this, Trent speaks of "the natural connection through which the parts of the Lord Jesus, who is risen already from the dead, who dies no more, are linked together."[91] The Body is never without the Blood, and the Blood is never without the Body.[92]

[90] St. Cyril of Jerusalem, *Catechetical Instruction*, lect. 22, no. 1.
[91] Council of Trent, Decree on the Eucharist, ch. 3.
[92] Cf. Vonier, *A Key to the Doctrine of the Eucharist*, 329–331.

The Most Holy Eucharist

Since Christ is present in this sacrament of the Eucharist by transubstantiation, by the change of one substance into another, he is present after the manner of a substance. The Council of Trent says that Christ's divinity is present after the Consecration "on account of its admirable hypostatic union with body and soul." So when Christ, having consecrated the wine in the chalice, gave it to his disciples to drink, each of them received the whole Christ, although the quantity of wine consecrated had been divided.

Another consequence of this principle is that the Real Presence lasts as long as the substance of bread and wine would have remained if transubstantiation had not taken place, that is, as long as the accidents of bread and wine remain. If the appearances of bread and wine cease to be present, then the sacrament no longer exists, nor does the Real Presence.[93]

Our Own Transformation through the Eucharist

Christ is really present in the Eucharist whether or not we believe in him or are open to him. But this offering of himself has to be met by faith if a life-giving encounter is to result. Although we rightly emphasize the conversion of the bread and wine in the Eucharist, it is ultimately the conversion of human hearts that God desires. Thus, in addition to bringing about the transformation of bread and wine into the Body and Blood of Christ, the Holy Spirit also comes to bring about a transformation of the lives of those who receive the Body of Christ. In this way we become more part of the Church, more united to our community.[94]

---

[93] Cf. Smith, "The Sacrament of the Eucharist," 863–867.
[94] *One Bread, One Body*, no. 53.

The Real Presence of Christ in the Eucharist

When Jesus presented his teaching on the Eucharist in Capernaum, the unbelieving Jews denied his divinity, denied his origin from God the Father, and held him to be an ordinary son of man, a son of Joseph, and so they denied that he was the true bread from heaven. More and more the Savior insisted that he was the true bread and demanded that they believe it. He showed them that faith was necessary if they wished to be nourished on this life-giving bread. He pointed out that such faith was as much a gift from the Father as is the bread itself which the Father would give them in his Son.

Undeterred by the Jews' lack of faith, he went on to set before them the mystery of the bread from heaven. He stated that he intended to give himself as the bread of eternal life and that he would give us his Flesh and Blood for our nourishment. Through the medium of his flesh, we were to be united to his person, and through his person to the Father, so that we might have life from Christ, as he has life from the Father.

Christ unites himself to us in the Eucharist as the spiritual nourishment of our soul and of our whole being. The Flesh of Christ is to nourish us, not as mere material flesh with the view of the life of the flesh, but as flesh steeped in the Spirit of God, building us up into a life that is at once divine and spiritual. By partaking of Christ's Flesh we are illuminated by the light of eternal truth. When we partake of the Eucharist, it nourishes us by conferring upon us the spark of divine life. In the Eucharist the Son unites himself to us in the most perfect way and gives us the power to become children of God.[95]

---

[95] Cf. Scheeben, *The Mysteries of Christianity*, 523–527.

Chapter 4

Priesthood

Christ's Eternal Priesthood

Jesus Christ, since he lives eternally, has an eternal priesthood. He took our nature in the womb of the Blessed Virgin Mary to be a mediator between God and man (cf. 1 Tim. 2:5), and after offering the sacrifice of his life, he is seated at the right hand of the Father, where "he lives always to intercede for us" (Heb. 7:25). With his unceasing priestly mediation in heaven he obtains pardon for our sins, which he expiated once and for all with his death on Calvary, and brings about the outpouring of the Holy Spirit, fruit of the Cross (cf. John 20:21–23).

Being made High Priest forever, Jesus offered himself to the Father as a most pleasing victim of infinite value. He willed to be simultaneously the Priest, the Victim, and the altar.[96] On Calvary, Jesus the High Priest is made a most acceptable offering of praise and thanksgiving to God and of propitiation for our sins.

---

[96] Cf. Roman Missal, Easter Preface 5.

At the same time Jesus continues exercising his priesthood on earth, through the members of his Mystical Body, partly through the common priesthood received in Baptism and partly through the ministerial priesthood, which confers on priests the faculty of acting *in persona Christi* principally in the celebration of holy Mass. Thanks to this ineffable mystery, we can receive our Lord in the Eucharist and can sanctify all human activities, uniting them to the offering of his sacrifice.

Christ is a priest indeed, not for himself but for us. It is in the name of the whole human race that he offers prayer and acts of homage to his eternal Father. He is also a victim, but a victim for us, because he substitutes himself for guilty mankind. St. Paul's exhortation, "Have this in mind among yourselves, which was in Christ Jesus," requires all Christians to reproduce in themselves the same sentiments that Christ had when he was offering himself in sacrifice—sentiments of humility, adoration, praise, and thanksgiving to his Father. We also ought to cultivate a spirit of self-denial in the ordinary circumstances of our lives, in expiation for our sins.[97]

Ministerial Priesthood

"You are a priest forever after the order of Melchizedek" (Ps. 110:4). The letter to the Hebrews gives us a precise definition of priesthood when it tells us that "every high priest chosen from among men is appointed to act on behalf of men in relation to God, to offer gifts and sacrifices for our sins" (Heb. 5:1). And so the priest, who is a mediator between God and men, is intimately connected with the sacrifice he offers; this is the principal act of worship whereby man adores his Creator.

---

[97] Cf. Pius XII, *Mediator Dei*, no. 85.

Priesthood

At the Last Supper, before his Passion, Jesus wanted to leave his beloved Spouse, the Church, a living sacrifice—a memorial of the sacrifice of his Body and Blood under the species of bread and wine. The Council of Trent tells us: "And since the sacrifice and the priesthood are so united by divine ordination that they have existed in every law, it must also be confessed that there is in that Church a new, visible and external priesthood into which the old has been translated."[98]

St. John Chrysostom points out:

> For the office of the priesthood is executed on earth, yet it ranks among things that are heavenly, and with good reason. For it was neither an angel nor archangel nor any other created power, but the Paraclete himself who established that ministry, and commanded that men yet abiding in the flesh should imitate the function of angels. Wherefore it behooves the priest to be as pure as if he stood in heaven itself amidst those powers.... For when you beheld the Lord immolated and lying on the altar, and the priest standing over the sacrifice and praying, and all the people purpled by that precious blood, do you imagine that you are still on earth amongst men, and not rather rapt up to heaven; and casting away all worldly thoughts from your mind, do you not contemplate with a clean heart and pure mind the things of heaven?[99]

The priest takes the place of Christ on earth: he has received Christ's power to forgive sins; he teaches men the way to

---

[98] Council of Trent, Decree on the Mass, ch. 1.
[99] St. John Chrysostom, *On Priesthood*, bk. 3, no. 4.

heaven; above all he lends his voice, his hands and his body to Christ at the most sublime moment of the Mass.[100]

The cooperation of the Church in the sacrifice is expressed above all through the ministry of the priest. He is only a minister, in the sense that he is at the service of Christ. In saying, "This is my Body" and "This is the chalice of my Blood," he renders present the Body and Blood of Christ, but he can pronounce these words only by virtue of the power he has received through priestly Ordination. This power of offering the eucharistic sacrifice in the name of Christ belongs exclusively to the priest, and not to any layperson, and it has been conferred upon him by the authority of the Church. In exercising this power in the name of the Church, he also exercises it in the name of Christ.

The offering of the eucharistic sacrifice, then, requires a specific commitment on the part of the ministerial priesthood. "The ministerial priest, by the sacred power which he has, forms and rules the priestly people; in the person of Christ he effects the Eucharistic sacrifice and offers it to God in the name of all the people."[101] The priest represents the people because he represents the person of our Lord Jesus Christ as head of all the members of the Mystical Body and he, the priest, offers himself for these members.[102]

Thus the redemptive work of Christ in the Sacrifice of the Mass is made present among men and women and encompasses the whole mystery of our salvation. "Holy Mass is the *centre* and

---

[100] Cf. St. Josemaría Escrivá, homily "A Priest Forever" (April 13, 1973), in *In Love with the Church* (London: Scepter 1989), no. 39.

[101] Vatican II, *Lumen gentium*, no. 10.

[102] Cf. Pius XII, *Mediator Dei*, no. 68.

the *root* of the spiritual life of the Christian,"[103] and of the entire Church, because it makes present to us the sacrifice of the Cross in all its integrity.

The sacredness of the Mass comes from the fact that it was a sacred rite through which Christ celebrated sacramentally the mystery of his Passion and Resurrection at the Last Supper. The words of the priest echo the words and action of Holy Thursday. As John Paul II points out: "The priest offers the Holy Sacrifice *in persona Christi:* this means more than offering 'in the name of' or 'in the place of' Christ. *'In persona'* means in specific sacramental identification with 'the eternal High Priest,' who is the Author and principal Subject of this Sacrifice of his, a sacrifice in which, in truth, nobody can take his place."[104]

In virtue of the powers received at Ordination, the priest performs at Mass a true sacrificial act that brings creation back to God. The priesthood is a great gift which Christ has given to his Church. The priest is

> a direct and daily instrument of the saving grace which Christ has won for us. If you grasp this, if you mediate on it in the active silence of prayer, how could you ever think of the priesthood in terms of renunciation? It is a gain, an incalculable gain. Our Mother Mary, the holiest of creatures—only God is holier—brought Jesus Christ into the world just once; priests bring him on earth, to our soul and body, every day. Christ comes to be our food, to give us life, to be, even now, a pledge of future glory.[105]

---

[103] St. Josemaría Escrivá, *Christ Is Passing By,* no. 87.

[104] Bl. John Paul II, Letter *Dominicae Cenae* (February 24, 1980), no. 8.

[105] St. Josemaría Escrivá, "A Priest Forever," no. 39.

The Most Holy Eucharist

What the faithful require of their priests is that they be always exemplary; that they be men of prayer; that they celebrate Mass lovingly; that they visit the sick; that they administer the sacraments with piety, especially the sacrament of Reconciliation; that they communicate the teaching of Jesus Christ and the Church with conviction; that they always be accessible and available to give advice. This priestly profile comes not only from formation and the working of grace, but also as a consequence of the prayers of the faithful. As St. Josemaría says: "Pray for the priests of today, and for those who are to come, that they may really love their fellowmen, every day more and without distinction, and that they may know also how to make themselves loved by them."[106]

Pope John Paul II, in his 1988 *Holy Thursday Letter to Priests*, says:

> As we celebrate the Eucharist at so many altars throughout the world, let us give thanks to the Eternal Priest for the gift which he has bestowed on us in the Sacrament of the Holy Orders. And in this thanksgiving may there be heard the words which the evangelist puts on Mary's lips on the occasion of her visit to her cousin Elizabeth: "the Almighty has done great things for me and holy is his name" (Lk 1:49). Let us also give thanks to Mary for the indescribable gift of the priesthood, whereby we are able to serve in the Church every human being. May gratitude also awaken our zeal!
>
> Let us unceasingly give thanks for this. Let us give thanks with the whole of our lives. Let us give thanks

---

[106] St. Josemaría Escrivá, *The Forge* (London: Scepter, 1988), no. 964.

with all our strength. Let us give thanks together with Mary, the Mother of Priests. "How can I repay the Lord for his goodness to me? The cup of salvation I will raise. I will call on the Lord's name" (Ps. 116:12–13).[107]

Through Ordination, priests are united in a "singular and exceptional way to the Eucharist." Priests derive from it and exist for it. Addressing priests John Paul II says: "Our Eucharistic worship both in the celebration of Mass, and in our devotion to the Blessed Sacrament, is like a life-giving current that links our ministerial or hierarchical priesthood to the common priesthood of the faithful, and presents it in its vertical dimension and with its central value. The priest fulfills his principal mission and is manifested in all his fullness when he celebrates the Eucharist.[108]

It is surely quite logical that if priests have a deep devotion to the Eucharist, the Church and the world[109] will benefit immensely. If the faithful see their priests spend time before the tabernacle while doing their meditation, or praying the Liturgy of the Hours, or paying a visit to the Blessed Sacrament, they will be encouraged to visit their church more frequently themselves.

The Priesthood of the Laity

The whole Church participates in the redemptive mission of Christ the Priest for it "is entrusted to all the members of the People of God, who through the sacraments of initiation have been made sharers in the priesthood of Christ, to offer to God a

[107] Bl. John Paul II, Holy Thursday Letter to Priests, 1988.
[108] Ibid.
[109] Bl. John Paul II, *Dominicae Cenae*, no. 3.

spiritual sacrifice and bear witness to Christ before men."[110] In *Christifideles laici*, John Paul II explains how laypeople participate in the mission of Christ the Priest:

> As a consequence of the grace and dignity of Baptism, the lay faithful participate, for their part, in the three-fold mission of Christ as Priest, Prophet and King. They are sharers in the *priestly mission* for which Christ offered himself on the Cross and continues to be offered in the celebration of the Eucharist for the glory of God and the salvation of humanity. Incorporated in Jesus Christ, the baptized are united to him and to his sacrifice in the offering they make of themselves and their daily activities (cf. Rom 12:1, 2). Speaking of the lay faithful, Vatican II says: "For their work, prayers and apostolic endeavors, their ordinary married and family life, their daily labor, their mental and physical relaxation, if carried out in the Spirit, and even the hardships of life if patiently borne — all of these become spiritual sacrifices acceptable to God through Jesus Christ (cf. 1 Pet 2:5). During the celebration of the Eucharist, these sacrifices are most lovingly offered to the Father along with the Lord's Body. Thus as worshippers whose every deed is holy, the lay faithful consecrate the world itself to God" (*Lumen gentium*, no. 34).[111]

All the lay faithful participate in Christ's priesthood, although in a manner different from that of priests. The faithful

---

[110] Alvaro del Portillo, *On Priesthood* (Chicago: Scepter, 1974), 20.

[111] Bl. John Paul II, Apostolic Exhortation *Christifideles laici* (December 30, 1988), 14.

should attend Mass with a deep spirit of reverence and should participate in the responses, prayers, and gestures. They can then offer to God, with the Sacrifice of the Mass, all their sufferings and disappointments, the demands of their work, their family and social responsibilities, and other concerns to be united with the sacrifice of Christ.

With a truly priestly soul they should strive to sanctify the world through the perfect exercise of their secular activities, seeking in everything the glory of God. In this way, offering their lives and their work through the Mass, they can make daily reparation for the sins of the world.

A priestly soul is proper to all Catholics since, through Baptism, "all of us have been made priests of our lives.... Everything that we do can be an expression of our obedience to God's will."[112] So in our morning offering we offer our day, our heart, and our work to the Lord.

Acting with a priestly soul requires frequently overcoming ourselves, going beyond the normal run of duty at times. It means doing battle with aspects of our character that need to be toned down or developed, because we see this is appropriate for the good of our neighbor. In this way we will make spiritual progress every day.

---

[112] St. Josemaría Escrivá, *Christ Is Passing By*, no. 96.

Chapter 5

The Incarnation, the Eucharist, and Freedom

The Incarnation and the Eucharist

What makes the eating and drinking of the Body and Blood of Christ possible is the primordial mystery of the Incarnation. In virtue of the Incarnation, Jesus defines himself as eucharistic bread: "I am the bread of life" (John 6:35); the divine person of Christ is itself the nourishment given to humanity for a new life. Christ is the bread of life only through the Body and Blood that belong to him. Still, it remains true that it is the Son of God as a person who offers himself as food and drink.

The Eucharist secures for humanity what was once accomplished through the work of redemption. This sacrament has a unique excellence because it contains not only the sacramental grace, but the very author of grace himself.

There is a close connection between the doctrine of the Eucharist and the Incarnation. The mystery of God's taking on a human nature is reproduced in the Eucharist, and therefore the Eucharist enables us to grasp more concretely the meaning and value of the Incarnation. Robert Sokolowski offers an insightful

explanation of the sacramentality of the Eucharist and its connection with the Incarnation:

> The choice of bread and wine as the embodiment of the
> memorial of our Redemption furnishes an image of the
> Incarnation: as the Son took on human flesh and assumed
> it into the life of God, so the common material elements
> of bread and wine become transformed into signs and
> vehicles of that same life. And the fact that bread and
> wine are food confirms the sacrament's involvement in
> the distribution of life. It is in being fed that our life is
> sustained. The Eucharist is the most material of all the
> sacraments; it establishes a sacramentality in eating. The
> bread and wine given to us to be consumed are palpable
> images of the life that is conveyed to us in and through
> the Church.[113]

This bond between the Eucharist and the Incarnation is
shown especially in the Gospel of St. John. The prologue tells
us that "the Word became flesh" (1:14), and in his discourse
in Capernaum, Jesus proclaims, "The bread that I shall give is
my flesh for the life of the world" (6:51). The use of the word
flesh to indicate both the Incarnation and the Eucharist is pregnant with meaning. Because Christ came on earth to give his
life for the world, the Incarnation finds its completion in the
Eucharist.

Jesus insists on this involvement of the divine person of the
Son in the eucharistic meal when he asserts: "For the bread of
God is that which comes down from heaven, and gives life to
the world" (John 6:33). The divine gift of the bread coincides

---

[113] Sokolowski, *Eucharistic Presence*, 37.

The Incarnation, the Eucharist, and Freedom

with the gift of the Incarnation. In the Consecration, the Son comes down from heaven and, in the eucharistic meal, gives life to the world. In this fashion, the Eucharist never ceases to renew the Incarnation.

In the Eucharist Jesus involves not only his Body and Blood, but his whole self. Thus, the eucharistic meal consists in his communicating his own life to us. It is a matter of communicating the divine life itself, the life possessed by the Son and placed at the disposition of all who are destined to share his Sonship. This is all contained in the declaration: "He who eats my flesh and drinks my blood has eternal life" (John 6:54).

The entire life of grace is the communication of this eternal life of the Son. But the communication occurs *par excellence* in the Eucharist. The act of eating and drinking represents a deeper penetration of Christ's life into the interior of the individual, a more complete assimilation of one's personal life to the higher life of the incarnate Son.[114] In the Blessed Eucharist our Lord gives to each one who receives him the very same life of grace that he brought into the world through the Incarnation.[115] "God has a Face. God has a name. In Christ, God was made flesh and gave himself to us in the mystery of the Most Holy Eucharist. The Word is Flesh. It is given to us under the appearances of bread and thus truly becomes the Bread on which we live. We live on Truth. This Truth is a Person: he speaks to us and we speak to him.[116]

Ronald Knox gives us another incisive perspective on the relationship between the Eucharist and the Incarnation:

114 Cf. *The Eucharist: Gift of Divine Life*, 15.
115 St. Thomas Aquinas, *Summa Theologica*, III, Q. 79, art. 3.
116 Benedict XVI, Homily, December 10, 2006.

The Most Holy Eucharist

In the Blessed Sacrament we have more than a continuation of what happened on Maundy Thursday, more than a continuation of what happened on Good Friday: it is a continuation of our Lord's whole life.... To be amongst us men, to make us, through his participation in our nature, participators in his, to bring heaven down to earth, Emmanuel, God with us—that is already something. And it is that divine condescension which is manifested to us in the thirty years of our Lord's hidden life, and most characteristically in the manger at Bethlehem.[117]

The Eucharist and Faith

The acclamation "The mystery of faith," said after the Consecration, is a reminder to us that a miracle has taken place on the altar, that the bread and wine have been changed into the Body and Blood of Christ. Only faith can make us assent to a miracle that totally transcends our capacity to grasp the infinite designs of God. Faith in the Eucharist is at the very core of our relationship with God. It is what Jesus asked for at Capernaum, but most of his disciples abandoned him when he asked them to accept that he would give his Body and Blood as food for their souls (cf. John 6:52–56).

We recall the incident when the woman with the issue of blood was cured by touching the hem of Jesus' garment and whose faith he praised (cf. Matt. 9:20–22). But in Communion we not only touch his garment but receive him totally, Body, Blood, soul, and divinity.

[117] Ronald Knox, *Heaven and Charing Cross* (London: Burns and Oates, 1935), 83–84.

The Incarnation, the Eucharist, and Freedom

After the Resurrection, when Thomas the Apostle confessed his faith in the risen Christ after touching the marks of the nails in his hands, Jesus gave Thomas a gentle rebuke: "Have you believed because you have seen me? Blessed are those who have not seen and yet have believed" (John 20:29).

Here Christ is again asking for total faith in the Eucharist. We are not to ask for more evidence about the eucharistic presence of Christ, nor are we allowed to accept it with a diluted faith. Catholic faith is eucharistic faith. If people have a sound faith in the Eucharist it will reflect itself in a real commitment to the other mysteries of the Faith. On the other hand, if Eucharistic faith is shallow, it will result in an anemic grasp of what we should believe. The Eucharist is the sum and summary of our faith: "Our way of thinking is attuned to the Eucharist, and the Eucharist in turn confirms our way of thinking."[118]

The Eucharist and Hope

The great hope that our lives will achieve their God-given plan comes from the words of Christ at Capernaum: "He who eats my flesh and drinks my blood has eternal life and I will raise him up on the last day" (John 6:54). The gift of the eucharistic Flesh and Blood penetrates the soul and guarantees the resurrection that will take place at the end of the world.

St. Paul has a slightly different perspective: "For as often as you eat this bread and drink the cup, you proclaim the Lord's death until he comes" (1 Cor. 11:26).

St. Ignatius of Antioch, writing to the church at Ephesus, tells us, as we have already seen, that "the Eucharist is the

---

[118] St. Irenaeus, *Adversus Haereses*, bk. 4, ch. 18, no. 5; cf. CCC, no. 1327.

medicine of immortality, the antidote for death, for living forever in the Eucharistic Christ."[119]

The Eucharist and Charity

During the Last Supper, Jesus spoke to his disciples about a "new commandment" he was giving them—"that you love one another as I have loved you" (John 13:34). The measure of their love for one another was, then, "as I have loved you." This was a very high standard. How could they measure up to it? Christ's response was to institute the Eucharist that very evening so that his disciples, and all his followers, would have the spiritual energy to give themselves without reserve, in response to Christ's infinite love for them. By nourishing ourselves with the Body and Blood of Christ we become united in a special way to our eucharistic Lord, and this makes it easier for us to practice charity at home, at work, and among our friends.

Christ, as St. John says, loved the Apostles "to the end" (13:1): "Greater love no man has than the man who lays down his life for his friends" (John 15:13). In saying this, Jesus wanted to make clear that his death on the Cross would be the supreme expression of his love. Because of the interrelationship of these events, it is easy for us to understand how the Eucharist is the ultimate expression of Christ's love for us.

Effects of the Mass

By his sacrifice on the Cross, Christ redeemed the whole human race. The grace through which the sinner's heart is converted to God and obtains forgiveness for guilt comes from his Passion. Likewise the satisfaction for the penalties due to sin

[119] St. Ignatius of Antioch, Letter to the Ephesians, 20.

springs from the same source. The merits of this sacrifice are infinite, immense; they have no limit; they extend to the whole of mankind, of every time and of every place.[120]

The Holy Sacrifice of the Mass possesses an infinitely effective value not only as praise, thanksgiving, and impetration, but also as propitiation. In every Mass we have access to the boundless redemptive power of the sacrifice of the Cross for the salvation of the entire world, for "as often as the sacrifice of the Cross is celebrated on the altar the work of our redemption is carried out."[121]

Holy Mass brings about pardon for venial sins. This is not the case with mortal sins, however. The sacrament of Penance is necessary for salvation for all those who have fallen into mortal sin after Baptism. So the propitiatory effectiveness of the Holy Sacrifice of the Mass does not consist in granting pardon from mortal sins but in directing sinners toward the sacrament of Penance, by moving their hearts to repentance through actual graces and, as a consequence, to prepare their souls for an encounter with Christ in the Eucharist.

Every Mass has an infinite value, even when the priest offering it has nobody but his server to accompany him. "From such a Mass an abundant treasure of special salutary graces enriches the celebrant, the faithful, the whole Church, and the entire world ... graces which are not imparted in the same abundance by the mere reception of Holy Communion."[122]

To the offering of the Church are united not only the intentions of the members here on earth, but also those who have already reached the glory of heaven, including the Blessed Virgin

[120] Cf. Pius XII, *Mediator Dei*, no. 94.
[121] Vatican II, *Lumen gentium*, no. 3.
[122] Paul VI, *Mysterium Fidei*, no. 32.

and all the saints. The Mass is also offered for the faithful departed who have died in Christ but who are not yet purified, so that they may be able to enter into the light and peace of Christ.

The Eucharistic Sacrifice and the Ordinary Life of the Catholic

The ends of the Mass are achieved in different ways and to a different extent. The ends that refer directly to God—namely, adoration, praise, and thanksgiving—are always produced infallibly and with all their infinite value, independently of our collaboration. This is true even when the Mass is celebrated without the presence of a single member of the faithful. God our Lord is praised infinitely every time the eucharistic sacrifice is celebrated and thanksgiving is offered up. This oblation, says St. Thomas, pleases God more than all the sins of the world offend him,[123] since Christ himself is the actual Priest who offers, as well as being the actual Victim who is offered in every Mass.

The other ends of the eucharistic sacrifice (propitiation and petition) which are for our benefit and are called the fruits of the Mass, however, do not in fact always achieve the fullness of which they are capable. These fruits—of reconciliation with God and of obtaining our petitions from him—could also be of infinite value. They too rest on the merits of Christ. We never actually receive these fruits to that perfect degree, however, since they are applied to us according to our personal dispositions. The more ardently and intently we take part in the Holy Sacrifice of the Altar, the greater the fruits of propitiation and petition we will receive. Christ's own prayer multiplies the

---

[123] Cf. St. Thomas Aquinas, *Summa Theologica*, III, Q. 8, art. 2.

value of our prayer to the extent that we unite our petitions and atonement to his in the Mass.

The Eucharist and Freedom

In the crucified and risen Christ shines forth the truth of the free gift with which Jesus, "having loved his own who were in the world, loved them to the end" (John 13:1). The Eucharist is the sacrament of this love. We should also remember that in the twentieth century, as during the first age of the Church, the Eucharist has been the bread, the Viaticum, of courage and martyrdom.[124]

The Church's eucharistic liturgy recalls the gift of the freedom with which Christ has set us free: "When the time had come to give his life for our liberation, he took bread...."[125]; "For when the hour had come for him to be glorified by you, Father most Holy, having loved his own who were in the world, he loved them to the end."[126] Jesus loves to the end, for only love can liberate. He brings the Passover to fulfillment with his redeeming death and his Resurrection, according to the words of St. Paul: "Christ, our Paschal lamb, has been sacrificed" (1 Cor. 5:7). In the gift of his Body and the outpouring of his Blood, Christ brings our liberation and redemption from sin; in the sacrifice of the New Covenant he expresses the fullness of our liberation and our salvation with the gift of the Spirit, and he summons us to the eternal Passover in his Kingdom.[127]

St. Irenaeus of Lyons presents the Eucharist from the standpoint of freedom. As a gift from the Lord, the Eucharist is an

---

[124] Cf. *The Eucharist and Freedom*, no. 9.

[125] Eucharistic Prayer of Reconciliation B.

[126] Eucharistic Prayer 4.

[127] Cf. *The Eucharist and Freedom*, no. 13.

offering of people who are free.[128] Even in the midst of persecutions, the first Christian communities understood and bore witness to the fact that the eucharistic celebration was the source of a great impetus to mutual charity.[129] Christian freedom begins by acknowledging our need for forgiveness. This is the only way to come to an authentic Christian transformation. The greatness of God and human finiteness seem to meet in the contemplation of the eucharistic mystery.

Before the Blessed Sacrament, contemplation of the mystery makes possible an intimate encounter with Christ, away from the bustle and superficiality that surround us. In modern times the dimension of mystery has been lost to a great extent. Because of the constant barrage of sound and visual images that assail us today, many, and especially young people, are in danger of losing the capacity to reflect—a condition exacerbated by the accelerated pace and activism of modern living. Hence there is a real need for reflection in the silence of prayer so that the soul can wonder at the deep truths of the Faith, especially the mystery of the Real Presence, and learn to adore. This is the great antidote to the superficiality that characterizes so much of human activity and discourse today. Only in such contemplation can we experience that true freedom which responds to God's love. By reflecting on the Eucharist we recognize that desires based on human freedom alone cannot by themselves reach fulfillment in this world. The deepest aspirations of the human heart will be satisfied only in a transcendent future.

Pope Benedict XVI sums up the relationship between the Eucharist and freedom as follows:

---

[128] Cf. St. Irenaeus, *Adversus Haereses*, bk. 4, ch. 18, nos. 1–2.
[129] Cf. *The Eucharist and Freedom*, no. 15.

The Incarnation, the Eucharist, and Freedom

The Eucharist ... is the real expression of that unconditional offering of Jesus for all, even for those who betrayed him. It was the offering of his Body and Blood for the life of mankind and for the forgiveness of sins. His Blood, a sign of life, was given to us by God as a covenant, so that we might apply the force of his life wherever death reigns due to our sins, and thus destroy it. Christ's Body broken and his Blood outpoured — the surrender of his freedom — became through these Eucharistic signs the new source of mankind's redeemed freedom. In Christ, we have the promise of definitive redemption and the certain hope of future blessings. Through Christ we know that we are not walking towards the abyss, the silence of nothingness, or death, but are rather pilgrims on the way to a promised land, on the way to him who is our end and our beginning.[130]

[130] Benedict XVI, Homily to Seminarians at World Youth Day, Madrid, August 20, 2011.

Chapter 6

Devotion at Mass and Holy Communion

Keeping the Lord's Day Holy

Sunday, as the commemoration of the Resurrection, should be a day of joy for individuals and families. This was the reaction of the Apostles when Christ appeared to them on Easter evening: "They disbelieved for joy" (Luke 24:41); "Then the disciples were glad when they saw the Lord" (John 20:20); "You will be sorrowful but your sorrow will be turned into joy" (John 16:20). Thus, to discover the full meaning of Sunday, we must rediscover this aspect of the life of faith. Joy should be a characteristic of every day of the week for us as children of God, but this should be especially so on Sundays as the day of the Risen Lord.[131]

Sunday is also a day of rest, which allows us to turn our hearts to God in a special way, allowing material cares to give way to spiritual values.

---

[131] Cf. Bl. John Paul II, Apostolic Letter *Dies Domini* (On Keeping the Lord's Day Holy), May 31, 1998, no. 57.

The Most Holy Eucharist

In his letter *Dies Domini*, John Paul II presented again the reasons Sunday should be observed with special reverence by Catholics. He said that the Lord's Day, as Sunday was called from apostolic times, was always given special attention in the history of the Church because of its close connection with Christ's victory over sin and death. It also recalls the last day, when he will come in glory (cf. Acts 1:11), and all things will be made new (cf. Rev. 21:5). It reflects the astonishment that came over the women who, having seen the crucifixion of Christ, found his tomb empty. It is an invitation to relive in some way the experience of the two disciples on the road to Emmaus, who felt their hearts "burning within them" as the Risen One walked with them on the road. The Resurrection of Jesus is the fundamental event upon which the Christian faith rests. Thus, in commemorating the day of Christ's Resurrection, not just once a year but every Sunday, the Church seeks to remind us of the one who is key to history and of our final destination.

John Paul II asked Christians to rediscover with new intensity the meaning of Sunday at the beginning of the third millennium. Changes in socioeconomic conditions have led to profound changes in social behavior and the character of Sunday. The concept of the "weekend" has become more widespread, and while that has many positive aspects, Sunday loses its fundamental meaning and becomes merely part of the weekend, rather than a day on which to celebrate. John Paul II asked Christians to avoid any confusion between the celebration of Sunday, which should be a way of keeping the Lord's Day holy, and the weekend, understood as a time of simple rest and relaxation.[132] "In the minds of many of the faithful, not only the

[132] Cf. *Dies Domini*, no. 4.

sense of the centrality of the Eucharist, but even the sense of duty to give thanks to the Lord and to pray to him with others in the community of the Church, seems to be diminishing."[133]

Because of this, John Paul II felt that it was necessary to recover the deep doctrinal foundations underlying the Church's precept of Sunday observance. As Vatican II reminds us, "Christian believers should come together, in order to commemorate the suffering, Resurrection and glory of the Lord Jesus, by hearing God's word and sharing the Eucharist, and to give thanks to God."[134]

John Paul II affirmed that Sunday should be arranged in such a way that it "allows people to take part in the Eucharist, refraining from work and activities which are incompatible with the sanctification of the Lord's Day, with its characteristic joy and necessary rest for spirit and body."[135]

Sunday is the day at the very heart of the Christian life, the day when Christians "open wide the door to Christ."[136] John Paul II asked all to rediscover Sunday: "Do not be afraid to give your time to Christ."[137] He said that time given to Christ is never lost, but is rather time gained.

John Paul II described different aspects of the Sunday duty. Looking back to the Old Testament, he saw it as a celebration of creation, in that God blessed the seventh day and made it holy (cf. Gen. 2:31). As the day on which man is at peace with God, with himself, and with others, Sunday allows us to look anew upon the wonders of nature and be caught up in that

[133] Ibid., no. 5.
[134] Vatican II, *Sacrosanctum concilium*, no. 106.
[135] *Dies Domini*, no. 67. Cf also CIC, 1247.
[136] John Paul II, Homily, October 22, 1978.
[137] *Dies Domini*, no. 7.

marvelous and mysterious harmony that, in the words of St. Ambrose, weds the many elements of the cosmos in a "bond of communion and peace" by "an inviolable law of concord and love."[138] Observing Sunday helps us to remember that the wonders of God should be acknowledged.

Sunday is the day on which Catholics observe the third commandment, "Remember to keep holy the Sabbath day." Because Jesus rose from the dead "on the first day after the Sabbath" (Mark 16:2, 9; Luke 24:1; John 20:1), Sunday gradually became the first day of the week for Christ's followers, and the distinction between Sunday and the Jewish Sabbath grew ever stronger in the mind of the Church.

Sunday is also the day that summons Christians to remember the salvation given us in Baptism. It is the day that tells us about life without end and renews hope of achieving eternal life.

For all these reasons Sunday is the day when our faith is renewed, especially when we make our profession of faith at Mass.

In 2003, John Paul II returned to this theme in his Apostolic Exhortation *Ecclesia in Europa*:

> Sunday should be sanctified by sharing in the Eucharist and by rest enriched with Christian joy and fellowship. It needs to be celebrated at the heart of all worship, an unceasing prefigurement of unending life, which reinvigorates hope and encourages us on our journey. There should be no fear, then, of *defending the Lord's Day against every attack and making every effort to ensure that* in the organization of labor *it is safeguarded*, so that it can be a day meant for man, to benefit all society. Indeed, were Sunday deprived of its original meaning and it were no

---

[138] *Dies Domini*, no. 67.

longer possible to make suitable time for prayer, rest, fellowship and joy, the result could very well be that "people stay locked within a horizon so limited that they can no longer see 'the heavens'. Hence, though ready to celebrate, they are really incapable of doing so" (*Dies Domini*, 4). And without the dimension of celebration, hope would have no home in which to dwell.[139]

The Eucharistic Assembly

On the basis of apostolic tradition, the Church has established a grave obligation to attend Mass on Sundays. On this day Christ's faithful are bound to come together into one place. They should hasten to the word of God and take part in the Eucharist, thus calling to mind the Passion, death, and Resurrection and glory of the Lord Jesus and giving thanks to God, "who has begotten them anew to a living hope through the Resurrection of Jesus Christ from the dead (1 Pet. 1:3)."[140]

From the very beginning of the Church, Christians have felt the need to acclaim Christ's Resurrection as a community. "The Eucharist feeds and forms the Church."[141] "The Sunday celebration of the Lord's Day and his Eucharist is at the heart of the Church's life."[142] This celebration brings to the fore the intimate connection between the Eucharist and the Church.[143] At each Mass, Christians relive "the experience of the Apostles on Easter evening when the Risen Lord appeared to them as they

[139] Bl. John Paul II, Post-Synodal Apostolic Exhortation *Ecclesia in Europa* (June 28, 2003), no. 82 (italics in original).
[140] Vatican II, Decree on the Liturgy, no. 106.
[141] Ibid., no. 32.
[142] CCC, no. 2177.
[143] Cf. John Paul II, *Ecclesia de Eucharistia*, no. 21–25.

were gathered together. In a certain sense the people of God of all times were present in the small nucleus of disciples."[144] Down through the centuries every generation of Christians hears at Mass the same words with which Christ greeted his disciples: "Peace be with you." "For Christian families, the Sunday assembly is one of the most outstanding expressions of their identity and their 'ministry' as 'domestic churches,' when parents share with their children at the one Table of the Word and of the Bread of Life."[145]

The family's practice of going to Sunday Mass together is a very powerful way of passing on the Faith to children. If parents explain the Mass to their children little by little, they will gradually open their children's eyes to the meaning and the mystery of the eucharistic sacrifice and thus help them understand the important reasons for the obligatory nature of the Sunday precept.

One of the consequences of fruitful attendance at Mass is a deeper sense of community with neighbors and those with whom we come in daily contact. The Sunday Mass has a striking communal aspect. The arrangement of the seating in the Church, the collections, the contribution of the choir, and the prayers of the faithful all help us realize that we are participating in a community event, while realizing at the same time that what is of importance is the personal relationship of our soul with Christ through prayer and the reception of the Eucharist.

The Mission We Receive in the Mass

At a deeper level, the effect of Sunday Mass should be to raise the apostolic consciousness of people. Vatican II's Decree

[144] *Dies Domini*, no. 33.
[145] Ibid., no. 36.

on the Lay Apostolate says: "For the faithful who have understood the meaning of what they have done, the Eucharistic celebration does not stop at the Church door."[146] Like the first Christians who gathered each Sunday to celebrate the Resurrection, today's faithful are called to evangelize and bear witness in their daily lives; thus the importance of the Dismissal at Mass. In Korea, at the end of Mass, the priest dismisses the congregation with the words, "Go out and evangelize the world." Perhaps it is because Korean Catholics have taken this instruction seriously that the Church in South Korea has shown such rapid growth, having increased from 250,000 in 1964 to 6.2 million Catholics in 2005.

The Code of Canon Law says that "on Sundays and other holy days of obligation the faithful are bound to attend Mass"[147] and adds that "those who deliberately omit this obligation commit a grave sin."[148] It is easy to understand why, if we keep in mind how vital Sunday is to the Christian life. John Paul II says that the Church cannot "settle for minimalism and mediocrity at the level of the faith."[149]

The spiritual and pastoral riches of Sunday that have been passed on to us by tradition are truly great. When it is fully understood the observance of Sunday becomes a synthesis of the Christian life. More than a precept, this observance should be seen as a need arising from the demands of living the Christian life. The Eucharist is the realization of the worship that humanity owes to God.[150]

[146] Vatican II, Decree on the Lay Apostolate, no. 3.
[147] CIC, 1247.
[148] CIC, 2181.
[149] *Dies Domini*, no. 52.
[150] Cf. ibid., no. 81.

The Most Holy Eucharist

No man can offer adequate praise and thanksgiving to God, but the Mass bridges the gulf so that Christ, by uniting us with his Mystical Body, the Church, through Baptism and by sharing with us his priesthood and making us co-offerers of himself in the Mass, enables us to reach from earth to the highest heavens, to give God a gift that is worthy of him and to offer him adoration and thanks.

Participating in the Mass

To obtain the fruits God wants to give us in each Mass, we must prepare ourselves for participation in the liturgical rites, conscious of what we are doing, with devotion and full collaboration.[151] "Never get used to celebrating or attending the Holy Sacrifice: in fact, do so with such devotion as you would if it were the only Mass of your life, knowing that Christ, God and Man, Head and Body, is always present, and together, therefore, with our Lord, the whole of his Church is offered."[152] Love for the Mass will express itself in a number of details: punctuality as a sign of courtesy, care of our appearance, the way we sit or kneel, and reverence and respect in the presence of God as a sign of faith and love, especially at the Consecration.

The Mass is the most pleasing thing we can offer to God. It is an opportunity to thank him for the many benefits we have received, to ask forgiveness for our sins, and to ask for all our spiritual and material needs.

We all have things we need to ask for. Lord, this illness … Lord, this sorrow … Lord, that humiliation I can't

---

[151] Cf. Vatican II, Decree on the Sacred Liturgy, no. 48.
[152] St. Josemaría Escrivá, Letter, March 28, 1955, in *In Conversation with God*, vol. 3, 324.

accept even for love of you ... We desire blessings, happiness and joy for the members of our household. We are saddened by the fate of those who suffer hunger and thirst for bread and justice; of those who undergo the anguish of loneliness; of those who at the end of their lives are facing death without an affectionate look or the help of a friend.

But it is sin which is the wretchedness that causes suffering, and it is the great world-wide malaise we have to remedy. It separates us from God and endangers souls with the prospect of eternal damnation. To bring men to eternal glory in the love of God—that was the essential desire of Christ when he gave up his life on Calvary, and that has to be our desire when we celebrate Mass.[153]

Our Lady can also help us in our participation in the Mass:

How could we take part in the sacrifice without remembering and invoking the Mother of the High Priest and Victim? Our Lady played such an intimate part in the priesthood of her Son during his life on earth that she is eternally united to the exercise of his priesthood. Just as she was present on Calvary, so she is present in the Mass, which is a prolongation of Calvary. She helped her Son on the Cross by offering him to the Father. In the sacrifice of the altar, the renewal of the sacrifice of Christ, she helps the Church to offer herself in union with her Head. Let us offer ourselves to Jesus through the mediation of Mary.[154]

[153] St. Josemaría Escrivá, *In Love with the Church*, 47–48.
[154] P. Bernadot, *Our Lady in My Life*, 233. Cf. Fernandez, *In Conversation with God*, vol. 3, 668.

The Most Holy Eucharist

The Offertory is a particularly appropriate moment for us to present our personal offerings to be united to the sacrifice of Christ. All that we do is worthwhile insofar as it is offered on the altar with Christ, who is at once Priest and Victim.

Preparation for Communion

Christ urges us to receive the Eucharist: "Truly, truly, I say to you, unless you eat the flesh of the Son of man and drink his blood, you have no life in you." The Church encourages us to receive our Lord every time we go to Mass, if we have the required dispositions.[155] St. Augustine tells us: "Live in such a way that you can receive every day."[156] In 1905, St. Pius X issued a decree that encouraged daily Communion, requiring but two conditions—being in the state of grace and having an upright and pious intention.[157] The Church also requires an hour of fasting beforehand as a sign of respect for the reception of the Eucharist.

Our Lord himself points out that, to share in the eucharistic banquet of eternal life, we must approach the altar clothed in the nuptial garment of sanctifying grace (cf. Matt. 22:12).[158] This requirement is perfectly logical since the bread we receive

---

[155] Cf. CCC, no. 1389.

[156] St. Augustine, *Sermon*, 4, 1.

[157] St. Pius X, *Sancta Tridentina Synodus* (1905).

[158] St. John Chrysostom upbraids the faithful of Antioch for their lack of supernatural outlook in preparing for Communion: "Is it not ridiculous, he asks, to be so meticulous about bodily things when the feast draws near, as to get out and prepare your best clothes days ahead ... and to deck yourself in your finest, all the while paying not the slightest attention to your soul, which is abandoned, besmirched, squalid and utterly consumed by desire?" (*Homily* 6).

is the very Flesh of the God-man, Christ. The soul, when it is bereft of grace, is spiritually dead and therefore incapable of absorbing spiritual food. We should go to confession whenever necessary, or even if only advisable, in order to receive Christ worthily.

Strictly speaking, no one is worthy to receive the Body and Blood of Christ. Like the centurion of Capernaum, a Christian becomes worthy by acknowledging his unworthiness: "Lord, I am not worthy that you should enter under my roof" (cf. Matt. 8:8). Our love for the Eucharist will express itself in efforts to cleanse our intellect, memory, imagination, and our affections before receiving the Blessed Sacrament. With St. Thomas Aquinas we can say to Jesus as we prepare to go to Communion:

> I come to the sacrament as a sick man to the physician who will save his life, as a man unclean to the fountain of mercy, as a blind man to the radiance of eternal light, as one poor and needy to the Lord of heaven and earth; praying that in thy boundless generosity you will deign to cure my sickness, wash my defilement away, enlighten my blindness, enrich my poverty, and clothe my naked-ness. May the Bread of angels, the King of kings and the Lord of lords be received by me with such humble rever-ence and devout contrition, such faith and purity, and such good resolutions as may assist in the salvation of my soul.[159]

In addition to purity of soul, the fruitful reception of Holy Communion requires that we have an adequate knowledge of the Faith, specifically of the doctrine regarding this noble

---

[159] St. Thomas Aquinas, *Roman Missal, Prayers before Mass.*

sacrament. St. Paul, referring to this sacrament, warns: "Anyone who eats and drinks without discerning the body eats and drinks judgment upon himself" (1 Cor. 11:29). We need to examine our faith to see how we prepare for Communion, when so many people neglect our Lord entirely. We have to receive him with the appropriate dispositions, with the faith and humility of the sick woman who approached Jesus to touch the hem of his garment (cf. Matt. 9:20–22). We should be able to say with Peter: "We have believed, and have come to know, that you are the Holy One of God" (John 6:69).[160]

We can increase our desire to receive our Lord in the Eucharist by keeping ourselves recollected before Mass and by making a spiritual communion, such as the following:

> My Jesus, I believe that you are present in the Most
> Holy Sacrament. I love you above all things, and I
> desire to receive you into my soul. Since I cannot at
> this moment receive you sacramentally, come at least
> spiritually into my heart. I embrace you as if you were
> already there and unite myself wholly to you. Never
> permit me to be separated from you. Amen.

In the eucharistic celebration, an attitude of adoration before Jesus, who has become present, precedes the Communion meal. This adoration helps to prepare us to receive the Body and Blood of Jesus with proper respect and veneration.

The Bread of Life

In his discourse at Capernaum, Jesus said: "Unless you eat the flesh of the Son of Man and drink his blood, you have no

---

[160] Cf. Francis Fernandez, *In Conversation with God*, vol. 2, 407.

life in you" (John 6:54). By means of eucharistic Communion, we become incorporated and identified with Christ, a process begun in Baptism and reinforced by Confirmation. Only by receiving the Blessed Eucharist do we communicate fully with the life of Christ and become one with him: "As the living Father sent me, and I live because of the Father, so he who eats me will live because of me" (John 6:57).

From the Eucharist flow all the graces and fruits of eternal life—for all humanity and for each individual soul—because in this sacrament "is contained the whole spiritual good of the Church, namely, Christ himself, our Pasch and living bread which gives life to men through his flesh—that flesh which is given life and gives life through the Holy Spirit."[161]

Msgr. Ronald Knox helps us to understand at a deeper level the incarnational aspect of Holy Communion:

> Our Lord came to be and to suffer; he also came to do. He went about doing good. When we receive Communion, we are made partakers of that same virtue which flowed from the incarnate Christ. We are reminded of that every time we go to Communion by the words the priest says when he holds up the host to our view. "Lord, I am not worthy that thou shouldest enter under my roof, but speak the word only, and my soul shall be healed." They are an echo of the words of that centurion who came to ask help from our Lord when his servant lay sick to death. "I will come and heal him" is our Lord's answer, and the centurion expostulates: Cannot the word that will bring healing be spoken from afar? What need of a visible presence or a personal contact to effect the mighty

---

[161] Vatican II, *Presbyterorum ordinis*, no. 5.

works of the Omnipotent? But the common practice of our Lord in his miracles is a continuous rebuke to that attitude. He will go to find the sufferer, he will touch, he will anoint, he will speak to him—why? Because he chooses so to condescend to our service. He could have healed the sick, cleansed the leper, raised the dead, without coming to earth at all; yet he came to earth to do it. He could communicate the grace which we receive through his Body and Blood without any sacramental medium; yet he makes himself present on our altars to do it. Is not this a God to serve?[162]

Considering the effects of this sacrament in the souls of those who receive it worthily will help us to draw more benefit from eucharistic Communion and from spiritual communions and, consequently, to progress steadily on the road to holiness. Thus there will be fulfilled in us what the Lord said in Capernaum: "He who eats my flesh and drinks my blood has eternal life and I will raise him up on the last day" (John 6:54). The Eucharist is the seed of immortality; it is the foundation for that great hope which fills our lives.

Holy Communion is so important for salvation that the Church commands—and it is a grave obligation—that the faithful receive Holy Communion at least once a year at Easter time and also when in danger of death. As a mother concerned for her children, the Church insistently recommends frequent Communion, so that Christians may draw strength from it to purify their daily faults and to prevent the grave sins to which human weakness is exposed.[163] This insistence of the Church

[162] Ronald Knox, *Heaven and Charing Cross*, 88–89.
[163] Cf. CCC, no. 1389.

is explained by the fact that the Eucharist contains all the treasures of wisdom and supernatural love, delivered by Christ to his holy Spouse, the Church, for the benefit of each of her members. In Holy Communion the Christian soul finds its center and its objective, the peak of life hidden with Christ in God to which St. Paul invites us (cf. Col. 3:3), the root of all our apostolic fruitfulness.

Accordingly, as St. Josemaría noted: "To communicate with the Body and Blood of our Lord is, in a certain sense, like loosening the bonds of earth and time, in order to be already with God in heaven, where Christ himself will wipe the tears from our eyes and where there will be no more death, or mourning, or cries of distress, because the old world will have passed away."[164]

In Holy Communion Christ himself, perfect God and perfect man, gives himself to us; he is mysteriously hidden, but he wishes to communicate divine life to us. When we receive him in this sacrament, his divinity acts on our soul by means of his glorious humanity. None of the people whom he cured—Bartimaeus the blind man, the lepers, the paralytic in Capernaum—were as close to Christ as we are every time we go to Holy Communion. The effects produced by that Living Bread, Jesus, in our soul are immeasurable and of infinite richness.

In Communion, the most holy Soul of Christ, who knows and loves us eternally and perfectly, pours out on our thirsty souls the infinite merits and satisfaction of his Passion; he sends us the grace and consolations of the Holy Spirit, and he leads us into his heart to transform us according to his holy sentiments and affections. One day a leper came to Jesus and asked that his

---

[164] *Conversations with Msgr. Josemaría Escrivá de Balaguer* (Manila: Sinag-Tala, 1987), no. 113.

skin be cleansed. Jesus stretched out his hand and touched him, saying, "I will. Be clean," and immediately the leprosy left him" (Luke 5:12-17). We can ask Jesus to cleanse us, and he will if we have faith: Christ just touched the leper, but in Communion we receive him totally—Body, Blood, soul, and divinity. Do we not have a right to expect that our reception of the Blessed Eucharist with the right dispositions will result in an increasing identification of our mind and heart with the sentiments of Christ?

The Eucharist sustains the spiritual life of our soul; that is, it maintains it in the grace of God and makes it more difficult for sin to dominate our soul.[165] St. Thomas Aquinas says that while material food changes into the one who eats it, spiritual food, on the other hand, changes a person who eats it into itself. Thus the proper effect of the Eucharist is the conversion of the man into Christ, so that he may no longer live, but that Christ may live in him.[166]

The Effects of the Sacrament

From Christ's discourse at Capernaum we see that the principal effect of receiving Holy Communion is life, supernatural life and eternal life (cf. John 6:27 ff.). This life, which promises us a share in the divine life, the life of grace, and enables us to have an intimate, personal friendship with God, gives a supernatural dimension to our everyday activities—work, family life, social involvement, recreation, and so forth—and enables us to discover Christ in those activities. As Jesus said to his Apostles at the Last Supper: "I am the vine, you are the

[165] Cf. CCC, no. 1393.
[166] St. Thomas Aquinas, *Commentary on Book IV of the Sentences*, d. 12, Q. 2, ad. 11.

branches. He who abides in me and I in him, he it is that bears much fruit" (John 15:5).[167]

Just as during his life on earth the healing touch of Christ's body gave sight to the blind and healed all manner of bodily diseases, so his life-giving humanity, sacramentally received by us, gives to our souls the life that makes us members of him and partakers of the divine nature. The eucharistic food assimilates us to Christ and transforms us. As our Lord said to St. Augustine: "It is not you who will change me into yourself, as the food of your flesh, but you will be changed into me."[168]

In relation to the fact that the Eucharist is the true food that gives the strength to live our Christian vocation, John Paul II points out: "It is only by means of the Eucharist that we are able to live the heroic virtues of Christianity, such as charity to pardon one's enemies, the love which enables one to suffer, the capacity to give one's life for another; chastity at all times of life and in all situations; patience in the face of suffering and the apparent silence of God in human history or our very own existence. Therefore, strive to always be Eucharistic souls so as to be authentic Christians."[169] The Eucharist gives unshakable perseverance in fulfilling our daily responsibilities.

The Holy Eucharist is not merely a food but is also a medicine. It serves as a prophylactic against grievous sin. In particular it quells concupiscence, especially in the area of impurity. The Eucharist responds to our every weakness. To those who complain of helplessness in the face of temptation, the eucharistic meal offers the guarantee of strength that belongs to Jesus himself.

[167] Cf. CCC, no. 1391.
[168] St. Augustine, *Confessions*, bk. 1, ch. 7, no. 10.
[169] Pope John Paul II, Homily, Castelgandolfo, August 19, 1979.

The Most Holy Eucharist

In the Eucharist we find the strength that sustains us because in it we find the Lord. It is a personal encounter in which Jesus gives himself and shares his effectiveness. As he did for the disciples of Emmaus, Christ gives meaning to our life; he gives back supernatural vision, he comforts us in our difficulties, and he fills us with apostolic desires. "I can do all things in him who strengthens me" (Phil. 4:10).

An effect of Holy Communion is, then, to maintain the life of God in the soul, freeing it from lukewarmness and spiritual routine. Without Holy Communion, spiritual vigor languishes; we would incur many venial sins and perhaps grave faults.[170] " 'Going to Communion every day for so many years! Anybody else would be a saint by now, you told me, and I ... I'm always the same!' 'Son, I replied, keep up your daily Communion, and think: what would I be if I had not gone?' "[171]

As long as we are on this earth, we will feel the inclination to sin, the *fomes peccati*, which tends to separate us from the right path. The Eucharist sustains our energies on our long journey toward God. It makes the yoke sweet and the burden light (cf. Matt. 11:30). It protects us against dangers and vacillations that try to separate us from the way, and it guides our pace. Each Communion brings a new wealth of grace, a light, and an impulse that give us charity and strength for the spiritual struggle, although at times we may not perceive it. As the sacrament of love, the Eucharist burns away the impurities of our soul, purifies it of venial sins, and sows in it the seed of eternal life.

Just as material food sustains life and enhances the health and vigor of the body, the Bread of Life increases our supernatural

---

[170] Cf. CCC, no. 1392.
[171] St. Josemaría Escrivá. *The Way* (Dublin: Scepter, 1968), no. 534.

life, while imparting to the soul a greater hunger for eternal goods. This increase in supernatural life signifies, in the first place, a more intense participation in the divine nature and a more effective inhabitation of the Three Divine Persons in the soul.

Receiving Communion also allows the theological virtues to increase in us.[172] Faith increases because in Communion we adhere to Christ, who is the truth, and we believe all the mysteries of his Trinitarian life and of his redemptive Incarnation. Our hope is strengthened for the imperishable goods that Christ has prepared for us and that he confirms in us unceasingly. The grace of the Eucharist is the seed of immortality that gives us strength to confront the daily struggle and to overcome whatever contradictions we experience. Communion helps us to grow in the perfect love of Christ, to love as good children of God. Our self-love is attenuated, and we come to feel a strong union with the whole Church. Nothing strengthens the Communion of Saints more than this sacrament.[173]

The eucharistic grace uplifts and delights us when we receive Communion with the right dispositions. The pleasure of Holy Communion is of an eminently spiritual nature. The spiritual joy that comes from the Eucharist is based on the possession of supernatural goods, known by the light of faith: the Real Presence of Christ within us, the appropriation of the merits of his life and death. Holy Communion is an anticipation of the eternal happiness of heaven because it allows us to possess God in this world, and it impels us with more contemplative ardor on the way to heaven.

---

[172] Cf. CCC, no. 1391.
[173] Cf. ibid., nos. 1394, 1395.

The Most Holy Eucharist

The Eucharist is the "pledge of our glorious resurrection and eternal happiness,"[174] according to the promise of Christ: "He who eats my flesh and drinks my blood has eternal life and I will raise him up at the last day" (John 6:53–54).

Holy Communion, given as Viaticum, prepares those in danger of death for that final journey into eternity. In this way they are strengthened by the body of Christ and receive the token of the Resurrection.

Since the Eucharist is the sacrament of unity, one of its effects is to unite us in the Mystical Body of Christ. As St. Paul says in this context, "Because there is one bread, we, who are many, are one body" (1 Cor. 10:17).[175]

The *Catechism* says that the Eucharist commits us to the poor. This is because to receive in truth the Body and Blood of Christ, we must recognize Christ in the poorest of his brethren. In *Deus Caritas Est*, Benedict XVI reminds us of the relationship between the Eucharist and practical charity: "The Eucharist draws us into Jesus' act of self-oblation. More than just statically receiving the incarnate *Logos*, we enter into the very dynamic of his self-giving."[176] "The Lord encounters us ever anew, in the men and women who reflect his presence, in his word, in the sacraments, and especially in the Eucharist. In the Church's liturgy, in her prayer, in the living community of believers, we experience the love of God, we perceive his presence and we thus learn to recognize that presence in our daily lives. He has loved us first and he continues to do so: we too, then, can respond with love."[177]

---

[174] Council of Trent, sess. 13, ch. 2.
[175] Cf. ibid., no. 1398.
[176] Benedict XVI, *Deus Caritas Est*, no. 13.
[177] Ibid., no. 17.

Devotion at Mass and Holy Communion

The degree to which we share in these benefits of the Eucharist depends on the quality of our dispositions and our desire for purification. Although the Church exhorts us to receive Communion frequently, we should not allow vanity to creep into our reception of the Blessed Eucharist, nor should we receive out of mere routine, because these would deprive us of many of the benefits to be gained from the Eucharist.

Communion is not a reward for the good and the perfect, but strength for the small and the weak. The knowledge of our weaknesses should lead us to seek strength in Communion. In this sacrament, as John Paul II says, "it is Christ himself who gives shelter to the traveler worn out by the roughness of the road. Christ comforts man with the warmth of his understanding and love. In the Eucharist there is the fulfillment of those sweet words: 'Come to me, all who labor and are heavy laden, and I will give you rest' (Matt 11:28). This personal and profound assurance is to be found in the divine Bread which Christ offers to us at the Eucharistic table. This is our final end as we travel the ways of this world."[178] If we are faithful, one day we will enter with him into heaven. *Ecce Panis angelorum, factus cibus viatorum, vere panis filiorum*: behold the bread of Angels, made into the food of travelers, truly the bread of the children.[179]

Encountering Jesus

Jesus Christ comes to us in the Blessed Eucharist as the Physician who heals the wounds in our soul caused by sin and concupiscence. Just before Communion, the priest turns to the congregation, and says: "Behold the Lamb of God, behold him

---

[178] Blessed John Paul II, Homily, 9 July 1980, Fortaleza, Brazil.
[179] Cf. Fernandez, *In Conversation with God*, vol. 4, 399.

The Most Holy Eucharist

who takes away the sins of the world. Blessed are those called to the supper of the Lamb." The first part of this text is taken from St. John's Gospel, where John the Baptist points out Jesus to two of his disciples, Andrew and John the Apostle. Our response —
"Lord, I am not worthy that you should enter under my roof, but only say the word, and my soul shall be healed"—echoes the words of the centurion who asked Christ to heal his servant. The centurion recognized Jesus as God and considered himself unworthy to have Jesus visit his home, but he believed that Jesus could heal his servant with a simple command. Because of the faith of the centurion, Jesus cured the servant from a distance. On the other hand, Christ always comes to us in Holy Communion, even though our souls are never sufficiently well disposed to receive him.

Ronald Knox says:

A matter for deep reflection is that the miracle of transubstantiation was performed just for you—just for me. He came and dwelt there just for you.... No secondary agent, no intermediaries, shall communicate to us the influence our souls need; he shall come to us himself. How he must love us to want to do that! How resolute he must be that nothing on his side should be wanting, that no loophole of excuse should be given us for refusing what he offers when he brings it himself! And we so blind, we so hesitating, we so neglectful—we so unwilling to give ourselves wholly to him who thus gives himself wholly to us![180]

[180] Ronald Knox, *Pastoral Sermons* (London: Burns and Oates, 1960), 306.

Devotion at Mass and Holy Communion

In front of the Blessed Sacrament, the words "Come to me, all you who labor and are heavy laden, and I will give you rest" (Matt. 11:28) acquire their deepest meaning. It is there, close to Christ, as we reflect on his power and his love for us, that our difficulties become more manageable, that the weight of our disappointments is lightened, that we recover our peace of soul, and that we are convinced that all the circumstances of our life are firmly in God's fatherly hands.

Thanksgiving after Holy Communion

As well as preparing for Communion, we should make a proper thanksgiving afterward. We should try to recollect our thoughts in a very personal dialogue with our eucharistic Lord during those minutes when he remains with us. We can thank him for the many favors we have received and ask for the many things of which we stand in need.

In our thanksgiving we must try to focus our attention on the presence of Jesus Christ within us. What Jesus desires from us at this time is a trusting dialogue. When we don't know what to say, we can read the prayers from a prayer book or a missal. Even distractions can improve our thanksgiving if we take the opportunity to apologize to our Lord for not being focused on him.

St. John Vianney says that "when we leave the altar rails we are as happy as the Magi would have been if they had been able to carry off the infant Jesus." And he continues:

> After each of your Communions, listen to our Lord present in your heart, converse with him, invite the Blessed Virgin to thank him for you, and keep recollected all day. The most elementary politeness and our own interest make thanksgiving a duty for us.

The Most Holy Eucharist

Converse for a while with Jesus Christ whom you are fortunate to possess in your heart, Body and Soul, as he was formerly during his life on earth. Ask him for all the graces you desire for yourself and others; the good God will not be able to refuse you anything if you offer him his Son, and the merits of his Passion and death.

Make your acts of thanksgiving after Holy Communion. Then invite the Blessed Virgin, all the angels and all the saints to thank God with you.[181]

"Abide in me, as I in you," Jesus says (John 15:4). To abide in Christ, to remain in him as he dwells in us, is an objective that corresponds to our most profound need and our most fundamental aspiration. St. Paul expressed his desire for happiness in the next world as follows: "My desire is to depart and be with Christ" (Phil. 1:23).

Living the Mass outside of Church

In our involvement in the Mass, let us recognize our dependence on God, Creator and Redeemer. With the liturgy of the Word and the liturgy of the Eucharist, the Mass leads us to contemplate the self-giving of Christ, and in this way it encourages us to be obedient to his instructions and commandments, to put our time and our efforts at the service of others, to moderate our reactions, to act with humility and rectitude of intention, doing everything in such a way that we can offer it on the altar, converting our entire day into a pleasing offering to God.

The Mass is the most important and the most fruitful of our encounters with God, the Father, Son, and Holy Spirit. The whole of the Trinity is present in the eucharistic sacrifice, and

[181] *The Eucharistic Meditations of the Curé of Ars*, 44.

participating in it is the best way of corresponding with divine love, the most pleasing to God. The Mass is the center and source of our spiritual life.[182] Everything we do finds its redeeming value in the Mass. Thus, in a certain way, our day becomes a prolongation of the Sacrifice of the Altar. Our existence and our activity are, as it were, the matter of the eucharistic sacrifice to which it is directed and in which it is offered. If we live the Holy Sacrifice with piety, with love, we will return home firmly disposed to show the vitality of our faith with deeds.[183]

[182] St. Josemaría Escrivá, *Christ Is Passing By*, no. 87; Vatican II, *Presbyterorum ordinis*, no. 14.
[183] Cf. Fernandez, *In Conversation with God*, vol. 3, 323.

Chapter 7

Adoration of the Eucharist

The Development of Eucharistic Adoration

In the Mass we express our faith in the Real Presence of Christ under the species of bread and wine by, among other ways, genuflecting or bowing deeply as a sign of adoration of the Lord. The Church has always encouraged devotion to the Eucharist, not only during Mass, but also outside of it, reserving consecrated Hosts with the utmost care, exposing them to the solemn veneration of the faithful, and carrying them in procession.[184]

It was faith in the Real Presence of Christ that led to devotion to Jesus in the Blessed Sacrament outside of Mass. In the first centuries of the Church the sacred species was reserved so that Communion could be taken to the sick and to those in prison awaiting martyrdom because they had confessed their faith. Gradually the faith of the people caused them to see the great treasure in the reservation of the Blessed Eucharist. The

[184] Cf. CCC, no. 1378.

Church has since been untiring in establishing and investing the Blessed Sacrament with more and more solemnity, homage, and devotion.

Corpus Christi

While Holy Thursday celebrates the institution of the Eucharist, the richness of the many events commemorated during those days does not allow adequate time to reflect on the greatness of the miracle of the Real Presence.

Thus it was that in 1241, in Liège, Belgium, our Lord appeared to St. Juliana, a cloistered nun who had a deep devotion to the Eucharist, and asked her to tell the local bishop to institute a public procession in honor of the Blessed Sacrament on the Thursday after Trinity Sunday. This good nun made known her request to the bishop of Liège, who was favorably impressed. The feast was approved in 1246 and was observed for the first time in Liège the following year, when the Blessed Sacrament was carried through the cities and towns of the diocese.

One of the people to whom St. Juliana first made known our Lord's desire for the Corpus Christi procession was Jacques Pantaléon, archdeacon of Liège, who subsequently became Pope Urban IV. She now urged the bishop of Liège to ask Urban IV to extend the celebration to the entire Church. Urban IV readily agreed and in 1264 published a beautiful document on the Eucharist, the Bull *Transiturus*, in which, having affirmed the love of the Savior for us as expressed in the Blessed Sacrament, he ordered the annual celebration of Corpus Christi on the Thursday after Trinity Sunday, at the same time granting many indulgences to the faithful for attendance at Mass and the divine office on that day. The *Transiturus* is rich with insights into the mystery of the Eucharist, such as the following:

Adoration of the Eucharist

O most excellent sacrament! O sacrament to be adored, venerated, worshipped, glorified, magnified with special praise, extolled with worthy hymns, honored by all kinds of study, accompanied by devout offerings, and guarded by sincere souls. O most noble memorial, to be entrusted to the innermost heart, firmly embraced by the soul, diligently reserved in the womb of the heart and in meditation, and sedulously examined by multitudes! We should celebrate continuously the memory of this memorial so that we may always be mindful of him whose memorial we know it to be, because the more frequently his gift and favor are looked upon, so much the more firmly are they kept in memory. Therefore, although this memorial Sacrament is frequented in the daily solemnities of the Mass, we nevertheless think it suitable and worthy that, at least once a year—especially to confound the lack of faith and the infamy of heretics—a more solemn and honorable memory of this sacrament be held.[185]

The pope asked St. Thomas Aquinas to compose the office and hymns of the Mass for this feast; these include such well-known hymns as *Pange Lingua, Lauda Sion Salvatorem, Panis Angelicus,* and O *Salutaris Hostia.* The custom of the Corpus Christi celebration was warmly recommended by Trent.[186]

St. Josemaría Escrivá says:

The Corpus Christi procession makes Christ present in towns and cities throughout the world. But his presence cannot be limited to just one day, a noise you hear and

---

[185] Cf. James T. O'Connor, *The Hidden Manna* (San Francisco: Ignatius Press, 1988), 194–195.

[186] Council of Trent, sess. 13, ch. 5.

then forget. It should remind us that we have to discover our Lord in our ordinary everyday activity. Side by side with this solemn procession, there is the simple, silent procession of the ordinary life of each Christian. He is a man among men who by very good fortune has received the faith and the divine commission to act so that he renews the message of our Lord on earth. We are not without defects; we make mistakes and commit sins. But God is with us and we must make ourselves ready to be used by him, so that he can continue to walk among men.[187]

At the Corpus Christi procession in Rome in the Jubilee Year 2000, Bl. John Paul II said: "With humble pride we will escort the Eucharistic sacrament through the streets of the city, close by the buildings where people live, rejoice and suffer; between the shops and offices where they work every day. We will bring it into contact with our lives beset by a thousand dangers, weighed down by worries and sorrows, subject to the slow but inexorable wear of time. As we escort him we will offer him the tribute of our hymns and prayers."[188]

If we take part in the Corpus Christi procession accompanying Jesus, we will be like those people who joyfully accompanied him during the days of his life on earth. If we see him pass through our streets exposed in the monstrance, we can tell him how much he means to us, we can thank him for the gift of our faith.

[187] St. Josemaría Escrivá, Christ Is Passing By, no. 156.
[188] Bl. John Paul II, Homily, June 22, 2000, to mark the opening of the International Eucharistic Congress in the Jubilee Year.

Adoration of the Eucharist

The Curé of Ars and
the Feast of Corpus Christi

For St. John Vianney, the Curé of Ars, the celebration of the feast of Corpus Christi was a unique occasion, not only in terms of splendor, but also as an expression of faith and love. For the Abbé Vianney it was one of the happiest days of the year. He encouraged the villagers to erect as many altars of repose as possible so as to multiply Benedictions in the parish. The procession was attended by a great crowd from the surrounding villages, as well as his own parishioners.

When he was in the company of priests St. John always tried to fade into the background, but on Corpus Christi he claimed the honor of carrying the monstrance in the procession. Walking under the canopy and clad in beautiful vestments, he advanced with great decorum with his eyes fixed on the Sacred Host.[189]

In his meditation on the Corpus Christi procession St. John Vianney says:

> Yes, Christians, rejoice! Your God is going to appear in your midst. This loving Savior is going to visit your squares, your roads and your houses. Everywhere he will shower the most abundant blessings. O fortunate houses before which he will pass! Happy the streets on which his sacred feet will tread.
>
> What does Jesus do when we carry him in procession? He is like a good king in the midst of his subjects, or a good father surrounded by his children, or a good

---

[189] Cf. Thomas J. McGovern, *Generations of Priests* (Dublin: Open Air, 2010), 170.

shepherd who visits his flock. Let us go with him with a lively faith, a firm hope and an atoning love.

Let us imagine, during this procession, the Savior going to Calvary. Some kick him, others heap injuries and blasphemies on him. How many profanations and sacrileges has he not suffered, during this long procession of nineteen centuries since the institution of the Blessed Eucharist until this day. Let us behave as a friend saddened by the afflictions of his friend, and thus show him a sincere friendship.

Yet the sense of joy always returns to the Curé:

What a wonderful day this is for us. This earth is about to become truly the image of heaven. The feasts and joy of heaven are going to come down to earth. Jesus is going to walk through our city. How can we help saying to ourselves when we repass the same way: "This is where my God passed by; this is the path he followed when he poured out his blessings on this parish." To gather up the graces that Jesus offers us on this feast day, let us follow him with docile attention to his word, with the deepest respect, and with a joy all heavenly.[190]

Worship of the Eucharistic Presence

As the implications of the Real Presence came to fruition in the minds of Christians, different forms of eucharistic worship grew in the Mass and Communion. The reservation of consecrated Hosts was, as we have seen, originally for the purpose of bringing Communion to the sick and to those who were absent.

[190] *The Eucharistic Meditations of the Curé of Ars*, 55–57.

Adoration of the Eucharist

Only during the Middle Ages, in the West, did there arise a more explicit worship of the Real Presence, with the emphasis on adoration. In the twelfth century the custom grew of elevating the Host after the Consecration. In the thirteenth century, the adoration of the Host developed outside of Mass along with popular attendance at processions of the Most Blessed Sacrament. In the fourteenth century, the use of exposition of the Host in the monstrance was introduced. Subsequently the Blessed Sacrament was exposed during the recital of the canonical hours. At the end of the fifteenth century, the Forty Hours' Adoration was initiated, in commemoration of the forty hours spent by our Lord in the tomb. During the Renaissance, tabernacles were erected on the main altars of churches.

Worship of the Real Presence outside of Mass

The development of worship of the Real Presence has represented a progress in consciousness of the wealth of the mystery of the Eucharist. It contributes to a better grasp of a sense of participation in the sacramental offering of Christ. It tends to concentrate greater attention on the person of the Savior in Communion.

Christ desired this response at the institution performed at the Last Supper. Pope Benedict XVI points out: "The One whom we adore is not some distant power. He has himself knelt down before us to wash our feet. And that gives to our adoration the quality of being unforced, adoration in joy and in hope, because we are bowing down before him who himself bowed down, because we bow."[191] This presence is an appeal to faith

---

[191] Cardinal Joseph Ratzinger, *God Is Near Us: The Eucharist, the Heart of Life* (San Francisco: Ignatius Press, 2003), 113.

and love. It is a wellspring of hope, given that the Eucharist associates us to the Passion of Christ "until he comes" (1 Cor. 11:26).

Christ's intention to develop the worship of his presence is more particularly evident in the promise made to the disciples before his definitive departure from the earth: "I am with you always, to the end of the world" (Matt. 28:20). This promise alludes to the name of God cited in Matthew 1:23: Emmanuel, "God with us." Knowing that his absence will cause them sorrow, Jesus guarantees his continuous presence, which will accompany them in the ordinary course of all of their days. In saying that it will be thus "to the end of the world," Jesus assures his disciples that his presence will accompany them in the great mission of evangelization of all the nations, which will come to an end only with the conclusion of the history of humanity.[192]

John Paul II emphasizes the direct relationship between prayer before the tabernacle and effective apostolic action:

> Closeness to Christ in silence and contemplation does not distance us from our contemporaries but, on the contrary, makes us attentive and open to human joy and distress and broadens our heart on a global scale. It unites us with our brothers and sisters in humanity and particularly with children, who are the Lord's dearly beloved. Through adoration, the Christian mysteriously contributes to the radical transformation of the world and to the sowing of the Gospel. Anyone who prays to the Savior draws the whole world with him and raises it to God. Those who stand before the Lord are therefore fulfilling an eminent

---

[192] Cf. *The Eucharist, Gift of Divine Life*, 119–120.

service. They are presenting to Christ all those who do not know him or are far from him; they keep watch in his presence on their behalf.[193]

Closeness to Christ in this way expands the heart to take in all human relations—friendships, joy and sorrow, the needs of people, the conversion of mankind.

Worship of the Eucharist

Paul VI asked the faithful to make a regular visit to the Blessed Sacrament. This is a sublime way of expressing our faith in the Real Presence of Christ in the Eucharist. We can reflect on the consolation our visit brings to the Heart of Christ, who has perhaps been waiting for hours for people to come and visit him. He wants to become our intimate friend. We would show little faith, or sense of gratitude, if we ignored his loving and generous presence in the tabernacle. Since the Eucharist is the cause of the unity of the Mystical Body, such visits are an appropriate occasion to pray for the Church and for the intentions of the Holy Father.[194]

J.R.R. Tolkien, reflecting on a period when he had nearly ceased practicing the Faith, intimates how he was rescued by "the never-ceasing, silent appeal of the Tabernacle, and the sense of starving hunger."[195] Writing to his son Michael about marriage, Tolkien, in a revealing account of his own soul, advises him:

[193] Bl. John Paul II, Letter to Bishop of Liège on the 750th anniversary of the first celebration of the feast of Corpus Christi, May 28, 1996.
[194] Paul VI, *Mysterium Fidei*, no. 66.
[195] J.R.R. Tolkien, *Letters*, ed. Humphrey Carpenter (London: G. Allen and Unwin, 1981), 340.

Out of the darkness of my life, so much frustrated, I put before you the one great thing to love on earth: the Blessed Sacrament.... There you will find romance, glory, honor, fidelity, and the true way of all your loves on earth, and more than that: Death: by the divine paradox, that which ends life, and demands the surrender of all, and yet by the taste (or foretaste) of which alone can what you seek in your earthly relationships (love, faithfulness, joy) be maintained, or take on that complexion of reality, of eternal endurance, which every man's heart desires.[196]

Tolkien's deep appreciation of the Real Presence was the foundation of his faith. It also had a profound influence on his literary philosophy.[197]

Jesus always awaits us in the Tabernacle. When we think of Christ present in there, his infinite love for us personally, and the fact that he stays with us to encourage and console us, to invite us to grow in friendship with him, we begin to appreciate why we should make at least one visit to the Blessed Sacrament at some time during the day.

In a 1996 letter to mark the 750th anniversary of the first celebration of the feast of Corpus Christi, John Paul II wrote to the bishop of Liège:

I encourage Christians regularly to visit Christ present in the Blessed Sacrament of the altar, for we are all called to abide in the presence of God, thanks to him who is

[196] Ibid., 53–54.
[197] Cf. Joseph Pearce, *Tolkien: Man and Myth: A Literary Biography* (London: HarperCollins, 1998).

with us until the end of time. In contemplation, Christians will perceive ever more profoundly that the paschal mystery is at the heart of all Christian life. This practice leads them to join more intensely in the paschal mystery, and to make the Eucharistic sacrifice, the perfect gift, the centre of their life in accordance with their specific vocation, for it "confers an incomparable dignity upon the Christian people";[198] in fact, during the Eucharist, we are welcomed by Christ, we receive his forgiveness, we are nourished by his word and his bread, we are then sent out on mission in the world; thus each one is called to witness to what he has received and to do the same for his brethren.

When we visit a church we should first kneel before the tabernacle, adore God, and thank him for his generosity. We can speak to him as the Apostles did and recount to him what concerns us and what gives us great joy, and we can thank him for being among us.

The Curé of Ars recommended that when we make a visit to the Blessed Sacrament we should open our hearts to receive God's blessings. To illustrate his point he told the following story:

When I first came to Ars, there was a man who never passed the Church without going in. In the morning on his way to work, and in the evening on his way home, he left his spade and pick-axe in the porch, and he spent a long time in adoration before the Blessed Sacrament. Oh! How I loved to see that! I asked him once what he

---

[198] Paul VI, *Mysterium Fidei*, no. 67.

said to our Lord during the long visits he made him. Do you know what he told me? "Eh, Monsieur le Curé, I say nothing to him; I look at him and he looks at me!" How beautiful, my children, how beautiful![199]

St. John Vianney says that we will find great joy and happiness in spending some time before the Blessed Sacrament to adore Christ and to "keep company with so great a friend."

Jesus Christ waits continually for us in the tabernacle, the living heart of churches and oratories. There he is exposed to the capricious love of men and women, their capacity to forget, their indifference, and also their contempt and profanation. Before this self-surrender of the Son of God, pained because of the brusqueness of our dealings with him and because of our indifference on so many occasions, we should repent of our sins, confess our belief in his humanity and divinity, and say with the Good Thief: "Remember me when you come into your kingdom" (Luke 23:42). Like the Good Thief we ask pardon for our sins and infidelities and for the sins of all humanity, especially the offenses against our Lord in the Eucharist.

Jesus is hidden there, wanting us to come to visit him, and to make our requests. "He wishes to see us near him, to tell us that he loves us, and wishes to load us with good things."[200] He remains in the Eucharist to console us and to offer us the rest that comes from his most lovable company.

Adoration in the First Place

John Paul II tells us: "The Eucharist is a priceless treasure: by not only celebrating it but also by praying before it outside of

[199] *The Eucharistic Meditations of the Curé of Ars*, 54.
[200] Ibid.

Adoration of the Eucharist

Mass we are enabled to make contact with the very wellspring of grace. A Christian community desirous of contemplating the face of Christ ... cannot fail to develop this aspect of Eucharistic worship, which prolongs and increases the fruits of our communion in the Body and Blood of the Lord."[201]

The saints are those who had an exceptional ability to penetrate the mystery of the Eucharist. St. Teresa Benedicta of the Cross (Edith Stein) wrote in one of her letters: "The Lord is present in the tabernacle in his Divinity and in his Humanity. He is not there for himself, but for us: for it is his joy to be with us. He knows that we, being as we are, need to have him personally near. As a result, anyone with normal thoughts and feelings will naturally be drawn to spend time with him, whenever possible and as much as possible."[202]

From the Tabernacle are derived, in the first place, fruits of personal sanctity: "Be a Eucharistic soul! If the centre around which your thoughts and hopes turn is the Tabernacle, then, my child how abundant the fruits of your sanctity and apostolate will be!"[203]

Christ in our midst, giving formation to morals and sustenance to virtue, comforting the sad, strengthening the weak. He encourages all who approach him to imitate him so that they may learn from his example to be gentle and lowly of heart, to seek not their own ends but God's. "Anyone, therefore, who bestows a singular devotion on the Eucharist and makes the effort to return a prompt and generous love to Christ, who has an infinite love for us, gains delight of heart and enjoyment to no

[201] Bl. John Paul II, *Ecclesia de Eucharistia*, no. 25.
[202] Quoted by Benedict XVI, in a homily in the Basilica of St. Anne in Altötting, September 11, 2006.
[203] St. Josemaría Escrivá, *The Forge*, no. 835.

small degree. He learns by experience and fully comprehends the great value of life hidden with Christ in God (cf. Col. 3:3), and the efficacy of engaging in conversation with Christ. Nothing on this earth holds more delight, nothing is more effective for covering the road to sanctity."[204]

Addressing the pilgrims of World Youth Day in Madrid during Eucharistic exposition, Pope Benedict encouraged them:

> Dear young people, in these moments of silence before the Blessed Sacrament, let us raise our minds and hearts to Jesus Christ, the Lord of our lives and of the future. May he pour out his Spirit upon us and upon the whole Church, that we may be a beacon of freedom, reconciliation and peace for the whole world.[205]

A Hidden God

Adoro te devote, latens Deitas — "Hidden God, I devoutly adore you" — is the first line of the famous eucharistic hymn attributed to St. Thomas Aquinas. Jesus promised: "I will remain with you always" (Matt. 28:20), but he does so hidden behind the disguise of transubstantiated bread.

We see Christ's humility in this hiddenness. It was part of God's plan that Jesus, like every child, remain hidden in his mother's womb for nine months. As he grew up in Nazareth and worked there as a carpenter, his divinity lay hidden until at age thirty he began his public life of preaching and healing. "The humility of Jesus: in Bethlehem, in Nazareth, on Calvary. But still more humiliation and more self-abasement in the most

---

[204] Paul VI, *Mysterium Fidei*, no. 67.
[205] Benedict XVI, Homily to World Youth Day pilgrims, August 20, 2011.

sacred host—more than in the stable, more than in Nazareth, more than on the Cross."[206]

In the Blessed Eucharist our senses are unable to perceive the Real Presence. We look at Jesus present in the tabernacle, perhaps just a few yards away, and we tell him that we know, through faith, that he is present—the same Jesus who was born in Bethlehem and grew up in Nazareth; the same Jesus who rose from the dead, ascended into heaven, and is now seated at the right hand of the Father.

St. John describes a very moving scene after the Resurrection when Thomas, after refusing to believe the testimony of the other Apostles, is confronted by the Risen Christ who elicits a deep act of faith from Thomas. He said to him, "Put your finger here and see my hands; and put out your hand and place it in my side; do not be faithless but believing" (John 20:27). Thomas responded immediately, "My Lord, and my God," expressing his faith in the Risen One. Our Lord replies, "Have you believed because you have seen me? Blessed are those who have not seen and yet believe" (John 20:28–29).

Jesus uses the occasion to emphasize that faith is a virtue that allows us to accept a truth that is a mystery, and that this is a blessed thing to do. He wants our faith to be manifest before the tabernacle, in our thoughts and words. "Build a gigantic faith in the Holy Eucharist. Be filled with wonder before this ineffable reality. We have God with us; we can receive him every day and, if we want to, we can speak intimately with him, just as we talk with a friend, as we talk with a brother, as we talk with a father, as we talk with Love itself."[207]

[206] St. Josemaría Escrivá, *The Way*, no. 533.
[207] St. Josemaría Escrivá, *The Forge*, no. 268; cf. Fernandez, *In Conversation with God*, vol. 4, 395.

The Most Holy Eucharist

St. Teresa of Avila wrote that when she heard the people say they wished they had lived when Christ walked on the earth, she would smile to herself, for she knew that we have him as truly with us in the Blessed Sacrament as people had him then, and wonder what more they could possibly want.[208]

And the holy Curé of Ars points out that our fortune is even greater than that of the people who lived with Christ during his life on earth, because they sometimes had to walk for hours or for days to find him, whilst we have him so close to us in every tabernacle.[209] "He is there as though behind a wall and from there he looks at us as though from behind the lattice (cf. Song 2:9). Even though we cannot see him he looks at us from that place where he is truly present, so that we may possess him, even though he conceals himself in order that we may seek him out. Until such time as we reach our celestial home, Jesus wants to surrender himself entirely to us, and to live united to us in this way."[210]

Everything in this world will come to an end—except the presence of Christ. As Ronald Knox describes it:

All the din and clatter of the streets, all the great factories which dominate our landscape are only echoes and shadows if you think of them for a moment in the light of eternity; the reality is in here, is there above the altar, is that part of it which our eyes cannot see and our senses cannot distinguish.... When death brings us into another world, the experience will not be that of one who falls asleep and dreams, but that of one who wakes

[208] St. Teresa of Avila, *The Way of Perfection*, ch. 34.
[209] St. John Vianney, Sermon on Maundy Thursday.
[210] St. Alphonsus Liguori, *The Practice of the Love of Christ*, ch. 2.

from a dream into the full light of day. Here, we are so surrounded by the things of sense that we take them for the full reality. Only sometimes we have a glimpse which corrects that wrong perspective. And above all when we see the Blessed Sacrament enthroned we should look up towards that white disc which shines in the monstrance as towards a chink through which, just for a moment, the light of the other world shines through.[211]

---

[211] Ronald Knox, *Pastoral Sermons*, 23.

Chapter 8

The Teachings of John Paul II on the Eucharist

In his very first encyclical, *Redemptor Hominis*, Pope John Paul II said:

> The Church lives by the Eucharist, by the fullness of this Sacrament, the stupendous content and meaning of which have often been expressed in the Church's Magisterium from the most distant times down to our own days. However, we can say with certainty that, although this teaching is sustained by the acuteness of theologians, by men of deep faith and prayer, and by ascetics and mystics, in complete fidelity to the Eucharistic mystery, it still reaches no more than the threshold, since it is incapable of grasping and translating into words what the Eucharist is in all its fullness, what is expressed by it, and what is actuated by it. Indeed the Eucharist is the ineffable Sacrament![212]

---

[212] *Redemptor hominis*, no. 20.

This is an original and striking statement that is rich enough to merit a chapter in its own right. In the following twenty-five years, John Paul II made many contributions to the theology of the Eucharist and drew out several practical conclusions in relation to eucharistic piety. In so doing, he provided many original ideas, not least the revealing of his own rich eucharistic devotion.

In this chapter I will focus on John Paul II's three main eucharistic documents: his letter *Dominicae Cenae* (The Lord's Supper; 1980), his encyclical *Ecclesia de Eucharistia* (The Eucharist and the Church; 2003), and his apostolic letter *Mane nobiscum Domine* (Stay with us, Lord; 2004). In the intervening years (1980–2003), John Paul II approved other eucharistic documents of the Congregation for Divine Worship and the Discipline of the Sacraments and gave innumerable addresses on the Eucharist, especially during his pastoral visits to many parts of the world.

DOMINICAE CENAE

Worship of the Eucharistic Mystery

In his 1980 letter *Dominicae Cenae,* John Paul II comments on the relationship between the Eucharist and the priest. "The Eucharist," he says, "is the principal and central *raison d'être* of the sacrament of the priesthood.... Through our ordination we are united in a singular and exceptional way to the Eucharist. In a certain way we derive *from* it and exist *for* it. We are also, and in a special way, responsible for it" (no. 2). He then describes how the Eucharistic devotion of the priest influences the laity. "Our Eucharistic worship, both in the celebration of Mass and in our devotion to the Blessed Sacrament, is like a life-giving current that links our ministerial or hierarchical priesthood to the common priesthood of the faithful, and presents it in its vertical dimension and with its central value" (no. 2).

The worship of the Eucharist, he says, is directed toward God the Father in the Holy Spirit through Jesus Christ and permeates the celebration of the eucharistic liturgy. "But," he adds, "it must fill our churches also outside the timetable of Masses" (no. 3). John Paul II's statement that eucharistic piety should fill our churches during the day shows his love and appreciation of the Real Presence. John Paul II was not only a theologian of the Eucharist but also had a profound personal devotion to it. He worked at his desk with the folding doors of his office opening out to the tabernacle in his private oratory. It was he who inaugurated the chapels for eucharistic devotion in the four principal Roman basilicas.

He was also responsible for the recovery of the Corpus Christi procession in 1979 in Rome, after a lapse of over a hundred years. It had been banned in 1870 after the loss of the Papal States, and the pope effectively became a prisoner of the Vatican. John Paul II carried the monstrance every year in that Corpus Christi procession until ill health prevented him from doing so, and then he traveled in a pope-mobile behind the monstrance mounted before him. To the surprise of many, tens of thousands of people of Rome came out each year to express their faith in the Real Presence of Christ in the Eucharist.

When John Paul II speaks to priests about worship of the Blessed Sacrament, he refers to personal prayer before the tabernacle, hours of adoration, periods of exposition, the Forty Hours' devotion, Benediction of the Blessed Sacrament, and Corpus Christi processions. He gives special mention to the feast of Corpus Christi, which had a particular significance for him during his years as Archbishop of Kraków. In order to get permission to hold the procession he had to fight many battles with the communist regime there. Yet he persevered successfully, as he considered it an exercise of basic human rights that people would be able to express their religious convictions publicly.

John Paul II refers to the deepening of eucharistic worship as *"proofs of that authentic renewal* which the [Second Vatican] Council set itself as an aim and of which they are *the central point."*[213] This is perhaps a perspective on Vatican II which we hadn't heard articulated before. There are perhaps few who realize that the "deepening of Eucharisic worship" is "the central point" of the program proposed by Vatican II. Certainly John Paul II had no doubt about this if he proposed that "churches should be filled outside the timetable of Masses."

In this context John Paul II makes a powerful plea to priests to deepen their worship of the Eucharist: "The Church and the world have a great need of Eucharistic worship. Jesus waits for us in this sacrament of love. Let us be generous with our time in going to meet him in adoration and in contemplation that is full of faith and ready to make reparation for the great faults and crimes of the world. May our adoration never cease."[214]

The Eucharist and Charity

Eucharistic worship constitutes the soul of the Christian life, that love of God and love of neighbor that finds its source in the Eucharist. The Eucharist, John Paul II says, educates us in this love, the love of the new commandment (cf. John

---

[213] *Redemptor hominis*, no. 20.
[214] Ibid.

13:35). In this way we grow in our appreciation of the dignity of each person; we become sensitive to the sufferings of others, to injustice, and are given the strength to redress suffering and injustice effectively. We must "learn to discover with respect the truth about the inner self of people" because it is here that "Christ comes into the hearts of our brothers and sisters and visits their consciences." Our image of others changes when we become aware of this reality.

Sacred Character

The absolute sacredness of the sacrificial rite cannot, John Paul II maintains, be diluted in any way by introducing profane elements, or by the modern tendency to "desacralize" everything. For this reason, he tells us, the Church has "a special duty to safeguard and strengthen the sacredness of the Eucharist. In our pluralistic and often deliberately secularized society, the living faith of the Christian community ... ensures respect for this sacredness.... This sense of the objective sacred character of the Eucharistic Mystery is so much part of the faith of the People of God that their faith is enriched and strengthened by it.[215]

John Paul II said of himself: "The celebration of the Eucharist continues being for me the most important and the most sacred moment of my day.... The Holy Mass is in an absolute way the centre of my life and of my day."[216]

The eucharistic celebration, which is the greatest and most elevated prayer, the supreme prayer of Christ the Priest and, with him, of the Church, encloses a divine force to transform

[215] Ibid., 8.
[216] Bl. John Paul II, Homily, October 27, 1995.

the world with the love of God. At the Last Supper Christ transformed bread and wine into his own Body and Blood; if we allow him to act, he can transform our own lives and that of those around us into something divine.

We should try to make a generous effort in our preparation for the Holy Sacrifice, so as to participate lovingly in it, and to give thanks afterward, instead of leaving quickly, so that we strive to make our day a prolongation of the Mass.

Sacrifice

In introducing a long section in *Dominicae Cenae* on the Eucharist as sacrifice, John Paul points out that "the Eucharist is above all else a sacrifice. It is the sacrifice of the Redemption and also the sacrifice of the New Covenant" (no. 9). By making this single sacrifice of our salvation present, man and the world, he says, are restored to God.

The priest in virtue of the powers received at Ordination performs a true sacrificial act that brings creation back to God. John Paul II affirms that the laity, who participate in the Eucharist, offer with the priest by virtue of their baptismal priesthood, their own spiritual sacrifices represented by the bread and wine from the moment of their presentation at the altar.

To emphasize the sacrificial nature of the Mass, John Paul II repeats some expressions from the Third Eucharistic Prayer: "Look, we pray, upon the oblation of your Church and, recognizing the sacrificial Victim by whose death you willed to reconcile us to yourself, grant that we, who are nourished by the Body and Blood of your Son and filled with his Holy Spirit, may become one body, one spirit in Christ. May this Sacrifice of our reconciliation, we pray, O Lord, advance the peace and salvation of all the world."

The Teachings of John Paul II on the Eucharist

The Table of the Bread of the Lord

John Paul II encourages priests to do all they can to safeguard the sacred dignity of the eucharistic mystery. Respect for the Eucharist requires that people come to receive properly prepared. However, he says, "Quite frequently, everybody participating in the Eucharistic assembly goes to Communion; and on such occasions, as experienced pastors confirm, there has not been due care to approach the sacrament of Penance so as to purify one's conscience" (no. 9).

This is a difficulty that has to be faced up to. Priests cannot be complicit in sacrilegious Communions. At funerals and weddings, some indication needs to be given about not participating in the Eucharist if people are not ready in as positive a manner as possible. We often see people present who haven't been at Mass for years or who are living in an illicit relationship. Priests can suggest to people who are not ready to receive Communion that they can approach the altar their arms crossed to receive a blessing rather than receiving Communion.

Priests are reminded by John Paul II to prepare well for the celebration of Mass, using the words of the instruction which the bishop gives the priest on the day of his ordination: "Accept the sacrifice of the holy people to be offered to God. Be conscious of what you are doing, imitate the events you are dealing with, and conform your life to the mystery of our Lord's cross."[217]

Priests, John Paul II reminds us, should take particular care of the way they handle the Body and Blood of the Lord, the way they distribute Holy Communion, and the way they perform the purifications. The priest's hands, by Ordination, become the

[217] Roman Pontifical.

135

direct instruments of Christ. Thus they have primary responsibility for the sacred species. John Paul II encourages priests to be faithful to the liturgical indications about saying Mass, about the use of approved liturgical texts, vestments, and so forth.

While the practice of receiving Holy Communion in the hand has been approved by the Holy See, John Paul II draws attention to instances of a deplorable lack of respect toward the eucharistic species that have been reported, cases which he says are imputable not only to the individuals concerned, but also to the pastors of the Church who have lacked the necessary vigilance regarding the formation of people in relation to the Eucharist (cf. no. 11).

The following words reflect the deep sense of sorrow John Paul II felt about liturgical abuses, which are also reported in *Inaestimabile Donum*,[218] a document issued in April 1980, just weeks after the publication of *Dominicae Cenae*. Clearly one document has to be read in the light of the other.

> As I bring these considerations to an end, I would like to ask forgiveness—in my own name and in the name of all of you, venerable and dear Brothers in the episcopate—for everything which, for whatever reason, through whatever human weakness, impatience or negligence, and also through the at times partial, one-sided and erroneous application of the directives of the Second Vatican Council, may have caused scandal and disturbance concerning the interpretation of the doctrine and the veneration due to this great Sacrament. And I

---

[218] Cf. Congregation of Divine Worship and the Discipline of the Sacraments, Instruction, *Inaestimabile Donum*, April 17, 1980.

pray the Lord Jesus that in the future we may avoid in
our manner of dealing with this sacred mystery anything
which could weaken or disorient in any way the sense
of reverence and love that exists in our faithful people.
(no. 12)

John Paul II affirms that the Eucharistic liturgy should not
be an occasion for dividing Catholics and for threatening the
unity of the Church. He asks the faithful to abandon all opposition and divisions, and to unite in this great mission of salvation which is both the price and the fruit of the Redemption.

Ecclesia de Eucharistia

On Holy Thursday 2003 Bl. John Paul II published his
encyclical on the relationship between the Church and the
Eucharist, *Ecclesia de Eucharistia*, in which he says that the Eucharist is at the center of the mystery of the Church.

What is the relationship between the Church and the Eucharist? This, John Paul II says, is summarized in the Vatican
II Decree on the Ministry and Life of Priests: "For in the most
blessed Eucharist is contained the Church's entire spiritual
wealth: Christ himself, our Passover and living bread. Through
his own flesh, now made living and life-giving by the Holy
Spirit, he offers life to men."[219]

At every celebration of the Eucharist, we are spiritually
brought back to the Paschal Triduum—to the events of the
evening of Holy Thursday, to the Last Supper and what followed it. John Paul II says the Church's "foundation and wellspring is the whole *Triduum Paschale*, but this is as it were

[219] Vatican II, Decree on the Ministry and Life of Priests, no. 5.

gathered up, foreshadowed and 'concentrated' forever in the gift of the Eucharist. In this gift Jesus Christ entrusted to his Church the perennial making present of the paschal mystery. With it he brought about a mysterious 'oneness in time' between the Triduum and the passage of the centuries" (no. 5).

The thought of what the Eucharist is fills Pope John Paul II with amazement and wonder. He says that the congregation should also be filled with amazement as it reflects on this great sacrament, but in a special way the consideration of the eucharistic mystery should fill the heart and mind of the priest, as he reflects on the extraordinary power God has placed in his hands at Ordination (no. 5). In his letter *At the Beginning of the New Millennium*,[220] he asks us to contemplate the face of Christ so as to be able to recognize him wherever he manifests his presence: "The Church draws her life from Christ in the Eucharist; by him she is fed, by him she is enlightened. . . . Whenever the Church celebrates the Eucharist, the faithful can in some way relive the experience of the two disciples on the road to Emmaus: 'their eyes were opened and they recognized him' (Lk 24:31)" (no. 6).

As spiritual food of the faithful, the Eucharist is, John Paul II says, the most precious possession the Church can have on her journey through history. This is why the Church has always emphasized the greatness of the eucharistic mystery and the reality of eating and drinking Christ's Body and Blood.

While John Paul II outlines the progress in eucharistic devotion in the Church since Vatican II, he also, with not a little disappointment, draws attention to the dark clouds of

---

[220] Bl. John Paul II, Apostolic Letter *Novo Millennio Ineunte* (January 6, 2001), nos. 16–18.

unacceptable doctrine and practice which have appeared. He points out how

> in some places the practice of Eucharistic devotion has been almost completely abandoned.... At times one encounters an extremely reductive understanding of the Eucharistic mystery. Stripped of its sacrificial meaning, it is celebrated as if it were simply a fraternal banquet.... Furthermore, the necessity of the ministerial priesthood, grounded in Apostolic Succession, is at times obscured and the sacramental nature of the Eucharist is reduced to its mere effectiveness as a form of proclamation.... How can we not express profound grief at all of this? The Eucharist is too great a gift to tolerate ambiguity and depreciation (no. 10).

John Paul II said that his hope was that *Ecclesia de Eucharistia* would effectively help banish the dark clouds of unacceptable doctrine and practice, so that the Eucharist would continue to shine all its radiant mystery (no. 10). It is clear, however, that he didn't consider the encyclical sufficiently detailed to adequately address the Eucharistic abuses which he outlined in paragraphs ten and fifty-two of the encyclical. Consequently, within a year of the publication of *Ecclesia de Eucharistia* he felt it necessary to authorize the issuance of a detailed instruction that would not only remove aberrations, but would also enhance all ceremonies in eucharistic practice. The Instruction, *Redemptionis Sacramentum*, of the Congregation for Divine Worship and the Discipline of the Sacraments, was published on March 25, 2004.

The Instruction reminds us that in the Eucharist is contained the whole spiritual wealth of the Church, namely, Christ our Paschal Lamb, and states that the purpose of the Instruction is to safeguard this great mystery of the Eucharist. Referring to what John Paul II says in *De Ecclesia de Eucharistia* about abuses (no. 10), the Instruction affirms that "it is not possible to be silent about the abuses, even quite grave ones, against the nature of the liturgy and the sacraments, as well as the tradition and authority of the Church, which in our day not infrequently plague liturgical celebrations in one ecclesial environment or another. In some cases the perpetration of liturgical abuses has become almost habitual."[221]

The Instruction says that the external observance of the liturgical norms published by the Church is not enough. Remedial action must therefore be illuminated by faith and charity, which unites us with Christ and teaches us to think as he himself does. It reiterates the point that John Paul II made in his encyclical: "Abuses contribute to the obscuring of the Catholic faith and doctrine concerning this wonderful sacrament" (no. 10).

Looking back to the 1980 Instruction, *Inaestimabile Donum*, from the perspective of the 2004 Instruction, *Redemptionis Sacramentum*, I think it is reasonable to infer that liturgical abuse was a permanent concern during the pontificate of John Paul II.

The Eucharist and Evangelization

One of the consequences of our receiving the Eucharist, John Paul II affirms, is that it spurs us on to make good use of our time and plants a living hope in our daily commitment to work. Yet while the Eucharist makes us look to the future, "this increases, rather than lessens our sense of responsibility

---

[221] *Redemptionis sacramentum*, no. 4.

for the world today."[222] It is in this world, John Paul II says, that Christian hope must shine forth. For this reason too, the Lord wished to remain with us in the Eucharist, making his presence in meal and sacrifice the promise of a humanity renewed by love (no. 20).

All who take part in the Eucharist should be committed to changing their lives and making them in a certain way completely "Eucharistic" (no. 20).

It is, John Paul II tells us, this fruit of a transfigured existence and a commitment to transforming the world in accordance with the Gospel that splendidly illustrates the eschatological tension inherent in the celebration of the Eucharist and in the Christian life as a whole (no. 20). This conviction of the transforming presence of the laity in the world imbued with a eucharistic spirit is one that John Paul II has articulated many times during his pontificate.

The Apostolicity of the Eucharist and the Church

Because the Eucharist builds the Church, and the Church confects the Eucharist, it follows that there is a profound relationship between the two (no. 26). In the way that the Church is one, holy, catholic, and apostolic, so in an analogous way the Eucharist has also each of these four characteristics. In keeping with John Paul's treatment of the topic, however, we will consider only the note of apostolicity of the Eucharist. Like the Church, the Eucharist also has its foundation on the Apostles, in that it was entrusted by Jesus to the Apostles. In continuity with the practice of the Apostles, in obedience to the Lord's

---

[222] Vatican II, Decree on the Church in the Modern World, no. 39; as quoted in *Ecclesia de Eucharistia*, no. 20.

command, the Church has celebrated the Eucharist through the centuries. The Eucharist is also apostolic in that it is celebrated in conformity with the faith of the Apostles, with the words they heard from our Lord's lips (no. 27).

The Eucharist is apostolic in another sense. Only the priest has the power to consecrate the Body and Blood of Christ. "The priest offers the Eucharistic sacrifice *in persona Christi*, in specific sacramental identification with the Eternal High Priest who is the author and principal subject of this sacrifice, a sacrifice in which, in truth, nobody can take his place" (no. 29). The power of the priest to offer this sacrifice infinitely transcends the power of the assembly. An ordained minister is essential to bring about the eucharistic consecration, so that no representative of the assembly can substitute for the priest.[223] The minister is a gift that the assembly receives through episcopal succession going back to the Apostles.

Priests and Vocations

John Paul II says that it is in prayer before the Blessed Sacrament that the most effective winning of vocations for the priesthood takes place. This is a devotion that, he affirmed, should be encouraged among the lay faithful, helping them to give effect to those words of Christ: "The harvest is great, but the labourers are few; ask the Lord of the harvest to send out more labourers into the harvest" (Luke 10:2). "Often it is the example of a priest's fervent pastoral charity which the Lord uses to sow and to bring to fruition in a young man's heart the seed of a priestly calling."[224] The lack of priests should cause the

---

[223] *Sacerdotium ministeriale.*
[224] Ibid.

community to pray with more fervor to the Lord to send more vocations.

John Paul II speaks with great sadness about Christian communities who do not have a priest to celebrate the Eucharist and the other sacraments. Their situation should bring them to implore God to send them priestly vocations.

I think it is probably true to say that John Paul II, by dint of his priestly example, his outgoing, attractive personality, and his devotion to the Eucharist, stirred up more vocations in the Church during his pontificate than any other individual has. Certainly vocations worldwide started to increase with his papacy.

The Dignity of the Eucharistic Celebration

An episode that serves as a prelude to the institution of the Eucharist is the anointing at Bethany. Mary, the sister of Lazarus, pours a flask of costly ointment over Jesus' head, and Jesus sees this act of anointing as an anticipation of the honor that his body will continue to merit even after his death (cf. Matt. 26:8; Mark 14:4; John 12:4). Like Mary of Bethany in using the expensive ointment, the Church does not fear extravagance in devoting her best resources to express her wonder and adoration at the unsurpassable gift of the Eucharist. The Church's awareness of which resources are worthy to use to celebrate the Eucharist has been refined over the centuries by the growth in appreciation of the ineffable gift of the Eucharist.

"In the wake of Jesus' own words and actions, and building upon the ritual heritage of Judaism, the Christian liturgy was born" (no. 48).

In this section of the encyclical, John Paul II develops the relationship between art and the Eucharist, and in this sense prepares the ground for many things that Benedict XVI would say in subsequent years on this topic.

The historical development of devotion to the Eucharist has, John Paul II says, led to ecclesial traditions that emphasize the grandeur of the event being celebrated. On this foundation a rich artistic heritage also developed. Architecture, sculpture, painting, stained glass, and music have found in the Eucharist, both directly and indirectly, a source of great inspiration. "It can be said that the Eucharist, while shaping the Church and her spirituality, has also powerfully affected 'culture,' and the arts in particular" (no. 9).

Church art in the East, the result of the Greco-Byzantine tradition, has, John Paul II affirms, preserved "a remarkably powerful sense of mystery, which led artists to see their efforts as creating beauty not simply as an expression of their own talents, but also as *a genuine service to the faith*" (no. 50).

Our Lady and the Eucharist

We are not surprised that John Paul II would finish off his encyclical with words of deep affection for our Lady in relation to the Eucharist, coupled with a penetrating theological analysis of her role in this context.

Mary can guide us toward the Eucharist, he says, because she herself had a profound relationship with it. In a certain sense she lived a eucharistic faith even before the institution of the Eucharist, when she carried Jesus Christ in her womb. Mary became, in a way, the first tabernacle for her Son, as she traveled from Nazareth to the hill country in Judea to visit her cousin Elizabeth (no. 53).

Thus, for the first nine months of her Son's existence, Mary lived physically very close to her Son, awaiting with a deep sense of expectation the day she would be able to contemplate his face. We can learn from Mary, John Paul II says, how to express our love for Jesus in our thanksgiving after Communion. "The Eucharist, while commemorating the Passion and the Resurrection, is also in continuity with the Incarnation. At the Annunciation Mary conceived God the Son in the physical reality of his Body and Blood, thus anticipating within herself what to some degree happens sacramentally in every believer who receives, under the signs of bread and wine, the Lord's Body and Blood" (no. 55).

We can be sure that Mary participated in the Eucharist celebrated by the first Christian community and referred to then as "the breaking of bread" (Acts 2:44). We can imagine the great love with which our Lady received her Son. Nobody can guide us like Mary in acquiring an appreciation of this mystery of faith. "*Ave verum corpus natum de Maria Virgine, vere passum, immolatum, in cruce pro homine!* ['Behold the true Body born of the Virgin Mary, who truly suffered and was sacrificed on the Cross for men']. Here is the Church's treasure, the heart of the world.... Our senses fail us: *visus, tactus, gustus in te fallitur*, in the words of the hymn *Adoro te devote*, which reminds us that faith alone in the words of Christ leads us to the centre of the Eucharistic mystery" (no. 59).

Mane nobiscum Domine

With *Mane nobiscum Domine* (October 7, 2004), his last apostolic letter, John Paul II set out to offer some basic guidelines as to how to live the Eucharistic Year (2004–2005), and to highlight the central place the Eucharist should enjoy in the life of the Church and the lives of Catholics.

The Most Holy Eucharist

The text invites us to "contemplate, praise, and adore"; to discover, to be conscious of the immense gift the Eucharist implies, and to translate this wonder into specific attitudes. As a summary of all this, John Paul II says at the end of his letter: "Rediscover the gift of the Eucharist as light and strength for your daily lives in the world, in the exercise of your respective professions amid so many different situations. Rediscover this above all in order to experience fully the beauty and the mission of the family" (no. 30).

John Paul II and the Family

How does John Paul II relate the Eucharist to the family? For the duration of his pontificate, and for many years before, he dedicated his best energies to persuading us of the truth and the richness of the Church's teaching on marriage and the family. His constant attention to this theme was a consequence of his conviction that stable marriages and happy family life were essential to human well-being and that, if this objective were achieved, many other evils in society would be eradicated. After he had completed his long series of talks on the theology of the body (1979–1984), he continued to give special attention to moral and pastoral questions related to marriage and the family. In his many journeys abroad, the affirmation of the Christian concept of the family was always high on his agenda. Indeed in 1984 he identified the defense of marriage and the family as his first pastoral priority,[225] because for him "the story of mankind and the history of salvation passes by way of the family."[226] A fundamental part of his program of evangelization

[225] Cf. Address, March 22, 1984.
[226] Bl. John Paul II, *Letter to Families*, no. 23 (February 2, 1994); see also *Familiaris consortio*, no. 86.

was geared toward making Christians rediscover once again the full implications of his exhortation: "Family, become what you are."[227]

During his pontificate we saw the publication of several important documents on the family, including *The Christian Family in the Modern World* [*Familiaris consortio*] (1981), the *Charter of the Rights of the Family* (1983), and the *Letter to Families* (1994). Familiarity with these writings of John Paul II will provide rich insights into his theology of the family.

He asks us to rediscover the gift of the Eucharist "in order to experience fully the beauty and the mission of the family." By referring to *Familiaris consortio*, John Paul II's *magnum opus* on the family, we discover how he sees the relationship between the Eucharist and the family:

> The Eucharist is the very source of Christian marriage. The Eucharistic Sacrifice, in fact, represents Christ's covenant of love with the Church, sealed with his blood on the Cross. In this sacrifice of the New and Eternal Covenant, Christian spouses encounter the source from which their own marriage covenant flows, is interiorly structured and continuously renewed. As a representation of Christ's sacrifice of love for the Church, the Eucharist is a fountain of charity. In the Eucharistic gift of charity the Christian family finds the foundation and soul of its "communion" and "mission": by partaking in the Eucharistic bread, the different members of the Christian family become one body, which reveals and shares in the wider unity of the Church. Their sharing in the Body of Christ that is "given up" and in his Blood

---

[227] *Familiaris consortio*, no. 17.

that is "shed" becomes a never-ending source of missionary and apostolic dynamism for the Christian family.[228]

This parallelism which John Paul II draws between the marriage covenant and the New and Eternal Covenant offers us a deep insight into the relationship between the Eucharist and marriage. It is the same parallel that St. Paul draws between the love of husband and wife and the love of Christ for his Church (cf. Eph. 5:23–33).

The Eucharist: the Center of the Church's Life

From the beginning of his pontificate, John Paul II said that the way of the Church is essentially eucharistic. Indeed from his very first encyclical, he pointed out that the Eucharist should become the center of the life of the Church and of individual Christians: "The essential commitment and, above all, the visible grace and source of supernatural strength for the Church as the People of God is to persevere and advance constantly in Eucharistic life and Eucharistic piety and to develop spiritually in the climate of the Eucharist."[229]

In addition to his previous discourses on the Eucharist, John Paul II felt the need to celebrate a Year of the Eucharist. It began with an International Eucharistic Congress in Guadalajara, Mexico, October 10–17, 2004, and ended in October 2005 with the Synod of Bishops in Rome, where the bishops devoted three weeks to the study of the theme "The Eucharist: source and summit of the life and mission of the Church."

John Paul II said he was also guided by another consideration in his writing of *Mane nobiscum Domine*: the future World

---

[228] *Familiaris consortio*, no. 57.
[229] *Redemptor hominis*, no. 20.

The Teachings of John Paul II on the Eucharist

Youth Day, scheduled for August 2005 in Cologne: "I would like the young people to gather around the Eucharist as the vital source which nourishes their faith and enthusiasm. A Eucharistic initiative of this kind has been on my mind for some time: it is a natural development of the pastoral impulse which I wanted to give to the Church, particularly during the years of preparation for the Jubilee and in the years that followed it" (no. 4).

Cologne was a great eucharistic event, as were those of Sydney and Madrid, following the blueprint established by John Paul II in previous World Youth Days.

The Jubilee Year 2000 was an especially Eucharistic one, with the primary focus on the International Eucharistic Congress held near Rome in June of that year. In preparation for the Jubilee, John Paul II also gave us the 1998 letter *Dies Domini* (On Keeping the Lord's Day Holy), in which he invited believers to rediscover the celebration of the Eucharist as the heart of Sunday.

The Eucharist: A Mystery of Light

In his apostolic letter on the Rosary, John Paul II explains in what sense the Eucharist is a mystery of light.[230] If all the mystery of Christ is light, this dimension is manifested above all in the years of his public life. The light that comes from the Eucharist is the testimony Christ gives of his love for humanity "to the end" (John 13:1), offering himself for us in the sacrifice of salvation. The light that comes from the Eucharist clarifies the rest of the mysteries of the life of Jesus, as they are contemplated in the Rosary.

---

[230] Bl. John Paul II, Apostolic Letter *Rosarium Virginis Mariae* (October 16, 2002), no. 21.

The Most Holy Eucharist

John Paul II reviews the mystery of the Eucharist as a mystery of faith and light, in its capacity to satisfy the desires of men. He sees the light that comes from the Eucharist in different perspectives. The apparition on the road to Emmaus, John Paul says, shows us that a primary aspect of the Eucharist is that it is a mystery of light. Jesus described himself as "the light of the world" (John 8:12), and this quality becomes manifest at different moments in his life, such as the Transfiguration and the Resurrection, when his divine glory shines forth. Yet in the Eucharist the divine glory remains veiled.

John Paul II describes how Christ, in meeting up with the two disciples on the road to Emmaus, explains the Scriptures to them, drawing them out of the darkness of sorrow, and awakening in them a desire to stay with him: "Stay with us Lord," they exclaimed (Luke 24:29). Jesus is light for these two disciples in the way he explains the Scriptures to them, showing them how they all point to Christ. They recognized him at table "in the breaking of bread." As John Paul II says, "when minds are enlightened and hearts are enkindled, signs begin 'to speak'. We are constantly tempted to reduce the Eucharist to our own dimensions, while in reality it is we who must open ourselves to the dimensions of the mystery" (no. 14).

In the Eucharistic hymn *Adoro te devote*, we are reminded that the complete hiddenness of Jesus in the Eucharist is an essential part of the mystery of the Blessed Sacrament, and, paradoxically, why it is at the same time a mystery of light. The Eucharist is light above all at Mass.

There is, John Paul II says, a particular need to cultivate a lively awareness of Christ's Real Presence, both in the celebration of Mass and in the worship of the Eucharist outside of Mass. The awareness of this presence is shown through the tone of voice, gestures, posture, and bearing. In this regard the importance of moments of silence both in the celebration of Mass and in Eucharistic adoration should be recalled. The Eucharist should always be treated with profound respect. If the priest acts in this way, the faithful will learn to adore with reverence: "Let us take time to kneel before Jesus present in the Eucharist, in order to make reparation by our faith and love for the acts of carelessness and neglect, and even the insults which our Saviour must endure in many parts of the world" (no. 18).

John Paul II suggests that there are four elements by which we become identified with Christ through the Eucharist: gratitude, the new evangelization, solidarity, and a spirit of service to the most needy.

Gratitude

This thanksgiving for the Eucharist is described as follows in the *Catechism of the Catholic Church*: "The Eucharist, the sacrament of our salvation accomplished by Christ on the Cross, is also a sacrifice of praise and thanksgiving for the work of creation. In the Eucharistic sacrifice the whole of creation loved by God is presented to the Father through the death and resurrection of Christ. Through Christ the Church can offer the sacrifice of praise and thanksgiving for all that God has made good, beautiful and just in creation and in humanity."[231]

Thanksgiving for God's gifts is expressed fully in the Eucharist. In every holy Mass we bless the Lord, God of the universe, offering him bread and wine, "which earth has given and human hands have made"; Christ has united his oblation of sacrifice to these simple elements.

[231] CCC, no. 1359.

John Paul II says that gratitude to God for his benefits, for all that we have and are, will not take away from the legitimate autonomy of earthly realities. In this context he continues:

> Christians ought to be committed to bearing more force-ful witness to God's presence in the world. We should not be afraid to speak about God and to bear proud wit-ness to our faith. The "culture of the Eucharist" pro-motes a culture of dialogue, which here finds strength and nourishment. It is a mistake to think that any public reference to faith will somehow undermine the rightful autonomy of the State and civil institutions, or that it can even encourage attitudes of intolerance.[232]

This is a powerful call to Christians to take on the apostolic responsibilities of their baptismal vocation in the secular world, sanctifying all earthly realities.

The New Evangelization

What place does the Eucharist occupy in the new evange-lization? The Eucharist is the center of the spiritual life of the Catholic and gives him the capacity to participate in the mis-sion of the Church. We read in *Ecclesia de Eucharistia*: "From the perpetuation of the sacrifice of the Cross and her communion with the Body and Blood of Christ in the Eucharist, the Church draws the spiritual power needed to carry out her mission. The Eucharist thus appears as both the *source* and the *summit* of all evangelization, since its goal is the communion of mankind with Christ and in him with the Father and the Holy Spirit."[233]

[232] CCC, no. 26.
[233] *Ecclesia de Eucharistia*, no. 22.

The Teachings of John Paul II on the Eucharist

In the last part of the letter *Mane nobiscum Domine*, the Holy Father makes explicit the consequences of the contemplation of the face of Christ: "The encounter with Christ, constantly intensified and deepened in the Eucharist, issues in the Church and in every Christian *an urgent summons to testimony and evangelization....* The dismissal at the end of each Mass is a charge given to Christians, inviting them to work for the spread of the Gospel and the imbuing of society with Christian values" (no. 24).

The Eucharist worthily received and with the desire to be one with Christ results in a commitment to evangelization. John Paul II describes this apostolic responsibility in more detail in *Dies Domini*:

Receiving the Bread of Life, the disciples of Christ ready themselves to undertake with the strength of the Risen Lord and his Spirit *the tasks which await them in their ordinary life.* For the faithful who have understood the meaning of what they have done, the Eucharistic celebration does not stop at the church door. Like the first witnesses of the Resurrection, Christians who gather each Sunday to experience and proclaim the Risen Lord are called to evangelize and bear witness in their daily lives. Given this, the Prayer after Communion and the Concluding Rite — the Final Blessing and the Dismissal — need to be better valued and appreciated, so that all who have shared in the Eucharist may come to a deeper sense of the responsibility which is entrusted to them. Once the assembly disperses, Christ's disciples return to their everyday surroundings with the commitment to make their whole life a gift, a spiritual sacrifice pleasing to God (cf. Rom 12:1). They feel indebted to their brothers and sisters because of what they have received in the celebration, not unlike the disciples of Emmaus who, once they had recognized the Risen Christ "in the breaking of bread" (cf. Lk 24:30–32), felt the need to return immediately to share with their brothers and sisters the joy of meeting the Lord (cf. Lk 24:33–35).[234]

The Eucharist not only provides the interior strength needed for this mission, but it also gives us the perspective for carrying it out: "Incarnating the Eucharistic 'plan' in daily life, wherever people live and work — in families, schools, the workplace, in all of life's settings — means bearing witness that human reality cannot be justified without reference to the Creator" (no. 26).

Solidarity and service of the needy

The Eucharist should also be a school of communion, peace, and solidarity (no. 27). It is not a question of an extrinsic imitation of Christ, but is fruit of the spiritual life that is born of the encounter with Christ through prayer and the sacraments.

John Paul II maintains that the service of the most needy is a proving ground for the eucharistic project, an idea that has also been articulated by Benedict XVI. In this service is reflected in great part the authenticity of the participation in the Eucharist celebrated in the community. "It is the impulse which the Eucharist gives to the community for *a practical commitment to building a more just and fraternal society*" (no. 28; italics in original). It refers to all the different kinds of poverty: hunger, disease, solitude, unemployment, and so forth, inviting Christian communities to a greater awareness in this regard.

[234] *Dies Domini*, no. 45.

The Teachings of John Paul II on the Eucharist

John Paul II draws our attention to the fact that "it is not by chance that the Gospel of St. John contains no account of the institution of the Eucharist, but instead relates the 'washing of the feet' (cf. 13:1–20)" (no. 28).

John Paul II draws a very challenging conclusion at the end of this section: "We cannot delude ourselves: by our mutual love and, in particular, by our concern for those in need we will be recognized as true followers of Christ (cf. Jn 13:35; Mt 25:31–46).This will be the criterion by which the authenticity of our Eucharistic celebrations is judged" (no. 28).

The Eucharist and Priests

All during his pontificate John Paul II gave special attention to the priests of the Church. Each year he sent them a letter for Holy Thursday, which he felicitously referred to as the "birthday of priests." He used these letters as an opportunity to encourage priests, to confirm them in their vocation, to deepen their appreciation of the gift God had given them, and to reinforce their love for the Mass and the Eucharist. He says that priesthood cannot be understood without the Eucharist: "It is our principal ministry, he says, and our greatest power is in relation to it. The Eucharist could not exist without us, but without the Eucharist we do not exist, or we are reduced to lifeless shadows. The priest therefore can never reach complete fulfilment if the Eucharist does not become the centre and root of his life, so that all his activity is nothing but an irradiation of the Eucharist."[235]

Nevertheless the centrality of the Eucharist in the life of the priest goes well beyond the sphere of personal devotion:

[235] Address, February 16, 1984, no. 2.

155

It constitutes the directing criterion, the permanent dimension of all his pastoral activity, the indispensable means for the authentic renewal of the Christian people. Therefore, if we want Christian love to be a reality in life; if we want Christians to be a community united in the apostolate and in the common attitude of resistance to the powers of evil; if we want ecclesial communion to become an authentic place of encounter, of hearing the Word of God, of revision of life, of becoming aware of the problems of the Church—every effort must be made to give the Eucharistic celebration its entire power to express the event of the salvation of the community.[236]

Recalling his experience as a priest for fifty years, John Paul II comments:

The priest is a man of the Eucharist. In the span of nearly fifty years of priesthood, what is still the most important and the most sacred moment for me is the celebration of the Eucharist. My awareness of celebrating *in persona Christi* at the altar prevails. Never in the course of these years have I failed to celebrate the Most Holy Sacrifice. If this has occurred, it has been due entirely to reasons independent of my will. *Holy Mass is the absolute centre of my life and of every day of my life.* It is at the heart of the theology of the priesthood, a theology I learned not so much from textbooks as from the living example of holy priests.[237]

[236] *Redemptor hominis*, no. 4.
[237] Address, October 27, 1995, no. 4 (italics in original).

He goes on to explain why offering the eucharistic sacrifice is totally rewarding even at a human level:

> In our world, is there any greater fulfilment of our humanity than to be able to re-present every day *in persona Christi* the redemptive sacrifice, the same sacrifice which Christ offered on the Cross? In this sacrifice, on the one hand, the very mystery of the Trinity is present in the most profound way, and, on the other hand, the entire created universe is "united" (cf. Eph 1:10)..... This is why in the thanksgiving after Holy Mass the Old Testament canticle of the three young men is recited: *Benedicite omnia opera Domini Domino.* For in the Eucharist all creatures seen and unseen, and man in particular, bless God as Creator and Father; they bless him with the words and the action of Christ, the Son of God.[238]

In *Dominicae Cenae*, John Paul II tells us that priests have a primary responsibility for the Eucharist for its consecration, its distribution, its reservation and adoration. As a consequence priests need to make a definite, generous commitment to spend time in prayer before the Tabernacle: "Never believe that the yearning for intimate conversation with the Eucharistic Jesus, the hours spent on your knees before the tabernacle, will halt or slow down the dynamism of your ministry. What is given to God is never lost for man. The profound demands of spirituality and the priestly ministry remain substantially unchanged throughout the centuries, and tomorrow, just as today, they will

[238] Bl. John Paul II, *Gift and Mystery: On the Fiftieth Anniversary of My Priestly Ordination* (London: Image Books, 1996), 73–74.

have their fulcrum and their reference point in the Eucharistic mystery."[239]

Conclusion

As John Paul II encourages us: "The Son of God became man for us and offered himself in sacrifice for our salvation. He gives us his Body and Blood as the food of a new life, of a divine life that is no longer subject to death. Through the words, 'Do this in remembrance of me', the infinite riches of salvation, including the power to rehabilitate human freedom destroyed by sin, are made available to humanity for all time."[240]

This same command, associated with the events of Calvary, surpasses the limits of history, allowing the person of Christ to accompany the new people of God on their journey until the end of time.[241]

The eucharistic liturgy is a preeminent school of Christian prayer, especially through adoration of the Blessed Sacrament, by which the faithful can enjoy the experience of the "abiding" love of Christ (cf. John 15:5).[242] In contemporary culture the dimension of mystery has been lost to a great extent, since activism is generally regarded as the only real form of fulfilled living. Yet because the human person can recognize his true self only in something beyond himself, that is, in the mystery of God, it is only in the truth about the Eucharist and its transcendence that we can fully discover and understand the mystery of our own being.

[239] Address, February 16, 1984, nos. 2, 3.
[240] Cf. Bl. John Paul II, Address at International Eucharistic Congress, Rome, June 25, 2000, no. 4.
[241] Cf. *The Eucharist and Freedom*, no. 14.
[242] Cf. John Paul II, Holy Thursday Letter to Priests, 1999, no. 6.

The Teachings of John Paul II on the Eucharist

John Paul II was a powerful promoter of devotion to the Blessed Eucharist all during his pontificate and opened our minds to appreciate the theological depth of this great mystery. His constant commitment to teaching us about this amazing sacrament derived from a deep conviction that love for the Eucharist will eventually lead us to the fullness of the faith, and to a profound love for the person of Christ.

Chapter 9

Benedict XVI's *Sacramentum Caritatis*

Pope John Paul II set the theme for the October 2005 Synod of
Bishops: "The Eucharistic Sacrifice, the source and summit of
the Christian life."[243] Due to his death in April 2005, however,
it was left to his successor, Benedict XVI, to write up the find-
ings of the synod in the document *Sacramentum caritatis*, which
was published on February 22, 2007.[244] This is a fundamental
and a very comprehensive document on the Eucharist and is
likely to be a main point of reference for studies of this sacrament for some time to come. We can also take it as a statement
of Benedict XVI's main ideas on the Eucharist. Consequently I

---

[243] Cf. Vatican II, *Lumen gentium*, no. 11.

[244] Benedict XVI links this new eucharistic document with
The Year of the Eucharist convoked by John Paul II for 2004–
2005. He also connects it with John Paul II's encyclical on
the Eucharist, *Ecclesia de Eucharistia*, and with his apostolic
letter *Mane nobiscum Domine*. Benedict pays warm tribute to
Ecclesia de Eucharistia, which he says is "a sure magisterial
statement of the Church's teaching on the Eucharist and a
final testimony of the central place that this divine sacrament
had in John Paul II's own life."

will devote this chapter to a study of *Sacramentum Caritatis* by way of a commentary on the text and, at the same time, make a summary of the main elements of the document.

Sacramentum caritatis deals with the Eucharist under three main headings: as a mystery to be believed (nos. 6–33); as a mystery to be celebrated (nos. 34–69); and as a mystery to be lived (nos. 70–93). In these three parts is a harmonic vision between dogma, liturgy, and the spiritual life. In this document we find a catechesis about the celebration of holy Mass, reflections about the repercussions of eucharistic life on social life, replies to some current pastoral problems, dogmatic expositions from the profound unity of the faith, and considerations in respect of the role of beauty in Revelation and the sacramental economy.

The Eucharist is the gift Jesus makes of himself, revealing to us God's infinite love for every human being. It is the sacrament which makes manifest that Christ's love caused him to lay down his life for us. In the same way Jesus continues in the sacrament of the Eucharist to love us "to the end" (John 13:1), offering us his Body and Blood for our spiritual nourishment. The great mystery of the Eucharist fills us with wonder as we reflect on the implications of this divine gift.[245] In this sacrament the

---

[245] Benedict XVI gives us one of his insights into the Eucharist as sacrifice in another source: "The Eucharist, as the presence of the cross, is the abiding tree of life, which is ever in our midst and ever invites us to take the fruit of true life.... To receive it, to eat of the tree of life, thus means to receive the crucified Lord and consequently to accept the parameters of his life, his obedience, his 'yes', the standard of our creatureliness. It means to accept the love of God, which is our truth—that dependence on God which is no more an imposition from without than is the Son's sonship. It is precisely this dependence that is freedom, because it is truth and love"

Benedict XVI's *Sacramentum Caritatis*

Lord truly becomes food for us, to satisfy our hunger for truth and freedom, to show us the truth about love, which is the very essence of God.

The Holy Spirit guides the Church in the orderly development of the ritual forms used to celebrate the Eucharist. The bishops at the synod said that the liturgical changes introduced as a consequence of Vatican II had to be "understood within the overall unity of the historical development of the rite itself, without the introduction of artificial discontinuities" (no. 3).

Benedict XVI comments that his objective in writing *Sacramentum caritatis* was to help the "Christian people deepen their understanding of the relationship between the Eucharistic mystery, the liturgical action, and the new spiritual worship which derives from the Eucharist as the sacrament of charity" (no. 5).[246] He also points out that it should be read alongside his first encyclical, *Deus Caritas Est*, in which he frequently mentions the sacrament of the Eucharist and stresses its relationship with Christian love.

I. A MYSTERY TO BE BELIEVED

Speaking the words "the mystery of faith" after the Consecration, the priest expresses his wonder at the substantial change of bread and wine into the Body and Blood of Christ — a reality that surpasses all understanding. "The Church's faith is

---

(Joseph Ratzinger, *In the Beginning: A Catholic Understanding of the Creation and the Fall* [Grand Rapids: Wm. B. Eerdmans Publishing Co., 1995], 76–77).

[246] In his book, *Christ Our Joy: The Theological Vision of Pope Benedict XVI* (San Francisco: Ignatius Press, 2006), Msgr. Joseph Murphy provides a very good summary of the eucharistic theology of Pope Benedict; see pp. 171–183.

essentially a Eucharistic faith, and it is especially nourished at the table of the Eucharist" (no. 6). The more lively the eucharistic faith of the people of God, the deeper their commitment to the life of the Church. The Church's history bears witness to this. Every great reform has in some way been linked to the rediscovery of belief in the Lord's Eucharistic presence.

The Institution of the Eucharist

The institution of the Eucharist takes place within a ritual meal commemorating the delivery of the Jews from the slavery of Egypt. This meal is a remembrance of the past but also the proclamation of a deliverance yet to come, a salvation that is more profound, more radical, more universal, more definitive (cf. no. 10). In instituting the Eucharist, Jesus anticipates and makes present the sacrifice of the Cross and the victory of the Resurrection. At the same time he reveals that he is the true sacrificial lamb and that his death is a supreme act of love and man's definitive deliverance from evil.

By his command to "do this in remembrance of me" (Luke 22:19; 1 Cor. 11:25) Christ expects the Church to receive this gift and, under the guidance of the Holy Spirit, to develop the liturgical form of the sacrament.

The substantial conversion of bread and wine into his Body and Blood introduces within creation the principle of a radical change, a sort of "nuclear fission" which penetrates to the heart of all being, a change meant to set off a process which transforms reality.[247] Thus, through the holy lives of Christians, nourished by the Eucharist, the entire world will be transformed.

---

[247] This is an analogy that Pope Benedict used before, in his address to the young people at World Youth Day in Cologne in August 2005.

The Holy Spirit plays a decisive role in the eucharistic celebration, in particular with regard to the transubstantiation of the bread and wine: "By the power of the Holy Spirit," writes St. John Damascene, "the transformation of the bread into the Body of Christ takes place."[248]

In instituting the Eucharist, Jesus spoke of "the new and eternal covenant" in the shedding of his Blood. This was the purpose of his mission on earth. John the Baptist, when he saw Jesus coming toward him, cried out: "Behold the Lamb of God, who takes away the sin of the world" (John 1:29). These same words are repeated at every celebration of the holy Mass when the priest invites the faithful to approach the altar: "Behold the Lamb of God, behold him who takes away the sins of the world. Blessed are those who are called to the supper of the Lamb" (no. 9).

The Eucharist and the Church

In the sacrifice of the Cross, Christ gave birth to the Church as his bride and his body (no. 14). There is therefore a causal connection between Christ's sacrifice, the Eucharist, and the Church. In a striking interplay we can say that the Eucharist builds the Church and that the Church makes the Eucharist. This is why Christian antiquity used the same words, *Corpus Christi*, to designate Christ's body born of the Virgin Mary, his Eucharistic body, and his ecclesial body.

The Eucharist constitutes the being and action of the Church, which is essentially communion. And this communion is expressed in its turn through the sacraments. Vatican II recalls "that all the sacraments, and indeed all the

---

[248] *De fide orthodoxo*, no. 13 (PG 94, 1139).

ecclesiastical ministries and works of apostolate, are bound up with the Eucharist and are directed towards it. For in the most blessed Eucharist is contained the entire spiritual wealth of the Church, namely Christ himself ... who gives life to humanity through his flesh.... Thus men and women are invited and led to offer themselves, their work and all creation in union with Christ."[249]

Thus Jesus asks us to participate in his self-surrender.

The Sacraments of Christian Initiation

The process of Christian initiation is directed to the reception of the Eucharist. It is our participation in the eucharistic sacrifice, which perfects within us the gifts given to us at Baptism. Receiving Baptism, Confirmation, and First Holy Communion are key moments not only for the individual receiving them but also for the entire family (no. 19).

Love for the Eucharist leads us to a growing appreciation of the sacrament of Reconciliation. We are surrounded by a culture that tends to eliminate the sense of sin, and that promotes a superficial approach that overlooks the need to be in the state of grace in order to approach Communion worthily (no. 20).

To achieve a fruitful participation in the Eucharistic celebration, in addition to Confession, the Church's liturgical tradition "requires that one be personally conformed to the mystery being celebrated, offering one's life to God in unity with the sacrifice of Christ for the salvation of the whole world" (no. 64).

Priests are recommended to be generous in devoting time to the confessional, and the practice of general absolution should

---

[249] Vatican II, Decree on the Ministry and Life of Priests, no. 5.

be limited exclusively to the cases permitted, since individual absolution is the only form intended for ordinary use (no. 21).

Holy Orders and the Eucharist

The intrinsic relationship between the Eucharist and the sacrament of Holy Orders emerges from Jesus' own words in the Upper Room: "Do this in memory of me" (Luke 22:19). The Eucharist and the priesthood of the New Covenant were instituted at the same time. As a consequence of Ordination, the priest can say, "This is my Body.... This is my Blood," acting in the person of Christ (no. 23).

The connection between the sacrament of the Eucharist and Holy Orders is seen most clearly in the Mass, when the priest presides in the person of Christ the Head.

Priestly Ordination is essential for the valid celebration of the Eucharist. Christ is present in his priest during the Mass. The celebrant also acts in the name of the whole Church when presenting to God the prayer of the Church and above all when offering the eucharistic sacrifice. As a consequence, priests should never put themselves or their opinions in the first place, but those of Jesus Christ. The priest is above all a servant of others and he must continually strive to be a sign pointing to Christ, a docile instrument in the Lord's hands. The priesthood, as St. Augustine said, is an *amoris officium* ("a labor of love"); it is the office of the good shepherd who offers his life for his sheep (no. 23).

Celibacy

In *Sacramentum caritatis*, Benedict XVI felt the need to reaffirm the profound meaning of priestly celibacy, as an expression of a total configuration to Christ. It is a profound identification with the Heart of Christ the Bridegroom, who gives his life for his Bride the Church. Benedict XVI goes on to say:

> In continuity with the great ecclesial tradition, with the Second Vatican Council and with my predecessors in the papacy, I reaffirm the beauty and the importance of a priestly life lived in celibacy as a sign expressing total and exclusive devotion to Christ, to the Church and to the Kingdom of God, and I therefore confirm that it remains obligatory in the Latin tradition. Priestly celibacy lived with maturity, joy and dedication is an immense blessing for the Church and for society itself. (no. 24)

Marriage

The Eucharist, as the sacrament of love, has a particular relationship with the love of man and woman united in marriage. Benedict XVI reminds us that Pope John Paul II often spoke of the nuptial character of the Eucharist and its special relationship with the sacrament of Matrimony. It is the sacrament of the Bridegroom and the Bride. Moreover, the entire Christian life bears the mark of the spousal love of Christ and the Church. The Eucharist strengthens the indissoluble unity and love of every Christian marriage. The mutual consent that husband and wife exchange in Christ, which establishes them as a community of life and love, also has a eucharistic dimension.

Indeed, in the theology of St. Paul, conjugal love is a sacramental sign of Christ's love for the Church, a love culminating in the Cross, the expression of his "marriage" with humanity and at the same time the origin and heart of the Eucharist (cf. Eph. 5:23–32) (no. 27).

If the Eucharist expresses the irrevocable nature of God's love in Christ for his Church, we can then understand why it implies, with regard to the sacrament of Matrimony, that indissolubility to which all true love necessarily aspires (no. 28). Benedict refers to the situation where divorced Catholics get married outside the Church as "a real scourge for contemporary society" (no. 29).

Eschatological Dimension of the Eucharist

After explaining the relationship between the Eucharist and the other sacraments, the document considers how the Christian life is an anticipation of the definite happiness of heaven (cf. no. 33).

In his discourse on the Eucharist in Capernaum, Jesus said: "He who eats my flesh and drinks my blood has eternal life and I will raise him up on the last day" (John 6:54). The Eucharist places in us the seed of eternal life. Participating in the Eucharist is a true foretaste of the final banquet of Heaven, celebrated in the joy of the Communion of Saints.

The eucharistic celebration, in which we proclaim that Christ has died and is risen and will come again, is a pledge of the future glory in which our bodies too will be glorified. It strengthens our hope in the resurrection of the body and the possibility of our meeting once again, face-to-face, those who have gone before us marked with the sign of faith. Mass is the privileged occasion to pray for the dead so that once purified they can come to enjoy the Beatific Vision (cf. no. 32).

By way of synthesis of the first part of the document we can say that the Christian life is called to be at all times a pleasing offering of oneself to God. Spiritual worship (cf. Rom. 12:1), radically new with respect to previous worship, consists in offering one's life with all that that implies, together with Christ, to God the Father.

II. A Mystery to Be Celebrated

In the second part of the document the Eucharist is presented as a mystery to be celebrated. It refers to an intrinsic connection between what is believed and what is celebrated. In the bread and wine we bring to the altar, all of creation is assumed by Christ the Redeemer to be transformed and presented to the Father.

The synod discussed at length the relationship between eucharistic faith and eucharistic celebration, pointing out the connection between the *lex orandi* ("the law of prayer") and the *lex credendi* ("the law of faith"): how we pray determines what we believe. It also emphasized the priority of the liturgical action. Both our faith and the eucharistic liturgy, however, have their source in the same event: Christ's gift of himself in the Paschal Mystery (no. 34).

Sacramentum caritatis explains that the Eucharist is a "mystery that has to be celebrated," and, to do so adequately and fruitfully, it is necessary to make an offering of one's own life in union with the sacrifice of Christ.

The Eucharist is both an offering and a sacrifice. Jesus does not simply give us something of himself but rather gives his entire life for us as the true Paschal Lamb: "He offers his own body and pours out his blood for us. He thus gives us the totality of his life and reveals the ultimate origin of his love" (no. 7).

Truly, whoever eats Christ lives for him. The eucharistic mystery helps us to understand the profound meaning of the Communion of Saints. Communion always and inseparably has

both a vertical and a horizontal sense: it is communion with
God and communion with our brothers and sisters. Both dimensions mysteriously converge.

Worship pleasing to God becomes a new way of living our
whole life, each particular moment of which is lifted up, since
it is lived as part of a relationship with Christ and as an offering
to God. The glory of God is the living man (cf. 1 Cor. 10:31).
And the life of man is the vision of God (no. 71).

Thus it is the Eucharist and spiritual worship which gives
unity of life to the Catholic in the Church and makes of our
lives an offering to God. As Benedict comments elsewhere:
"The Lord is near us in our conscience, in his word, in his personal presence in the Eucharist: this constitutes the dignity of
the Christian and is the reason for his joy."[250]

Beauty and the Liturgy

The relationship between creed and worship is evidenced
in a particular way in the beauty of churches and altars, sacred
vestments, sacred vessels, church furnishings, and so forth. This
beauty is an expression of the splendor of truth. Christ allows
his beauty to be glimpsed in the liturgy, where the truth of God's
love attracts us, delights us, and transforms the dark mystery
of death into the radiant light of the Resurrection. Here the
splendor of God's glory surpasses all worldly beauty. The memorial of Jesus' redemptive sacrifice contains something of that
beauty which Peter, James, and John beheld when the Master
was transfigured before their eyes (cf. Mark 9:2) (no. 35).

The Eucharist, as the nucleus of spiritual worship, gives form
to the Christian life with all its dimensions and beauty:

[250] Ratzinger, *God Is Near Us*, 106.

Like the rest of Christian revelation, the liturgy is inherently linked to beauty: it is the *veritatis splendor*. The liturgy is a radiant expression of the Paschal mystery, in which Christ draws us to himself and calls us to communion.... The beauty of the liturgy is part of this mystery.... It is a sublime expression of God's glory and, in a certain sense, a glimpse of heaven on earth. Beauty, then, is not mere decoration, but rather an essential element of the liturgical action, since it is an attribute of God himself and his revelation. (no. 35)

The Eucharistic Celebration

St. Augustine, speaking specifically of the eucharistic mystery, stresses the fact that Christ assimilates us to himself:

The bread you see on the altar, sanctified by the word of God, is the Body of Christ. The chalice, or rather, what the chalice contains, sanctified by the word of God, is the Blood of Christ. In these signs, Christ the Lord willed to entrust to us his Body and the Blood which he shed for the forgiveness of our sins. If you have received them properly, you yourselves are what you have received.[251]

Consequently our objective in receiving the Eucharist is not just to demonstrate our reverence for the sacrament, but rather to take on the personality of Christ, to become other Christs. The Eucharist, then, brings about a profound unity between us and Christ.

The Church celebrates the Eucharistic sacrifice in obedience to Christ's command, based on her experience of the risen

[251] St. Augustine, *Sermo* 227.

Lord and the outpouring of the Holy Spirit. For this reason, from the beginning, the Christian community gathered for "the breaking of bread" on the Lord's Day (no. 37).

Holy Mass: A Divine Action

In the holy Mass we situate ourselves on Calvary, beside the Cross, where Jesus died for our sins, participating actively in his redemptive sacrifice. The Son of God—as he himself revealed to Nicodemus—had been sent into the world, not to judge the world "but that the world might be saved through him" (John 3:17). The New Testament repeats this and the Church confesses it solemnly: Christ was born and lived on this earth; he died on the Cross and rose again "for us men and for our salvation." The greatness of divine mercy, the love of God for men, such that words are incapable of expressing it, has been revealed on the Cross, where the Son of God gave his life once and for all.

According to the living design that guided all the history of salvation, each time the Eucharist is celebrated, the glorious and risen Lord continues renewing and making present in history, through the hands of the priest, this self-giving love for men: "In the bread and in the wine, under whose appearance Christ gives himself to us at the Paschal supper, all the divine life comes to us and is given to us in the form of the Sacrament" (no. 8).

How can we not be moved by so great an expression of the love of God for men? How can we not feel a loving impulse to make the Mass the center of our day? How do we not marvel at the invitation to unite all our actions to the sacrifice of Calvary, in such a way that they acquire an infinite value as part of the work of redemption?

The Most Holy Eucharist

The Art of Celebration

Since the priest is the "steward of the mysteries of God" (1 Cor. 4:1) he has a particular responsibility to ensure that the liturgy is celebrated according to the indications of legitimate Church authority and to the liturgical norms laid down for the celebration. The liturgical texts contain riches that have preserved and expressed the faith and the experience of the people of God. Equally important is attentiveness to words and music, gestures and silences, movement and liturgical colors of vestments. By its nature the liturgy operates on a different level of communication which enables it to engage the whole human person (cf. no. 38).

We have already noted the profound connection between beauty and the liturgy. This should ensure attentiveness to every work of art placed at the service of the celebration. Church architecture and the furnishings of the sanctuary, such as the altar, the crucifix, the tabernacle, the ambo, and the celebrant's chair deserve special attention from an artistic point of view (no. 41).

In the course of her two thousand years, the Church has created, and still creates, a significant patrimony of music and song. The introduction of musical genres that fail to respect the meaning of the liturgy should be avoided. Gregorian chant is the chant proper to the Roman liturgy.

Aspects of the Liturgy

It is necessary to reflect on the inherent unity of the rite of Mass. There is an intrinsic bond between the word of God and the Eucharist. Listening to the word of God creates a deeper faith in the Eucharist. The liturgical proclamation of the word of God should be entrusted to well-prepared readers (no. 44).

Vatican II emphasized the active, full, and fruitful participation of the faithful in the eucharistic celebration.[252] *Sacrosanctum concilium* clarified that the word *participation* does not refer to mere external activity during the celebration; it has to be understood on the basis of a great awareness of the mystery being celebrated and its relationship to daily life: "The *ars celebrandi* ['the art of celebrating'] is the best way to ensure their *actuosa participatio* ['active participation']. The *ars celebrandi* is the fruit of faithful adherence to the liturgical norms in all their richness; indeed, for two thousand years this way of celebrating has sustained the faith life of all believers, called to take part in the celebration as the People of God, a royal priesthood, a holy nation (cf. 1 Pet. 2:4–5, 9)" (no. 38).

To participate effectively in the Eucharist, we offer our lives to God in unity with the sacrifice of Christ for the salvation of the whole world. The faithful need an education in eucharistic faith to enable them to live faithfully what they celebrate. The synod affirmed that the best education in the Eucharist is the Eucharist itself celebrated well (no. 55).

Verum Corpus Natum ex Mariae Virgine

Jesus took his flesh and blood totally from Mary; he had no human father. Therefore, when we approach the Eucharist, we should bear in mind this special relationship which the Eucharist has with the Blessed Virgin. Mary, as John Paul II commented, was the first "tabernacle" for Jesus; she carried him with her for nine months before giving him to the world.

She is the *tota pulchra*, the all-beautiful, for in her God's glory shines. Through the intercession of the Blessed Virgin

---

[252] Vatican II Decree on the Liturgy, no. 48.

Mary, Benedict asks that the Holy Spirit enkindle within us the same ardor experienced by the disciples on the road to Emmaus and renew our "eucharistic wonder" through the splendor and beauty radiating from the liturgical rite, the efficacious sign of the infinite beauty of the holy mystery of God.

In Mary most holy, we see perfectly fulfilled the sacramental way in which God comes down to meet his creatures and involves them in his saving work. Mary is the great believer who places herself confidently in God's hands, abandoning herself to his will. This mystery deepens as she becomes completely involved in the redemptive mission of Jesus (cf. 33).

Reverence for the Eucharist

A measure of the effectiveness of catechesis on the Eucharist is the increased level of reverence in the presence of the Eucharist as reflected in postures, genuflections, kneeling during the central moments of the eucharistic celebration, and eucharistic adoration. In the Eucharist the Son of God comes to meet us and desires to become one with us. Eucharistic adoration is simply the natural consequence of the eucharistic celebration, which is itself the Church's supreme act of adoration. Our principal attitude should be one of adoration, recognizing the Body of Christ (no. 66).

Eucharistic adoration is strongly recommended, both individually and in community. The personal relationship that the individual believer establishes with Jesus present in the Eucharist constantly points beyond itself to the whole communion of the Church and nourishes a fuller sense of membership in the Body of Christ. Processions with the Blessed Sacrament on the feast of Corpus Christi and on other occasions, The Forty Hours' devotion, and so forth are all recommended (no. 68).

III. A MYSTERY TO BE LIVED

Jesus said in his discourse at Capernaum, "If any one eats of this bread he will live forever" (John 6:51). Thus eternal life begins in us even now, thanks to the transformation effected in us by the gift of the Eucharist. "He who eats me will live because of me" (John 6:57). Hence the Eucharist becomes the principle of life within us and the form of our Christian existence. By receiving the Body and Blood of Christ we become sharers in the divine life in an ever more conscious way. It is not the eucharistic food that is changed into us, but rather we who are mysteriously transformed by it. Christ nourishes us by uniting us to himself. By a total self-offering of ourselves, our work, and our day, everything is united to Christ. Hence the intrinsically eucharistic nature of Christian life begins to take shape: "There is nothing authentically human—our thoughts, our affections, our words and deeds—that does not find in the sacrament of the Eucharist the form it needs to be lived to the full.... The worship of God in our lives cannot be relegated to something private and individual, but tends by its nature to permeate every aspect of our existence" (no. 71).

For the Eucharist really to have a more effective influence on the world,

> The Christian faithful need a fuller understanding of the relationship between the Eucharist and daily living. Eucharistic spirituality is not just participation in Mass and devotion to the Blessed Sacrament. It embraces the whole of life. It must be acknowledged that one of the most serious effects of secularisation is that it has relegated the Christian faith to the margins of life as if it were irrelevant to everyday affairs. The futility of this

way of living—as if God did not exist—is now evident to everyone. Today there is a need to discover that Jesus is not just a private conviction or an abstract idea, but a real person whose becoming part of human history is capable of renewing the life of every man and woman. Hence the Eucharist, as the source and summit of the Church's life, must be translated into spirituality, into a life lived "according to the Spirit." ... An integral part of the Eucharistic form of Christian life is a new way of thinking. (no. 77)

Living in Accordance with the Lord's Day

We have already reviewed John Paul II's letter *Dies Domini*. Because Benedict XVI adds new nuances to the topic, however, I think it is worthwhile to review them.

The significance of the Eucharist was clearly grasped by the early Church. St. Ignatius of Antioch expressed this truth when he called Christians "those living in accordance with the Lord's Day." The phrase of the great Antiochean martyr highlights the connection between the reality of the Eucharist and everyday Christian life. St. Ignatius' phrase—"living in accordance with the Lord's Day"—also emphasizes that this holy day becomes paradigmatic for the whole week, because it is the day when they received the Eucharistic form that their lives were meant to have (no. 72).

The synod, in light of the vital principle that the Eucharist imparts to the Catholic, reaffirmed the importance of the Sunday obligation for all the faithful. The life of faith is endangered when we lose the desire to share in the celebration of the Eucharist. To lose a sense of Sunday as the Lord's Day is symptomatic of the loss of a sense of Christian freedom, the freedom of the children of God. Sunday gives rise to a Christian meaning of life and a new way of experiencing work, life, and death. On Sundays then, it is fitting that the Church organize activities of the Christian community: social gatherings; faith-formation classes; programs for children, young people, and adults; pilgrimages; charitable works; and different moments of prayer. Even if we can fulfill the Sunday obligation on Saturday evenings, we need to remember that it is Sunday itself that is meant to be kept holy, lest it end up as a day empty of God (cf. no. 73).

Meaning of Rest and Work

The day of the Lord is also a day of rest from work. Christians, with reference to the Jewish tradition, have seen the Lord's Day as a day of rest from daily exertions, emancipating them from a possible form of enslavement. "Work is of fundamental importance to the fulfilment of the human being and to the development of society. This must always be organised and carried out with full respect for human dignity, and must always serve the common good" (no. 74).

People shouldn't allow themselves to be enslaved by work or to idolize it. On the Lord's Day the Christian rediscovers the communal dimension of his life as one who has been redeemed.

The Eucharist and Mission

Having participated fully in the eucharistic celebration, it is necessary to give witness to it as a Christian:

> The more ardent the love for the Eucharist in the hearts of the Christian people, the more clearly will they recognise the goal of all mission: *to bring Christ to others*. Not just a theory or a way of life inspired by Christ, but

the gift of his very person. Anyone who has not shared the truth of love with his brothers and sisters has not yet given enough. The Eucharist, as the sacrament of our salvation, inevitably reminds us of the unicity of Christ and the salvation that he won for us by his Blood. The mystery of the Eucharist, believed in and celebrated, demands a constant catechesis of the need for all to engage in a missionary effort centred on the proclamation of Jesus as the one Saviour. (no. 86)

In his homily inaugurating his Petrine ministry, Benedict XVI said that "there is nothing more beautiful than to be surprised by the Gospel, by the encounter with Christ. There is nothing more beautiful than to know him and to speak to others of our friendship with him" (no. 84). When we apply these words to the Eucharist they acquire a greater significance. The Eucharist by its very nature demands to be shared with all; we cannot keep such a treasure to ourselves. The laity has to transmit a living faith, not just information about the Faith. After eucharistic Communion, the first experience of mission is the example of our own life. The Eucharist is the force, the strength of Catholic witness which therefore comes to be an expression of Catholic devotion.[253]

The Eucharist: Life of the Catholic in the World

The Eucharist is offered to man as nourishment of truth, love, and life. It is bread broken for the life of the world. This,

[253] In this context it is interesting to note that Benedict XVI since approved two additional dismissal texts for the end of Mass: "Go to announce the Gospel of the Lord" and "Go in peace, glorifying the Lord with your lives."

Sacramentum caritatis tells us, has immediate social implications. Inasmuch as it makes present sacramentally the self-giving of Christ, the Eucharist enables us to extend his compassion, mercy, and love. This means that we have to look at people with the eyes of Christ, to treat them with the compassion of Christ. Each Catholic community has, therefore, to open itself out to *all* to give them their "broken bread," so that the world may be a more just and more fraternal place. "We have to become 'bread that is broken' for others, and to work for the building of a more just and fraternal world. Keeping in mind the multiplication of the loaves and fishes, we need to realize that Christ continues today to exhort his disciples to become personally engaged: 'You yourselves give them something to eat' (Matt. 14:16). Each of us is truly called, together with Jesus, to be bread broken for the life of the world" (no. 88).

As Benedict XVI said in his first encyclical, "I cannot possess Christ for myself; I can belong to him only in union with all those who have become, or who will become, his own. A Eucharist which does not pass over into the concrete practice of love is intrinsically fragmented" (no. 84).[254]

The priest has the task of explaining the relationship between the Eucharist and social commitment. Because the Eucharist is the sacrament of communion and love, the walls of enmity and confrontation have to be thrown down, and we have to seek the restoration of justice, reconciliation, and pardon. We shouldn't remain passive when confronted with unjust inequalities or with those who lack the basic necessities of life. "The Lord Jesus, the bread of eternal life, spurs us to be mindful of situations of extreme poverty. The food of truth demands

---

[254] *Deus Caritas Est*, no. 14.

that we denounce inhumane situations.... The alms collected in our liturgical assemblies are an eloquent reminder of this, and they are also necessary for meeting today's needs" (no. 90).

Another social consequence of the Eucharist is that "all who partake of the Eucharist must commit themselves to peace-making in our world scarred by violence and war, and today in particular, by terrorism, by economic corruption and sexual exploitation" (no. 89).

In a particular way, the Catholic laity, formed at the school of the Eucharist, are called to assume their specific political and social responsibilities to try to find solutions to these problems (cf. no. 91).

The Eucharist projects an intense light on human history and on the cosmos, and so it can bring about a real change in the way we look at history and the world.

The Eucharist and the Evangelization of Cultures

The presence of Jesus Christ is capable of engaging every cultural reality and bringing to it the leaven of the Gospel. The Eucharist becomes a criterion for our evaluation of everything that Christianity encounters in different cultures.

Because of the universal implications of the Eucharist it is clear that the eucharistic mystery puts us into dialogue with the various cultures, but also in some way challenges them. We must be committed "to the evangelization of cultures, conscious that Christ himself is the truth for every man and woman and for all human history" (no. 78).

The synod fathers emphasized that the Catholic faithful need a fuller understanding of the relationship between the Eucharist and their daily lives and pointed out that spirituality is not limited to participation in the Mass and devotion to the

Blessed Sacrament, but that it embraces the whole of life. The Eucharist meets each of us as we are and makes our concrete existence the place where we daily experience the radical newness of the Christian life.

In the first place, Pope Benedict points out, it is the lay faithful who are called to live this spiritual worship which is pleasing to God, precisely in the ordinary conditions of life, as indicated in John Paul II's 1988 Apostolic Exhortation *Christifideles laici*, on the vocation and mission of the laity in the Church and in the world. This is why *Sacramentum caritatis* says:

> The laity should cultivate a desire that the Eucharist have an even deeper effect on their daily lives, making them convincing witnesses in the workplace and in society at large. I encourage families in particular to draw inspiration and strength from this sacrament. The love between man and woman, openness to life, and the raising of children are privileged spheres in which the Eucharist can reveal its power to transform life and give it its full meaning.... I exhort all lay faithful, and families in particular, to find ever anew in the sacrament of Christ's love the energy needed to make their lives an authentic sign of the presence of the Risen Lord. (nos. 79, 94)

There is a parallelism between what Benedict says here about the family and what John Paul II said in *Familiaris consortio*.[255]

Conclusions

Catholic life has an essential eucharistic form, allowing us to offer spiritual worship to God. The celebrated Eucharist has

---

[255] Cf. *Familiaris consortio*, no. 57.

a transforming effectiveness on the ordinary life of the Catholic and on the world, since it renews the sacrifice of the Cross. At the same time this effectiveness depends on the response of Catholics: on their witness and on their mission, on their charity and their promotion of justice.

Thus the life of grace is a priority in catechesis for this mature Christianity so that the rejection of sin is the first objective in the spiritual life. By means of an effective participation and full engagement in the eucharistic celebration on Sundays, Christian life is nourished, and the faithful leave Mass with a sense of mission. In this way the Eucharist becomes the sacrament of love with its transforming energy to bring about real communion with men.

In summary, as Benedict says: "The Eucharist makes us discover that Christ, risen from the dead, is our contemporary in the mystery of the Church, his body. Of this mystery of love we have become witnesses. Let us encourage one another to walk joyfully, our hearts filled with wonder, towards our encounter with the Holy Eucharist, so that we may experience and proclaim to others the truth of the words with which Jesus took leave of his disciples: 'Lo, I am with you always, until the end of the world' (Mt 28:20)" (no. 97).

We can see the continuity in the eucharistic magisterium of John Paul II and Benedict XVI. With *Sacramentum caritatis*, Benedict completed a Eucharist project begun by John Paul II. We have also seen during the years of Benedict's pontificate many expressions of his own eucharistic devotion, which he used as teaching opportunities, such as his preaching in Hyde Park in London (September 2010) before the exposed Blessed Sacrament or at the Solemn Exposition of the Eucharist in Madrid for World Youth Day (August 2011), before two million young people. This eucharistic concern is also expressed in the quality of the vestments used, the music, and the reverence of the papal ceremonies in Rome, or whenever Benedict travels to places outside the eternal city.

Chapter 10

The Eucharistic Liturgy[256]

The identification of the priest with Christ finds its supreme expression in the celebration of the eucharistic sacrifice.[257] When he takes the bread in his hands and says, "This is my Body," the priest challenges himself to the deepest possible involvement in the redemptive sacrifice of Christ, while ensuring the historical continuity of the Incarnate Word among men and women today.

As a result of his Ordination the priest's most important task is the celebration of Eucharistic sacrifice. Since it is primarily through the sacramental ministry that the work of redemption is carried out, the priest needs to have a profound knowledge of all those elements which constitute the liturgical action in order to facilitate its salvific effectiveness. Devout celebration of the liturgy has always had a profound influence on the piety of the faithful, but this is particularly necessary at the present time, when authoritative voices have articulated considerable

---

[256] The material in this chapter is taken mainly from chapter 12 of my book *Priestly Identity: A Study in the Theology of Priesthood* (Dublin: Wipf and Stock Publishers, 2002).

[257] Cf. St. Thomas Aquinas, *Summa Theologica*, III, Q. 82, art. 1.

concern about irregularities and a loss of the sense of reverence in liturgical celebrations.[258]

John Paul II warned against the tendency of dumbing down the liturgy in the interests of intelligibility. "Conscious participation" he tells us, calls for proper instruction in the mysteries of the liturgy, but, he asserts, "*It does not mean a constant attempt within the liturgy itself to make the implicit explicit*, since this often leads to a verbosity and informality which are alien to the Roman rite and end by trivializing the act of worship. Nor does it mean the suppression of all subconscious experience, which is vital in a liturgy that thrives on symbols that speak to the subconscious just as they speak to the conscious."[259]

---

[258] "I am convinced that the crisis in the Church that we are experiencing today is to a large extent due to the disintegration of the liturgy, which at times has even come to be conceived of *etsi Deus non daretur*: in that it is a matter of indifference whether or not God exists and whether or not He speaks to us and hears us. But when the community of faith, the world-wide unity of the Church and her history, and the mystery of the living Christ are no longer visible in the liturgy, where else, then, is the Church to become visible in her spiritual essence? Then the community is celebrating only itself, an activity that is utterly fruitless. And, because the ecclesial community cannot have its origin from itself but emerges as a unity only from the Lord, through faith, such circumstances will inexorably result in a disintegration into sectarian parties of all kinds — partisan opposition within a Church tearing itself apart. This is why we need a new Liturgical Movement, which will call into life the real heritage of the Second Vatican Council" (Cardinal Joseph Ratzinger, *Milestones: Memoirs 1927–1977* [San Francisco: Ignatius Press, 1998], 148–149).

[259] Bl. John Paul II, Address, October 9, 1998, no. 3 (italics in original).

The Eucharistic Liturgy

The challenge now, he affirms is to move beyond the misunderstandings and to return to a deeper appropriation of the universal, the vertical and the eternal aspects of the liturgy, that is, to a greater appreciation of the cosmic and eschatological dimensions of Catholic worship.[260]

In an interview in the year 2000, Cardinal Ratzinger made some trenchant comments about the state of the liturgy:

> The Second Vatican Council undoubtedly had in mind organic growth and renewal [of the liturgy]. But we have to see clearly that today there are widespread tendencies toward conducting simple dismantling and reassembly—and they are thereby doing something that cannot be reconciled with the nature of the liturgy. We do at least need a new liturgical consciousness, to be rid of this spirit of arbitrary fabrication. Things have gone so far that Sunday liturgy groups are cobbling together the liturgy for themselves. What is being offered here is the work of a few clever and hardworking people who have made something up. But what I encounter in that is no longer the Wholly Other, the Holy One being offered to me, but rather the cleverness and the hard work of a few people. And I notice that this is not what I am looking for. It's too little, and it is something else.
>
> The most important thing today is that we should gain respect for the liturgy and for the fact that it is not to be manipulated. That we learn to know it again as the living entity that has grown up and has been given to us, in which we take part in the heavenly liturgy. That we

[260] Cf. ibid., no. 2.

do not seek self-fulfillment in it but rather the gift that comes to us.[261]

Old Testament Liturgy

The Church reads the books of the Old Testament in the light of the Paschal event to discover the testimony they bear to the history of salvation. This has implications not only for the theology, but also for the liturgy of the New Covenant. The institution of the Passover feast, the making of the Sinai covenant, and the establishment of religious worship for the people of Israel find their fulfillment in the liturgy instituted by Christ.

Liturgical legislation was an essential element of the Sinaic covenant. Since the Chosen People were to be "a priestly kingdom and a holy nation" (Exod. 19:6), the whole of life was to come under the influence of religion and be sanctified. The Mosaic religion in fact inculcated a profound reverence for God—his majesty was symbolized by the extraordinary care exercised in the preparation of the Hebrew cult with reference to the sanctuary, the Ark, and the Holy of Holies. The need for absolute ritual purity impressed on the Hebrews this sense of God's sanctity. There was a clear perception among the Israelites of the need for redemption and of the offering of sacrifice for this purpose. By means of the different sacrifices—holocaust, peace and sin offerings, and so forth—the Hebrew people would now be able to glorify the God who delivered them from Egypt.

---

[261] Joseph Cardinal Ratzinger, *God and the World: A Conversation with Peter Seewald* (San Francisco: Ignatius Press, 2000), 414–415.

The Eucharistic Liturgy

In the Old Testament we find detailed instructions given by Yahweh to Moses relating to every aspect of the liturgy of the covenant—the feasts, the sanctuary, prescriptions about the different types of sacrifice (cf. Exod. 25–31). Here too we encounter comprehensive legislation about the ordination of priests, the different liturgical rites—nothing is left to chance, nor is there any scope for personal innovation. The book of Leviticus prefigures what becomes a reality in the New Testament. Many of its passages, particularly in the letter to the Hebrews, use Leviticus as a reference point. The minute details as regards design and dimensions, and the specific indications about the quality of materials, fabrics, and furniture to be used in the construction of the Tabernacle, emphasize on the one hand the transcendence of God and on the other his closeness to his people. At the same time we see that the liturgy of the Old Covenant is fulfilled in the New with several points of continuity—listening to the word of God, offering sacrifice, praying the psalms in the Divine Office, the tabernacle as the locus par excellence of God's presence among men.

It is salutary to reflect on the fact that all these indications were given directly by God himself for a liturgy which was infinitely inferior to that of the Christian era. Under the old dispensation Temple worship was focused on the sacrifice of mere animals. However, in the cult of the New Covenant, where the principal act of worship is the renewal of the sacrifice of the Son of God, we intuit how much more worthy the liturgical arrangements for the celebration of the eucharistic sacrifice should be. It is a revealing lesson for us on the importance of everything the Church lays down about the liturgy, especially the celebration of the Eucharist. As we are reminded in *Dominicae Cenae*: "The Eucharist is a common possession of the whole Church as the sacrament of her unity. And thus the Church has the strict duty to specify everything that concerns participation in it and its celebration."[262]

What is obvious too is that the liturgy of the Old Testament is not a humanly crafted worship; it is made present through God's revelation to Moses. Consequently authentic liturgy implies that it is God himself who reveals how best we can worship him.[263] In the same way that Scripture is a work inspired by the Holy Spirit and an expression of God's self-revelation, so also the liturgy is a work of God and an integral part of the living Tradition of the Church, which has to be transmitted and interpreted with the same fidelity and attention as the word of God.

Many of the current criticisms of the liturgy relate to the need for a deeper sense of reverence and transcendence, and the elimination of informality, improvisation, and overemphasis on horizontal engagement. There is also an increasing awareness that this will not come about without the recovery of a more profound sense of the eschatological dimension of the liturgy expressed in church music, art, and design. Reflection on the ideas of redemption, transcendence, holiness, and splendor that characterized the Old Covenant worship will also help to reclaim whatever may have been lost to the liturgy through too humanistic an interpretation of how divine worship should be offered to God.

The Catechism and the Renewal of the Liturgy

The teaching of the Catechism of the Catholic Church fosters a clear perception of the transcendent nature of the liturgy.

---

[262] Bl. John Paul II, *Dominicae Cenae*, no. 12.
[263] Cf. Ratzinger, *The Spirit of the Liturgy*, 21–22.

The Eucharistic Liturgy

Here we find the best insights of the Liturgical Movement and the permanently valid elements of this tradition.[264] The *Catechism* makes its own the definition and description of the liturgy contained in *Sacrosanctum concilium*:

> The liturgy then is rightly seen as an exercise of the priestly office of Jesus Christ. It involves the presentation of man's sanctification under the guise of signs perceptible by the senses and its accomplishment in ways appropriate to each of these signs. In it full public worship is performed by the Mystical Body of Jesus Christ, that is, by the Head and his members. From this it follows that every liturgical celebration, because it is an action of Christ the priest and of his Body which is the Church, is a sacred action surpassing all others. No other action of the Church can equal its efficacy by the same title and to the same degree.[265]

While the liturgy has an essentially Trinitarian dimension, the priest will be particularly conscious of the christological aspect.[266] Christ, now seated at the right hand of the Father,

---

[264] Cf. Cardinal Joseph Ratzinger, *A New Song for the Lord* (New York: The Crossroad Publishing Company, 1997), 133.

[265] CCC, no. 1070, quoting SC 7 §2–3.

[266] "In the liturgy of the New Covenant every liturgical action, especially the celebration of the Eucharist and the sacraments, is an encounter between Christ and the Church. The liturgical assembly derives its unity from the "communion of the Holy Spirit," who gathers the children of God into the one Body of Christ. This assembly transcends racial, cultural, social—indeed all human affinities. The assembly should prepare itself to encounter its Lord and to become "a people well disposed" (CCC, nos. 1097, 1098).

acts through the sacraments he instituted to communicate his grace, making present his own Paschal Mystery. He always associates the Church with himself in offering worship to the Father.[267]

The ordained priesthood, which is at the service of the priesthood of all the baptized, guarantees that it really is Christ who acts in the sacraments. By means of the apostolic power transmitted from one generation of bishops to the next, the priest is the sacramental bond which ties the liturgical action to the words and actions of Christ, the source and foundation of the sacraments.[268] In this way the priest sees himself inserted by divine gift and grace into the source of that spiritual energy which is the Paschal Mystery, entrusted with the responsibility to channel these graces to souls in the most effective manner possible.

[267] Cf. CCC, nos. 1084–1089. "The liturgy is not celebrated by the individual, but by the body of the faithful. This is not composed merely of the persons who may be present in the church; it is not the assembled congregation. On the contrary, it reaches out beyond the bounds of space to embrace all the faithful on earth. Simultaneously it reaches beyond the bounds of time, to this extent, that the body which is praying upon earth knows itself to be at one with those for whom time no longer exists, who, being perfected, exist in Eternity. Yet this definition does not exhaust the conception of the universality and the all-embracingness which characterise the fellowship of the liturgy. The entity which performs the liturgical actions is not merely the sum total of all individual Catholics. It *does* consist of all those united in one body, but only in so far as this unity is of itself something, apart from the millions which compose it. And that something is the Church" (Romano Guardini, *The Spirit of the Liturgy* [London: Sheed and Ward, 1937], 37–38).
[268] Cf. CCC, no. 1120.

The Eucharistic Liturgy

The Sacramental Character of the Liturgy

In everyday life signs and symbols serve an important function. Because we are social beings we need to communicate with each other through language, gestures and actions. The same holds true for our relationship with God. He speaks to us through his visible creation, and these realities in turn can be a means for man to offer worship to God. The liturgy of the Church presupposes and sanctifies elements from creation and human culture, conferring on them the dignity of signs and causes of grace. This is the basis of the sacramental principle — as a creature of body and soul man perceives spiritual realities through signs and symbols. In the Old Testament the Chosen People received from God distinctive signs that marked their liturgical life. These included purifications, anointings, sacrifices of crops and animals, but especially the Passover meal. In the sacraments of the New Covenant, Christ gives natural elements such as water, oil, bread, and wine a new supernatural dimension so that they transmit specific graces when they are taken up into the liturgical action and specified by the consecrating words.[269] Thus all the signs and actions of the liturgy

---

[269] Cf. ibid., 1145–1152. As Romano Guardini points out: "In the liturgy the faithful are confronted by a new world, rich in types and symbols, which are expressed in terms of ritual, actions, vestments, implements, places, and hours, all of which are highly significant.... The people who really live by the liturgy will come to learn that the bodily movements, the actions, and material objects which it employs are all of the highest significance. It offers great opportunities of expression, of knowledge, and of spiritual experience; it is emancipating in its action, and capable of presenting a truth far more strongly and convincingly than can the mere word of mouth" (*The Spirit of the Liturgy*, 70, 84).

should lead to the mystery beyond the visible. Since Pentecost, it is through the sacramental signs of the Church that the Holy Spirit carries on the work of sanctification.

Through the words, actions, and symbols that constitute the scheme of every celebration, the Holy Spirit puts the faithful and ministers in living relationship with Christ, Word and Image of the Father, so that they can insert into their own life the meaning of what they hear, contemplate, and carry out.

St. Thomas tells us that the liturgy expresses in concrete images what it is difficult for the mind to grasp.[270] To maintain and encourage the perception of the liturgy as sacramental, it is celebrated with ceremonial language, is punctuated by symbolic actions, and is focused on the transcendence of the redemptive action of Christ. "It speaks measuredly and melodiously; it employs formal, rhythmic gestures; it is clothed in colors and garments foreign to everyday life; it is carried out in places and at hours which have been co-ordinate and systematized according to sublimer laws than ours. It is the highest sense of the life of a child, in which everything is picture, melody and song."[271]

In the liturgy "man, with the aid of grace, is given the opportunity ... of really becoming that which according to divine destiny he should be and longs to be, a child of God."[272] Devel-

---

[270] Cf. *Summa Theologica*, I-II, Q. 101, art. 2, obj. 2, ad. 2.

[271] Guardini, *The Spirit of the Liturgy*, 101–102.

[272] Ibid., 102. "Such is the wonderful fact which the liturgy demonstrates: it unites art and reality in a supernatural childhood before God. That which formerly existed in the world of unreality only, and was rendered in art as the expression of mature human life, has here become reality. These forms are the vital expression of real and frankly supernatural life. But this has one thing in common with the play of the child and the life of art — it has no purpose,

oping this analogy Pope Benedict says that the liturgy should be a reminder that "we are all children, or should be children, in relation to that true life towards which we yearn to go." In this sense the liturgy should be a prelude to eternal life, "a rediscovery within us of true childhood, of openness to greatness still to come, which is still unfilled in adult life.... Thus it would imprint on the seemingly real life of daily existence the mark of future freedom, break open the walls that confine us, and let the light of heaven shine down upon earth."[273]

If there is faith in the sacramental reality, a conviction grows that something happens which is altogether exceptional — Christ has become really present among us. Because man wants to transcend himself, the solemnity of the liturgy appeals to something deep in his soul, raising his mind and heart to the contemplation of the divine and the infinite.[274]

but it is full of profound meaning. It is not work, but play. To be at play, or to fashion a work of art in God's sight — not to create but to exist — such is the essence of the liturgy. From this is derived its sublime mingling of profound earnestness and divine joyfulness. The fact that the liturgy gives a thousand strict and careful directions on the quality of the language, gestures, colours, garments and instruments which it employs, can only be understood by those who are able to take art and play seriously" (Guardini, *The Spirit of the Liturgy*, 102–103).

[273] Ratzinger, *The Spirit of the Liturgy*, 14.

[274] This is why a priest is not doing his congregation any favors when, in the interests of a supposed community bonding, he greets them with a cheery "good morning" from the altar. From the very beginning of the liturgy he thus sends a signal to the congregation that they are participating in something almost trite and banal. It undermines the conviction that they have come to participate in a divine action, confusing the distinction between the sacred and the profane.

The Most Holy Eucharist

The early Christians had a deep conviction that when celebrating the *Dominicum* they were participating in something of such an exalted nature that the catechumens were required to depart the assembly before the liturgy of the Eucharist proper began. Only those who had the fullness of the Faith could remain and adore.[275]

The main reason some people, especially the young, find the Mass is boring or meaningless is a failure to grasp the sacramental character of the sacred actions. It is only through faith that the meaning signified by the words is perceived as objective reality. This is to recognize that Christ's true Body is present at Mass, and that the nourishment of soul which comes from communicating with it derives not from a sense of community, but exclusively from the power of God in the Eucharist.[276] A true and deep sense of the sacramental is one of the best defenses against the desacralization of the liturgy.

One great danger with regard to liturgy, however, is routine—we cannot allow the sacred encounter to become just a habitual exercise for us lest we lose reverential fear. Our presence before God in the liturgy should be one of reverence and a sense of wonder, knowing that we are in the presence of the eucharistic Christ, with his Body, Blood, soul, and divinity.

The Eschatological Dimension of the Liturgy

A fundamental element of the Christian theology of worship is the perception that Christ is the Lamb of God who takes away the sin of the world. When John the Baptist used this

[275] Cf. Georges Chevrot, *Our Mass* (London: Burns and Oates, 1948), 189.
[276] Cf. Josef Pieper, *In Search of the Sacred* (San Francisco: Ignatius Press, 1991), 28.

description to identify Jesus for two disciples (cf. John 1:29–31) he was well aware of the Old Testament references that prefigured the true Lamb (cf. Exod. 12:6–7; Isa. 53:7), Christ, the victim in the sacrifice of Calvary. This is why St. Paul says, "Christ, our paschal lamb, has been sacrificed" (1 Cor. 5:7). The book of Revelation presents Jesus victorious and glorious in heaven as the sacrificed lamb (cf. Rev. 5:6–14), surrounded by saints, martyrs, and virgins (cf. Rev. 7:9, 14; 14:1–5) who offer him the praise and glory due to him as God (cf. Rev. 7:10). Through Christ's sacrifice the heavenly liturgy is made present in the world.

This essentially eschatological nature of the liturgy, which is a basic point of reference for the Church's liturgy, is richly developed in the documents of Vatican II:

> In the earthly liturgy we take part in a foretaste of that heavenly liturgy which is celebrated in the Holy City of Jerusalem toward which we journey as pilgrims, where Christ is sitting at the right hand of God, Minister of the holies and of the true tabernacle. With all the warriors of the heavenly army we sing a hymn of glory to the Lord; venerating the memory of the saints, we hope for some part and fellowship with them; we eagerly await the Savior, our Lord Jesus Christ, until he our life shall appear and we too will appear with him in glory.[277]

A wider dogmatic base is given to this understanding of the liturgy in *Lumen gentium*:

> It is especially in the sacred liturgy that our union with the heavenly church is best realized; in the liturgy,

---

[277] *Sacrosanctum concilium*, no. 8.

through the sacramental signs, the power of the Holy Spirit acts on us, and with community rejoicing we celebrate together the praise of the divine majesty, when all those of every tribe and tongue and people and nation (cf. Apoc. 5:9) who have been redeemed by the blood of Christ and gathered together into one Church glorify, in one common song of praise, the one and triune God. When, then, we celebrate the Eucharistic sacrifice we are most closely united to the worship of the heavenly Church; when in the fellowship of communion we honor and remember the glorious Mary ever virgin, St. Joseph, the holy apostles and martyrs and all the saints.[278]

Do priests normally celebrate Mass with this vision of the liturgy? Is this the kind of worship that the faithful usually experience on Sundays? In all honesty we would have to say that this eschatological dimension is rarely transmitted with the clarity and significance given it by Vatican II.

There are historical reasons for this. The cultural and social dynamic of the post–Vatican II years led to a secularization of eschatological themes. Excessive importance was given to liturgy as a service to culture and society, often resulting in its reductive instrumentalizaton for narrowly socially conscious ends.[279]

A greater awareness of this eschatological dimension of the liturgy will allow the priest to celebrate Mass with a deeper spirit of its transcendence and thus avoid the danger of parish worship being reduced to the human dimensions of the local

[278] *Lumen gentium*, no. 50.
[279] Cf. M. Francis Mannion, "Liturgy in the Third Millennium," in *Priest and People* (December 1999): 459.

community. If people understand that every Mass is a participation in the eternal liturgy which is celebrated in heaven, it will evince a deeper sense of reverence and promote the conviction that the Eucharist is truly a pledge of future glory. Since the true glory of the liturgy is to be "a window onto the eternal Trinitarian love,"[280] everything that goes on in the sanctuary should be in function of this noble objective.

Churches and the Mass

In churches of East and West we find the great masterpieces of art—in painting, sculpture, and stained glass—reflecting this eschatological vision of the liturgy. With the secularization caused by post-Enlightenment thinking, the culture lost its anchorage in the eternal truths and this loss of reference is clearly reflected not only in secular art, but in many of the churches that are built today. Minimalist spaces, banal exteriors, and disfigured religious art reflect a jarring discontinuity with the accumulated artistic wisdom of the past. Because Christianity is a historical religion, as such it must identify itself with the past to bring Christ into the present: "Jesus Christ is the same yesterday, today, and forever" (Heb. 13:8). New and original work should be inspired by this tradition so as to connect artistic and architectural contributions of previous and future generations.[281]

A church should reflect the fact that it provides an environment for the most sacred and sublime action that takes place on this earth. People behave with respect and reverence

[280] Aidan Nichols, *The Service of Glory* (Edinburgh: T. and T. Clark Publishers, Ltd., 1997), 7.

[281] Cf. Duncan Stroik, "Displaced Tabernacles," in *Crisis* (June 2000): 27.

when they are conscious of being in a sacred place. In contemporary culture, which has been infected with "the virus of desacralization,"[282] the concept of the sacred is becoming less clear and needs to be affirmed in more specific language. Hence the requirement at present to emphasize rather than dilute the tradition of Christian art and architecture so that churches immediately communicate the sense of being a sacred place.

The fact that a church is built to surround an altar on which is reenacted the sacrifice of Calvary is what distinguishes it from every other type of building where people gather. The history of the liturgy shows how the insight and ingenuity of the Christian people down through the centuries has developed many styles of church architecture. From a conviction of faith as to what happens there, certain boundary lines are laid down as regards physical orientation, furniture, and behavior. While such markers will have a clear significance in relation to the local culture, at the same time, because the celebration of the liturgy has a common universal dimension, it is not surprising that some elements of church architecture are reflected in every nation. Nor is it surprising that for a Christian people, who live by faith and see the Mass as the center of existence, the challenge of church architecture would inspire buildings of permanent artistic merit. Vatican II has reaffirmed this aspiration: "Holy Mother Church has always been the patron of the fine arts and has ever sought their noble ministry, to the end especially that all things set apart for use in divine worship should be worthy, becoming, and beautiful, signs and symbols of things supernatural.[283] ... Thus in the course of the centuries she has

[282] Cf. Pieper, In Search of the Sacred, 26.
[283] Sacrosanctum concilium, no. 122.

brought into existence a treasury of art which must be preserved with every care."[284]

The worship of God unites people and gives their being together its true liturgical meaning. Throughout history this transcendental bonding has taken place in the sacred space set aside for worship, whether in the Temple or the synagogue of the Old Testament or, under the New Covenant, in an oratory, church, or cathedral. There is a strong parallel between the liturgical arrangements of the sacred places of the two covenants since, in both, people came together to hear the word of Scripture and to seal the covenant by means of sacrifice.[285] Christianity has also learned from the Temple liturgy how to surround the holy place of the sanctuary with signs of reverence that befit the mysterious presence of God. When the Jewish synagogue had to be reshaped for Christian worship, we see both a continuity and a newness in the relationship of the Old Covenant to the New.[286]

One of the challenges of liturgical reform is the recovery of the sense of reverence in churches. Why do many people no longer genuflect when passing in front of the tabernacle? Witness, too, the chatter before Mass that is common in many churches. This loss of the sense of the transcendent is due to several factors, not least a dilution of faith in the Real Presence of Christ in the Blessed Sacrament. Church design that gives priority to functionalism over beauty does little to encourage people to remain to pray. Certainly *Lumen gentium* envisages a higher architectural concept when it uses metaphors such as "the dwelling place of God among men," "the holy temple," "the image of the Holy City," and "the New Jerusalem" to

[284] Ibid., no. 123.
[285] Cf. Ratzinger, *The Spirit of the Liturgy*, 63.
[286] Cf. ibid., 75.

describe a church building.[287] Sacred architecture should make the world of the spirit perceptible through material construction. Thus John Paul II affirms that the church should be

> a worthy place for prayer and sacred functions both for its good order, cleanliness, the neatness with which it is maintained, and for the artistic beauty of its environment, which has a great importance for the way it forms and inspires prayer. For this reason the Council recommends that the priest "properly cultivate liturgical knowledge and art" (*Presbyterorum ordinis*, 5). I have called attention to these aspects because they too belong to the complex picture of a good "care of souls" on the part of priests.[288]

Gothic Cathedrals

During the fall of 2009, Pope Benedict XVI devoted some of his Wednesday audience addresses to a consideration of theologians of the Middle Ages. In this context he included a presentation about the art of Gothic cathedrals.[289] He said that Christian faith, which was deeply rooted in the men and women of these centuries, not only gave rise to masterpieces of theological literature, but also "inspired one of the loftiest creations of universal civilization: the cathedrals, true glory of the Middle Ages."[290] For almost three centuries, beginning in the eleventh, Europe witnessed an extraordinary artistic and

---

[287] Cf. *Lumen gentium*, no. 6.
[288] John Paul II, Address, May 12, 1993, no. 6.
[289] Benedict XVI, Address, November 18, 2009.
[290] Apart from Gothic there are also some spectacular Romanesque and Norman cathedrals.

architectural development, especially in relation to its ecclesiastical buildings.

Pope Benedict XVI pointed out a number of factors that contributed to this rebirth. First of all, historical conditions were more favorable in that there was greater political security; there was also a constant increase in population, with the development of cities and wealth. Thirdly, stonemason-architects found increasingly elaborate technical solutions to expand the dimensions of buildings, ensuring at the same time their stability and artistic design. However, Benedict affirmed, it was primarily due to the spiritual zeal of monasticism, then in full expansion, that abbey churches were erected, where the liturgy would be celebrated with dignity and solemnity, where the faithful could remain to pray, attracted by the veneration of the relics of the saints, the object of countless pilgrimages. In this way Romanesque churches and cathedrals were born, "characterized by their longitudinal development along the naves to house numerous faithful; very solid churches, with thick walls, stone vaults and simple and essential lines."

In the twelfth and thirteenth centuries, beginning in the north of France, technical advances allowed another type of architecture to develop for the construction of sacred buildings: the Gothic style. This style had two new characteristics that distinguished it from the Romanesque—a vertical thrust and vibrant luminosity. "Gothic cathedrals," Benedict affirmed, "were a synthesis of faith and art expressed harmoniously through the universal and fascinating language of beauty, which still today awakens wonder." With the introduction of ribbed and pointed vaults, supported by robust pillars and buttresses, it was possible to raise notably the height of these churches. The upward thrust of the Gothic was an invitation to prayer; the architectural lines were an expression in stone of souls longing for God. The enclosing walls were punctuated and embellished by large, colorful stained-glass windows, which, scene by scene, provided a catechetical instruction for the people. From these colorful windows, a cascade of light was shed on the faithful, narrating the history of salvation and inviting them to be part of that history.

The people were catechized not only by means of the radiant light from the windows, but also by means of the lavish sculptures in the cathedrals which illustrated the content of the liturgical year. This statuary represented episodes from the Gospels, especially the suffering Christ, which was able to inspire piety and repentance of sins. As Pope Benedict points out: "With their faces full of beauty, tenderness, intelligence, Gothic sculpture of the thirteenth century reveals a happy and serene piety which is pleased to emanate heartfelt and filial devotion to the Mother of God, seen at times as a young, smiling and maternal woman, and represented primarily as the sovereign of heaven and earth, powerful and merciful."

The faithful who filled the Gothic cathedrals found in them images of the saints who were models of Christian life and intercessors before God. Here, too, they discovered representations of work in the fields, in the sciences, and in the arts, which helped them offer their secular activities in the place where the liturgy was celebrated.

Benedict reminded his audience of two great truths. Firstly, the works of art reflected in the Romanesque and Gothic cathedrals are incomprehensible if one does not take into account the religious soul that inspired them. Secondly, "the forces of the Romanesque style and the splendor of the Gothic cathedrals remind us that the *via pulchritudinis*, the way of beauty, is a privileged and fascinating way to approach the mystery of God." This beauty is a reflection of the splendor of God, of the Eternal Word made flesh.

Benedict XVI concluded his address with these words: "Gradually, Gothic architecture replaced the Romanesque, adding height and luminosity to the previous style. The Gothic cathedral translates the aspirations of the soul into architectural lines, and is a synthesis between faith, art and beauty which still raises our hearts and minds to God today. When faith encounters art, in particular in the liturgy, a profound synthesis is created, making visible the Invisible."

Munificence and Splendor in the Liturgy

Liturgy down through the ages has not just been a vehicle for reverence, worship, and prayer. It has also manifested another aspect, that of "abundance and enthusiasm, of generosity and almost extravagance."[291] The liturgy has in fact inspired many of the highest expressions of Western culture in architecture, metalwork, painting, stained glass, and sculpture. It was motivated by the conviction that the sacred action of the liturgy transcended all other human activity and was therefore deserving of the richest expressions of man's artistic imagination and skill. Hence we see why Christ would praise the generosity of the woman who used a flask of expensive ointment to prepare his body for burial. He described what she did as "a beautiful thing," and he promised that her story would be told wherever the Gospel was preached (cf. Mark 14:3–9; Matt. 26:6–13).

What is also striking about the Mosaic liturgy is the largesse and splendor that characterized everything related to the

---

[291] Cf. Pieper, *In Search of the Sacred*, 43.

worship of Yahweh. We see this particularly in the instructions Moses received from God for the construction of the Ark and the Tabernacle, which were to be the physical expression of Yahweh's presence among the Chosen People (cf. Exod. 25–31). The plates and dishes, flagons and bowls used in the sacrifices were to be of pure gold (cf. Exod. 25:23–30). The seven-branch candlestick was clearly a work of exceptional craftsmanship (cf. Exod. 25:31–40). Not only were the candle snuffers to be fashioned of gold, but also the very trays on which they rested. The Tabernacle was to be made of silver.

The tabernacle in which the Blessed Sacrament is reserved takes the place previously occupied by the Ark of the Covenant and is the complete fulfillment of what it represented — it is the new Holy of Holies. The centrality of the Ark to the sanctuary, its beauty of design, and the reverence with which it was held by the Chosen People are all pointers to the very special consideration that should be given to the artistic, architectural, and liturgical presentation of the tabernacle in the churches of the New Covenant. If the Ark housed merely the symbolic presence of Yahweh, how much more significant is the new Holy of Holies, which contains the Real Presence of the Incarnate Son of God. In the revised *General Instruction of the Roman Missal*, there is a renewed emphasis on the need for the tabernacle to have a prominent location in churches.[292]

When we come to the question of the priest's vestments in the Old Testament, we find a description of garments designed for beauty and glory (cf. Exod. 28). They are to be made of the richest material and only by the most accomplished craftsmen. The quality of vestments worn by the Temple priests points to

---

[292] Cf. *General Instruction of the Roman Missal*, 315.

the significance of vestments for the celebration of the liturgy of the New Covenant. The visible appearance of the priest on the altar, the way he is vested, the reverence of his approach to the liturgy—all this can have a profound effect on the people present at Mass. This is because liturgical vestments took their specific form, not because of any practical need stemming from their specific use, but as a consequence of historical association and the cultural environment. And yet they proclaim loud and clear that, for a certain span of time, their wearer is speaking and acting, *not* as the individual named and described on his driver's license, but *in persona Christi*.[293] Vestments are a reminder of that Pauline image of "putting on Christ" (Gal. 3:7). They

> are a challenge to the priest to surrender himself to the dynamism of breaking out of the capsule of self and being fashioned anew by Christ and for Christ. They remind those who participate in the Mass of the new way that began with Baptism and continues with the Eucharist, the way that leads to the future world already delineated in our daily lives by the sacraments.[294] ... The liturgical vestment has a meaning that goes beyond that of external garments. It is an anticipation of the new clothing, the risen Body of Jesus Christ, that new reality which awaits us when the "earthly" tent is taken down and which gives us a "place to stay." (Cf. John 14:2)[295]

In this context we can understand more clearly why neglecting to wear appropriate liturgical vestments is one of the abuses reprobated by Church authority.

[293] Cf. Pieper, *In Search of the Sacred*, 73.
[294] Ratzinger, *The Spirit of the Liturgy*, 217.
[295] Ibid., 219.

The Most Holy Eucharist

Participation of the Laity in the Liturgy

The participation of the laity in the liturgy is one of the most visible consequences of the liturgical renewal since Vatican II. Being a priestly people, called to offer spiritual sacrifices, they are empowered to participate actively in the liturgy. The Mass for them, as for priests, is the "root and centre"[296] of the spiritual life. Thus their very vocation demands a profound participation in the eucharistic sacrifice. However, a deep understanding of what the Mass is about is the basis of any meaningful involvement in it. But this is not something that can be improvised. As John Paul II advises: "*Conscious participation* calls for the entire community to be properly instructed in the mysteries of the liturgy lest the experience of worship degenerate into a form of ritualism."[297]

The *Catechism of the Catholic Church* provides a wealth of teaching about this central element of the Faith, which the priest does well to communicate to his people if they are to appreciate what full and conscious participation in the liturgy means.[298] Without this knowledge, without this transcendental approach to the liturgy, there is a danger that the Mass will be seen in a reductive manner by the participating congregation, often no more than a way of celebrating its own cultural and religious identity rather than the objective historical realization of the Redemption accomplished by Christ on the Cross.[299]

---

[296] *Presbyterorum ordinis*, no. 14.
[297] Address to U.S. Bishops, October 9, 1998, no. 3, in *L'Osservatore Romano*, October 14, 1998 (italics in original).
[298] Cf. CCC, 1077–1186, 1322–1405.
[299] Cf. Aidan Nichols O.P., *Looking at the Liturgy* (San Francisco: Ignatius Press, 1996), 55.

The Eucharistic Liturgy

In this context Pope John Paul II clarified a point that had been a bone of contention—the precise implications of the council's call for a "full, conscious and active participation in the liturgy."[300] Full participation, he tells us, means that every member of the community has a part to play in the liturgy. Failure to respect the different roles of priest and people, however, could "lead to a *clericalizing* of the laity and a *laicizing* of the priesthood."[301]

What does the "active participation" in the liturgy, affirmed by Vatican II, mean? Ratzinger explains that unfortunately this *participatio actuosa* was quickly misunderstood to mean something external, entailing a need for general activity, as if as many people as possible should be visibly engaged in action. Since "participation" refers to a principal action in which everyone has a part, we must first of all determine what that central action (*actio*) is in which people are supposed to take part. Basically this is the Eucharistic Prayer, which forms the core of the liturgical celebration. But the Eucharistic Canon is much more than speech—it is *actio* in the highest sense, the *actio divina* (divine action) of God. Because of his ontological bonding with Christ, the being of the priest is mysteriously appropriated by the Word Incarnate and the event of Calvary is re-presented on the altar in an unbloody manner by means of the words, "This is my Body," "This is my Blood" spoken through the mouth of the priest. This is the distinctive character of the Christian liturgy by comparison with that of the Old Testament. God himself acts and does what is essential.[302]

[300] *Sacrosanctum concilium*, no. 14.
[301] Address, October 9, 1998, no. 3 (italics in original).
[302] Cf. Cardinal Joseph Ratzinger, *The Spirit of the Liturgy*, San Francisco 2000, pp. 171–173.

For the laity, active participation in the liturgy is expressed primarily by uniting with the Sacrifice of the Mass their efforts to sanctify daily work, family life, and social commitments.[303] Their participation in the liturgy is more complete when they draw from it the spiritual energy they need to evangelize the culture, bringing Christ and the values of the Gospel into every aspect of human activity.[304] The essential role of the liturgy for the laity is, then, to make them a priestly people in the middle of the world, to activate their capacity to be witnesses to Christ in the home and at work and, in this way, to sanctify temporal realities. "The true liturgical action is the deed of God, and for that very reason the liturgy of faith always reaches beyond the cultic act into everyday life, which must itself become "liturgical," a service for the transformation of the world. Much more is required of the body than carrying objects around and other such activities. A demand is made on the body in all its involvements in the circumstances of everyday life.[305]

John Paul II underscores the relationship between authentic liturgical renewal and effective evangelization: "In so far as developments in liturgical renewal are superficial or unbalanced, our energies for a new evangelization will be compromised; and in so far as our vision falls short of the new evangelization our liturgical renewal will be reduced to external and possibly unsound adaptation. The Roman rite has always been a form of worship that looks to mission." Even with the dismissal, the community is sent out to evangelize the world in obedience to Christ's command (cf. Matt. 28:19–20).[306]

---

[303] Cf. *Lumen gentium*, 34.
[304] Cf. *Dies Domini*, 45.
[305] Ratzinger, ibid., pp. 175–176.
[306] Address, October 9, 1998, no. 4.

The Eucharistic Liturgy

Our Posture during Mass

Because we believe that Christ is present in the Eucharist, it has always seemed the appropriate posture to kneel before it:

> Kneeling does not come from any culture—it comes from the Bible and its knowledge of God. The central importance of kneeling in the Bible can be seen in a very concrete way. The word *proskynein* (to kneel) alone occurs fifty-nine times in the New Testament, twenty-four of which are in the Apocalypse, the book of the heavenly liturgy which is presented to the Church as the standard for her own liturgy.... St. Luke tells us that Jesus prayed on his knees. This prayer, the prayer by which Jesus enters his Passion, is an example for us, both as a gesture and in its content.[307]

Our behavior should give to inner recollection and reverence an outward bodily expression. Earlier, Communion used to be received kneeling, which made perfectly good sense. Nowadays it is done standing. But this standing, too, should be standing in reverence before the Lord.

The attitude of kneeling ought never to be allowed to disappear from the Church. It is the most expressive physical expression of Christian piety, by which, on the one hand, we remain upright, looking out, gazing on him, but on the other hand, we nonetheless bow down.[308]

Genuflecting reverently before the tabernacle is a way of atoning to Jesus for the insults he suffered on the night of his Passion when the Roman soldiers made him a mock king.

[307] Ratzinger, *The Spirit of the Liturgy*, 184–187.
[308] Ratzinger, *God and the World*, 409–410.

Others should learn from the care with which we genuflect that we have faith in the Real Presence of Christ in the tabernacle. Likewise, the priest should genuflect with profound reverence during Mass or when crossing in front of the tabernacle.

In this context it is worth noting the comments of Cardinal Antonio Cañizares, Prefect of the Congregation for Divine Worship and the Discipline of the Sacraments. Asked whether Catholics should receive Communion in the hand or on the tongue, he recommended that they "should receive Communion on the tongue and while kneeling." Receiving Communion in this way, the cardinal continued, "is the sign of adoration that needs to be recovered. I think the entire Church needs to receive Communion while kneeling. In fact, if one receives while standing, a genuflection or profound bow should be made, and this is not happening. If we trivialize Communion, we trivialize everything, and we cannot lose a moment as important as that of receiving Communion, of recognizing the real presence of Christ there, of the God who is the love above all loves."[309]

> Adoring the God of Jesus Christ, who out of love made himself bread broken, is the most effective and radical remedy against the idolatry of the past and of the present. Kneeling before the Eucharist is a profession of freedom: those who bow to Jesus cannot and must not prostrate themselves before any earthly authority, however powerful. We Christians kneel only before God or before the Most Blessed Sacrament because we know and believe that the one true God is present in it, the God who created the world and so loved it that he gave his Only Begotten Son (cf. Jn 3:16). We prostrate ourselves before

[309] Catholic News Agency, July 28, 2011.

a God who first bent over man like the Good Samaritan to assist him and restore his life, and who knelt before us to wash our dirty feet. Adoring the Body of Christ means believing that there, in that piece of Bread, Christ is really there, and gives true sense to life, to the immense universe as to the smallest creature, to the whole of human history as to the most brief existence. Adoration is prayer that prolongs the celebration and Eucharistic Communion and in which the soul continues to be nourished: it is nourished with love, truth, peace; it is nourished with hope, because the One before whom we prostrate ourselves doesn't judge us, does not crush us but liberates and transforms us.[310]

Silence in the Liturgy

Active participation in the liturgy does not, however, preclude "the active passivity of *silence, stillness and listening*: indeed it demands it."[311] John Paul II explains the nature of this *active* silence as follows: "Worshippers are not passive, for instance, when listening to the readings or the homily, or following the prayers of the celebrant, and the chants and music of the liturgy. These are experiences of silence and stillness, but they are in their own way profoundly active. In a culture which neither favors nor fosters meditative quiet, the art of interior listening is learned only with difficulty."[312]

[310] Benedict XVI, Homily, May 22, 2008, Solemnity of Corpus Christi.
[311] John Paul II, Address, October 9, 1998, no. 3 (italics in original).
[312] Ibid. Romano Guardini's comments in this context are interesting: "It is in this very aspect of the liturgy that its didactic

The Most Holy Eucharist

It is in this sense that the pope says the liturgy has to be countercultural in an environment where activism is regarded as the essence of being and living.[313] A commentator on this address that John Paul II gave to a group of American bishops has aptly said:

> If we are to foster the awe, reverence, and adoration through which we may know the Word of Christ, then we must love, and not fear silence and stillness in the Mass and in our life. From silence comes the Word. From silence God spoke and created the world. From silence he spoke to Mary and came to dwell in her womb. From silence he sent his Holy Spirit at Pentecost to lead the Church. Meditative quiet, as the Pope laments, is neither favored nor fostered in our culture. Yet there is no getting around the simple fact that only in stillness do we learn to listen with the interior ear. Only in stillness can we build the habit of listening, a habit that, when impeded by the jangle of noise, can never develop. Only in stillness do we

---

aim is to be found, that of teaching the soul not to see purposes everywhere, not to be too conscious of the end it wishes to attain, not to be desirous of being over clever and grown-up, but to understand simplicity in life. The soul must learn to abandon, at least in prayer, the restlessness of purposeful activity; it must learn to waste time for the sake of God and to be prepared for the sacred game with sayings and thought and gestures, without always immediately asking "why?" and "wherefore?" It must learn not to be continually yearning to do something, to attack something, to accomplish something useful, but to play the divinely ordained game of the liturgy in liberty and beauty and holy joy before God" (*The Spirit of the Liturgy*, 106).

[313] Address, October 9, 1998, no. 3.

calm down enough to sense the Lord's presence. Only in stillness do we find out that the Lord loves us and that we are made to love him. Silence, then, is not a den of terror; it is rather the place where we fall in love.[314]

It is surely no accident that increasing numbers of people are trying out different techniques of meditation in search of a spirituality to empty the mind of all that clogs it up. This may well be due to the fact that the way the liturgy is celebrated today frequently fails to provide that silence which is so manifestly necessary in the spiritual life. John Paul II reminds us that only a liturgy that produces a "silence filled with the presence of him who is adored" can respond to the demands and the goals of the Christian life.[315]

It is instructive to note how the revised rite promotes the value of silence in preparation for Mass: "Even before the celebration itself, it is praiseworthy for silence to be observed in church, in the sacristy, and adjacent areas, so that all may dispose themselves for the sacred rites which are to be enacted in a devout and fitting manner."[316]

Music and the Liturgy

While prayerful silence is an integral part of the liturgy, song is also required to give integral human expression to joy, sorrow, consent, and complaint, in order to fulfill the vocation to worship and glorify God.[317] The Hebrew people found it necessary

---

[314] Anne Husted Burleigh, "Common Wisdom," in *Crisis* (January 1999): 58.

[315] Cf. John Paul II, Address, May 3, 1996, no. 5.

[316] *General Instruction of the Roman Missal*, 45.

[317] Cf. Ratzinger, *A New Song for the Lord*, 100.

to sing the psalms to give fuller expression to their prayer and glorification of Yahweh. These chants, with a new christological interpretation, found continuity in the early Church as a means to praise God for the gift of the Paschal Mystery. This, in a very real sense, is the beginning of the tradition of Christian liturgical music.[318]

Vatican II's Constitution on the Sacred Liturgy strongly recommends that the treasury of sacred music should be preserved and cultivated with great care and that Gregorian chant should be given pride of place in liturgical services.[319] We are reminded by the *Catechism* that song and music serve their liturgical function when they fulfill certain criteria: that they constitute beauty expressive of prayer; that the music involves participation by the congregation at the designated times; and that it reflects the solemn character of the celebration. In this way liturgical music and song give glory to God and sanctify the faithful.[320] While exceptionally some churches have man-

---

[318] Ratzinger draws out the implications of this basic reference: "Artistic creation as the Old Testament sees it is something completely different from what the modern age understands by creativity. Today creativity is understood to be the making of something that is completely one's own and completely new. In comparison with this, artistic creativeness in the book of Exodus is seeing something together with God, participating in his creativity; it is exposing the beauty that is already waiting and concealed in creation. This does not diminish the worth of the artist, but is in fact its justification.... For church music this means that everything the Old Testament has to say about art—its necessity, its essence, and its dignity—is concealed in the *bene cantare* of the psalms" (*A New Song for the Lord*, 103).

[319] Cf. *Sacrosanctum concilium*, nos. 114, 116.

[320] Cf. CCC, no. 1157.

aged to maintain this tradition, it is hardly an exaggeration to say that there is considerable dissatisfaction with the state of contemporary Church music. The sense of beauty and art has often given way to banality and mediocrity in an effort to try to be more "meaningful."

Sacrosanctum concilium, as already noted, encourages the use of Gregorian chant. But is this form of music still relevant to contemporary culture? In this context, Pope John Paul II warned against the abandonment of Latin, and especially Gregorian chant, in the liturgy in the interests of intelligibility. Why? Because "if subconscious experience is ignored in worship, an affective and devotional vacuum is created, and the liturgy can become not only too verbal but also too cerebral." The genius of the Roman rite, he concludes, is that "it feeds the heart and the mind, the body and the soul."[321] Chant thus penetrates the heart where it goes to the core of our being, engaging with the image of the Creator and Redeemer in us. Chant dilates the sacred text and allows it to disclose its specifically theological value.[322]

It has been pointed out that when a certain spirit of worldliness entered into the liturgy, one of the first things that came under attack was the tradition of sacred music and liturgical chant.[323] It is necessary to rediscover this tradition, not out of a sense of nostalgia for the past but rather because the modern experiment in liturgical music has hardly been successful in

---

[321] Address, October 9, 1998, no. 3.

[322] Cf. Mark-Daniel Kirby, "Sung Theology: The Liturgical Chant of the Church," in Stratford Caldecott, ed., *Beyond the Prosaic* (Edinburgh: T &T Clark, 1998), 130.

[323] Cf. Stratford Caldecott, "The Spirit of the Liturgical Movement," in *Beyond the Prosaic*, 157.

helping people to pray. Rapidly emptying churches, especially the exodus from Sunday worship of the younger generation, which this music was supposed to attract and hold, suggests that the opposite is the case.[324] It is surely not without significance that in recent years Gregorian chant has been rediscovered as popular music on a massive scale outside of the Church. Consequently, it is perhaps not surprising to note that in the revised rite, even in the context of Mass in the vernacular, we are told that "because the faithful from different countries come together ever more frequently, it is desirable that they know how to sing at least some parts of the Ordinary of the Mass in Latin, especially the profession of faith and the Lord's Prayer."[325]

Liturgical Improvisation

The supernatural unity which is generated as a consequence of the celebration of the eucharistic sacrifice is what gives rise to the sense of Christian community. One of the dangers, however, with liturgical praxis today is the tendency to engender a sense of community as an end in itself. This is a self-defeating exercise since "it is by acceptance through faith of our composition into a supernatural unity through a pre-existing rite that community is engendered, not by devising of new or adapted rites that have the creation of community as their immediate

---

[324] The point has been made that "Deprived of the sacred, sometimes without even knowing what it is they instinctively miss, many abandon religious practice. A whole generation of young people is growing up believing that the essential purpose of the liturgy is didactic; they get bored quickly and stay away" (Mark Drew, "The Spirit or the Letter? Vatican II and Liturgical Reform," in Caldecott, *Beyond the Prosaic*, 51).

[325] *General Instruction of the Roman Missal*, 41.

end. Like happiness, community is not produced by aiming at it directly; rather, it is a vital, indirect consequence of immersion in other things."[326]

This is because fidelity to the system of signs, symbols, and actions is the means of being integrated into the liturgical tradition. It is an affirmation of the universality of the Church. Liturgical improvisation on the part of the priest is, therefore, an action of the individual only, disconnected from the official prayer and worship of the Church.[327] In his review of twenty-five years of liturgical innovation, John Paul II lays down a clear marker: "The Liturgy belongs to the whole body of the Church. It is for this reason that it is not permitted to anyone, even the priest, or any group, to add, subtract or change anything whatsoever on their own initiative. Fidelity to the rites and to the authentic texts of the Liturgy is a requirement of the *Lex orandi,* which must always be in conformity with the *Lex credendi.* A lack of fidelity on this point may even affect the validity of the sacraments."[328]

---

[326] Nichols, *Looking at the Liturgy,* 43.

[327] Cf. Pieper, *In Search of the Sacred,* 41.

[328] John Paul II, Apostolic Letter *Vicesimus Quintus Annus* (December 4, 1988), no. 10. The trend to downgrade ritual caused by the assimilation of particular philosophical influences has been compounded to some extent by what is happening in society in general. Here we see a slackening of family ties, an excessive emphasis on freedom as individualism disconnected from objective truth, and the leveling, if not rejection, of hierarchical structure. Coupled with this is a growing amnesia about traditional values due to a lack of any real bonding with the past, with consequent ignorance about the need to hand on something of value to future generations. All this leads to lack of appreciation if not contempt for rite and ritual; cf. Nichols, *Looking at the Liturgy,* 74.

Because the core of the mystery of Christian worship is the sacrifice of Christ offered to the Father, it is essential, John Paul II reminds us, "that in seeking to enter more deeply into the contemplative depths of worship the inexhaustible mystery of the priesthood of Jesus Christ be fully acknowledged and respected."[329] The priest clearly has a special responsibility to guarantee this authentic dimension of the liturgy. He has to be seen not just as one who presides, or as the inventor or producer of the liturgy, but above all as one who acts in the person of Christ.[330] The revised rite reminds the priest that to be truly a servant of the liturgy he should be faithful to all the details of the ceremonies as laid down.[331]

Cosmic Dimension of the Liturgy

Historically the cosmic dimension of the liturgy is more explicit in the Eastern Christian tradition. The intention to recover this perspective for the West, however, is clearly indicated in the *Catechism of the Catholic Church*. In its section on the liturgy we read about those who take part in the service of praise of God and the fulfillment of his plan:

> "Recapitulated in Christ," these are the ones who take part in the service of praise of God and the fulfillment of his plan: the heavenly powers, all creation (the four living beings), the servants of the Old and New Covenants (the twenty-four elders), the new People of God (the one hundred and forty-four thousand), especially the martyrs "slain for the word of God", and the all-holy

[329] Address, October 9, 1998, no. 2.
[330] Cf. ibid.
[331] Cf. *General Instruction of the Roman Missal*, 24.

Mother of God (the Woman), the Bride of the Lamb, and finally "a great multitude which no one could number, from every nation, from all tribes, and peoples and tongues."[332]

Redemption involves the whole of creation where all things have to be made new, as St. Paul dramatically describes it in his letter to the Romans (8:19–24). Reestablishment of the order willed by God, bringing the whole world to fulfill its true purpose to give glory to God, is part of the mission of the Holy Spirit. But God wants man to cooperate with him in the renewal of creation. As we have already seen, it is particularly the vocation of laypeople, called to sanctify the world, to impregnate all temporal realities with the spirit of Christ and in this way allow creation to give true glory to the Father.[333]

Because of the different influences—philosophical, cultural, social—that have had the effect of diluting the eschatological and doxological aspects of liturgy, it is not surprising that in recent decades there have been complaints about the loss of the sense of mystery, dignity, and solemnity in Catholic worship. In an increasingly secularized culture, we need to recover a deeper sense of the eschatological dimension of worship if it is to engage and unfold to the full the expectations for liturgical renewal of Vatican II. Since the visual is an extremely important part of the message and the sentiments that the liturgy is meant to convey, detailed attention to ceremony that reflects the ethos of participation in a profoundly mysterious action is also an integral part of the renewal desired by *Sacrosanctum*

[332] CCC, no. 1138.
[333] Cf. *The Navarre Bible: Romans and Galatians* (Dublin: Four Courts Press, 1990), 117.

concilium.[334] Clearly the priest has a central role to play in making this vision a reality in the life of the community he serves. But it has to start with a personal assimilation of this vision and the effort to appropriate it in his own spiritual life.

---

[334] A very practical help for celebrating the liturgy with reverence and dignity is *Ceremonies of the Modern Roman Rite*, by Peter J. Elliott (San Francisco: Ignatius Press, 1994).

Chapter 11

A History of Fidelity to the Mass

From the arrival of St. Patrick in Ireland in 431 to the middle of the sixteenth century, devotion to the Blessed Eucharist was a significant characteristic of the Irish people.[335] During that time, they practiced their religion in peace until tragic events on their neighboring island in the sixteenth century caused a religious war in Ireland which was not settled until the granting of Catholic emancipation in 1829 and even beyond.

At the beginning of the Reformation in Germany Henry VIII was a loyal son of the Church and in fact wrote a book against the Lutheran errors—*A Defense of the Seven Sacraments against Luther*—for which he was rewarded with the title Defender of the Faith by Pope Leo X, a title which ironically is still sported on British coins.

Henry was married to Catherine of Aragon (1509) but had no male heir. He was concerned about the future of the Tudor dynasty, but about this time Anne Boleyn, a lady-in-waiting to

---

[335] Fr. Augustine, O.F.M. Cap., *Ireland's Loyalty to the Mass* (Dublin: Sands and Co., 1933), 11.

Catherine, took his fancy. Henry convinced himself that his marriage to Catherine was invalid because she had previously been married to Arthur, his elder brother. He petitioned Rome for a decree of nullity but without success. Henry's response was secretly to marry Anne, who was by then pregnant, in January 1533.

In 1534 the Act of Supremacy was passed by Parliament which severed England's ancient connection with Rome, and Henry was declared Supreme Head on Earth of the Church in England. In recognition of Henry's new status, people were required to take an oath that effectively denied the supremacy of the pope.

Shortly after this, Henry, through his chancellor, Thomas Cromwell, brought about the suppression of the monasteries so that he could replenish his empty coffers and those of many other hangers-on as well. This was the first expression of Henry's concerted attack on the Church.

In one fell swoop Henry not only destroyed monasticism in England, but by so doing eliminated the hospitality and social services that the monasteries provided for the people. This operation showed how callous Henry was not only toward the Church but toward the people of England as well.

In July 1536 the Irish parliament, not without great opposition, passed the Act of Supremacy declaring Henry Supreme Head of the Church in Ireland. As in England, people could be compelled to take an oath, which the Act of Supremacy required. Refusal to do so could mean death, as it did in the case of St. John Fisher and St. Thomas More in England. The new archbishop of Dublin, an apostate monk from England, wrote to Thomas Cromwell that he could persuade no one to take Henry's side.

Although Henry broke with Rome, he still retained his loyalty to the Mass. However, the newly appointed archbishop of Canterbury, Thomas Cranmer, who was installed by Henry without reference to Rome, was a Lutheran at heart and was only biding his time to eliminate the Mass from the Church of England and replace it with a communion service.

In 1539 the suppression of 382 Irish monasteries was put into effect, and the spoils were allotted to Henry's courtiers and favorites.[336] This also involved the closure of the schools for the education of priests.

When Henry died in 1547 he was succeeded by his son, the ten-year-old prince Edward VI. Cranmer now had his opportunity to bring about the destruction of the Mass in the liturgy of the fledgling *Ecclesia Anglicana*. He knew he would have to proceed with caution. He first introduced a vernacular service in 1549; any reference to the sacrificial aspect of the Mass was expunged from the text. The English faithful revolted, but the insurrection was cruelly put down. The next two years were a period of vigorous propaganda in favor of the new service, which replaced the altar with a communion table. A second prayer book appeared that was absolutely devoid of any idea of the Real Presence and every suggestion of sacrifice.

The innovations attempted in England found no real support in Ireland. The priests continued to say Mass and the people to assist at it as before. Some of the bishops and political authorities tried to impose the new regime, but without success.

[336] Cf. Cardinal Patrick Moran, *The Catholics of Ireland under the Penal Laws of the Eighteenth Century* (London: Catholic Truth Society, 1899), 104.

During Edward VI's reign (1547–1553), the bishop of Meath, Edward Staples, wrote to the Lord Deputy that "all the people are up against me," when he tried to substitute for the Mass the "Book of the Reformation." He wrote about a brave lady whose child he christened. The lady had named the boy Edward, but now she returned asking how she might change his name because she didn't want him "to bear the name of a heretic."

Another gentleman forbade his wife from having their child confirmed by Staples, saying that his child would not be confirmed "by one who denied the Sacrament of the Altar." Openly in the marketplace in Navan, the people said they would not go to hear the bishop preach "for fear they should learn to be heretics."[337]

In 1551 the saying of Mass was made a penal offense. The Irish bishops presented a bold front and refused to accept the imposition of the Book of Common Prayer—the new handbook of liturgical services.

The young Edward died after six years (1553), during which time little had been achieved in implementing the "Reform" in Ireland. In fact, under Mary Tudor (1553–1558) a lot of the lost ground was recovered. The Mass was restored, and this caused great rejoicing. However, the sun was only to shine for a little time on the Mass, due to the early death of Mary.

Elizabethan Persecution

Elizabeth I (1558–1603) succeeded Mary and was quick to introduce more Protestant elements into the religious services.

---

[337] Helena Concannon, *The Blessed Eucharist in Irish History* (Dublin: Browne and Nolan, 1932), 214.

She abolished the Mass by an act of Parliament, thereby eliminating in one fell swoop what had been the core of religious and social life in England for over a thousand years.

In 1560 the Irish Parliament passed the Act of Uniformity by which the Book of Common Prayer was imposed on all and the people were commanded to attend Protestant services on all Sundays and holy days under pain of a heavy fine. The Catholic faithful were not intimidated by this legislation. They fought it with various weapons and engaged in vigorous opposition. The people left the churches empty and flocked to the oratories of the private houses of the wealthy merchants and the castles of the nobles; there priests and people had Mass as of old.

An attempt was made on one occasion to force the children, sons of great Irish lords, for whom they were held in Dublin Castle as hostages, to go to the Protestant service. Not being strong enough to resist the physical compulsion that was exercised to bring them to the church, the youngsters planned to make a row: "They set up a great shouting and bawling when the ministers commenced their hymns and music, preventing them being heard, and obstructing the heretical observance; nor did they desist until they were carried out of the church and sent back to their former prison, whence they were never again summoned to the heretical rites."[338]

Outside of the Dublin area, known as the Pale, there was no political machine to enforce these laws. Yet Elizabeth was determined to destroy the old religion in Ireland, as well as its Gaelic language and customs.

[338] Ibid., 226; cf. Philip O'Sullivan, *Catholic History*, vol. 2, bk. 4, ch. 27.

During this period, Irish priests, having been ordained in one of the many continental seminaries — Valladolid, Salamanca, Rheims, Nantes, Louvain, Rome — arrived back in Ireland by stealth. There was a price on their heads, yet they saw it as their first responsibility to provide holy Mass and the sacraments for a persecuted people. Many, of course, were martyred.

Bishop William Walsh took over from the heretic Staples in the diocese of Meath during the reign of Queen Mary. After Elizabeth succeeded, Walsh preached against the Book of Common Prayer, for which he was clapped in prison. He refused the Oath of Supremacy and said publicly that he would never participate in a Protestant service. For thirteen years he was kept in the dungeons of Dublin Castle. In all his lengthy martyrdom, prayer was his only recourse, and as he himself avowed, he received many spiritual consolations. Some friends persuaded the authorities to connive at his escape, and they arranged a passage for him on a ship bound for Nantes. He died in Alcalá in Spain in 1577.

In 1576, four hundred people were hanged in the South of Ireland for refusing to accept the new religion. Others were treated by fire and sword or had their lands robbed. But they still resisted. What is striking is that this vigorous resistance did not weaken with the passage of time. People still crowded into churches for the Mass.

The Englishman Sir William Drury, one of the chief administrators of Ireland, introduced new venom into the attack on the Mass. In 1579 two Franciscans fell into his hands. Interrogated before Drury, they confessed their loyalty to the Mass and the Catholic Faith. They were condemned to the rack, had needles thrust under their nails, and their arms and legs were broken with hammers. After this they were hanged from a tree, where their bodies were left suspended for four days as target practice for the bullets of the soldiers.[339]

Despite the Acts of Supremacy and Uniformity, and the rejection of the claims of the pope as treasonable, despite persecution and death, the Irish people refused to abandon the faith that had been theirs for over a thousand years. Reports to London from the Dublin authorities speak about "Massing in every corner," Masses in churches, in houses—these were the crimes with which the country was charged.

The Irish dispatched agents to Rome to ask for help to carry on a religious war for the recovery of their churches and for freedom of public worship. In 1580 an expedition under James Fitzmaurice Fitzgerald arrived in Smerwick Harbor, on the south coast of Ireland, and took over the ancient fort of Dun-an-Oir.

What Ireland was fighting for was best described by the brave Fitzmaurice Fitzgerald:

> The cause for which we are waging this war is the glory of God, to whom we are striving to restore the outward rite of sacrifice and the visible honor of our holy altars, which heretics have impiously overturned; it is the glory of Christ to whose sacraments heretics blasphemously deny the power of conferring grace ...; it is the glory of the Catholic Church which in the teeth of Sacred Scripture the heretics lyingly assert to have become obscured and consigned to oblivion in recent centuries; whereas our salvation chiefly depends on the name of God, who

[339] Cf. Fr. Augustine, *Ireland's Loyalty to the Mass*, 50.

sanctifies us by Christ's sacraments and on the preservation of the unity of the Church.[340]

The theological richness of this declaration leaves us in no doubt that educated Irish people were fully aware of the heretical content of the new Anglican religion being exported from England.

There were about eight hundred troops, mostly Spanish and Italian, in Fitzmaurice Fitzgerald's army. When the English troops arrived they massacred the Roman expedition, but a few people were singled out for special attention. These included a priest, an Irish gentleman named Plunkett, and an Englishman named Walsh. They were told that if they would only acknowledge the queen as head of the Church they would be freed. They rejected every inducement, however, saying they were prepared to die in defense of their faith. When all efforts to change their minds failed, they were led to a forge, where their arms and legs were broken in three places. The priest however, was subjected to an additional torture—his thumbs and forefingers were cut away because, as his executioners said, they had been so often used in the consecration of the Eucharist and touched it. They bore their torments with Christian patience and at length were hanged and then cut to pieces.[341]

At this time Dermot O'Hurley, a priest who had been professor of philosophy at the University of Louvain for about twenty-five years, was teaching canon and civil law at the seminary of Rheims. Having been called to Rome he learned that

[340] Myles V. Ronan, *Reformation in Ireland under Elizabeth* (London: Longmans, 1930), 619.
[341] Cf. John O'Rourke, *The Battle of the Faith in Ireland* (Dublin: J. Duffy, 1887), 26

he had been appointed archbishop of Cashel by Gregory XIII. He was consecrated archbishop in September 1581. He now had to decide how best to return to Ireland in secret to begin his pastoral responsibilities. Government spies were watching at every port since "Rome-runners" were a precious capture and papal bulls brought a rich reward. The bearer of a papal bull giving jurisdiction over a diocese was guilty of high treason, the penalty for which was imprisonment and death.

The newly consecrated bishop was aware of this, but, fortified by the blessing of the pope, he set off for Ireland. Disguised probably as a seaman he landed safely at Skerries in north County Dublin. He entrusted a box containing the papal bull of his appointment, his episcopal robes, vestments, pyxes, chalice, and the rest of his belongings to the care of the captain of a merchant ship, hoping to be able to pick them up at Waterford.

The merchant ship was captured and the belongings confiscated. O'Hurley was eventually captured in 1583, brought to Dublin, and thrown into the dungeon of Dublin Castle, where he was held for six months. On Holy Thursday of 1584 he was brought before the justices and promised pardon if he would deny the supremacy of the pope and take the oath that denied this supremacy, but he boldly refused to do what the lord justices asked him. Tied to a trunk of a tree he was beaten cruelly. Then his boots were filled with pitch, his feet were inserted into them, and the pitch was set alight. Even though the flesh melted and the bones were exposed, O'Hurley still bravely refused to deny his faith. We can only imagine how much he suffered.

He was returned to prison and after a few weeks was brought before the justices again. This time they tried blandishments, offers of ecclesiastical preferment, and the gracious favor of the queen—but all to no purpose. Fearing a public trial, the justices obtained permission to proceed against O'Hurley by martial law. He was sentenced to be hanged, and the judgment was put into effect on June 20, 1584, at the spot where Merrion Row and Ely Place now meet in Dublin city center.[342]

At this time several priests were put to death simply for saying Mass. One priest was hanged in his own church, opposite the high altar. Another was hanged and quartered in 1597.

The execution of Archbishop O'Hurley was meant to strike terror into the other "Rome-runners" and Mass-priests then in Ireland. But the priests remained firm, exasperating the authorities in Dublin Castle. In 1584 an order was issued that all priests should be exterminated. A priest by his very existence was judged to be guilty of high treason; he was condemned to be hanged, cut down while yet alive, disemboweled, burned, and beheaded.[343]

A 1607 report from the Lord Deputy to the Privy Council in London offers a glimpse of the situation at that time:

The priests land here secretly in every creek and port of the realm (a dozen sometimes together) and afterwards disperse themselves in several quarters in such sort that every town and county is full of them, and most men's minds are infected with their doctrine and seditious persuading. They have so gained the women that they are in a manner all of them recusants. Children and servants are wholly taught and catechized by them, esteeming the same, as in truth it is, a sound and safe foundation of their synagogue. They withdraw many from the [Protestant]

[342] Cf. Fr. Augustine, *Ireland's Loyalty to the Mass*, 55–58.
[343] Cf. ibid., 58.

church, that formerly had conformed themselves, and others of them of whom good hope had been conceived, they have made altogether obstinate, disobedient and contemptuous.

Most of the Mayors and principal officers of the cities and corporate towns, and justices of the peace of this country refuse to take the Oath of Supremacy as is required by statute. The people in many places resort to Mass in greater multitudes, both in town and country, than for many years past, and if it chance that any priest known to be factious and working be apprehended, men and women will not stick to rescue the party. Such as are conformed and go to church are everywhere derided and oppressed by the multitude.[344]

The surest way to expel the Mass was to destroy the priests—that was the policy of Dublin Castle, the center of British authority in Ireland. But although hunted like wild beasts, imprisoned and starved, tortured and executed, they could not be so easily exterminated. By careful hiding they were able to say Mass now and then in private houses for the faithful, who were previously notified of the meeting place and who came to confess, hear Mass, and receive the Blessed Eucharist.

Red Hugh O'Donnell, one of the Gaelic leaders, constantly kept a priest with him to offer Mass. Whenever he set out on a journey or prepared for battle, or whenever he was threatened with any danger, he observed a fast, confessed his sins, assisted at Mass, and received Holy Communion. He was certainly in

[344] Lord Deputy and Council to Privy Council, October 27, 1607 (Cal. Doc. Ireland, 1606–1608, p. 310) in Concannon, *The Blessed Eucharist in Irish History*, 295–297.

grave danger in 1599. The Elizabethan forces were trying to break the hold of O'Donnell and O'Neill on the north of Ireland and bring it within the control of Dublin Castle. O'Donnell encouraged his officers and troops for the forthcoming battle. He said they were fighting for their homes and their altars against the soldiers of a heretic queen. His army assisted at Mass the day before, and O'Donnell and his chief officers received Communion. Victory in the battle went to O'Donnell's men. For them it was the power of the Mass that gave them the upper hand.[345]

The religious persecution in Ireland during Elizabeth's long reign produced a rich crop of martyrs, some two hundred or more. In addition there were many who suffered imprisonment in filthy dungeons that often hastened their death. While many of these were laypeople, the majority were priests who were hated with a special virulence as ministers of the holy Mass.

On one occasion soldiers made a sudden attack on a Cistercian monastery in County Limerick and massacred forty monks and their abbot in their church before the Blessed Sacrament. Other priests were dragged from the altar while saying Mass, while many were slain within the sanctuary itself.

Hope for Better Things

When Elizabeth died (1603), there was great hope among the Irish that her successor, James I, a son of Mary Queen of Scots, would grant greater freedom of worship and allow them to assist at Mass openly. People, especially in Munster, took peaceful re-possession of the churches and enthroned the Blessed Eucharist. In some places processions with the Blessed Sacrament were held, in many cases attended by the whole population, as

[345] Cf. Fr. Augustine, *Ireland's Loyalty to the Mass*, 62–64.

an expression of their faith and their love for their eucharistic King. In Waterford, High Mass was celebrated in the cathedral. When the bells were rung the whole population answered the summons and walked in procession after the Blessed Sacrament amid great scenes of emotion. When the procession returned to the cathedral a *Te Deum* was sung by the choir.

When news of these doings reached the Lord Deputy, Mountjoy, he was not at all pleased and set out for Waterford. After the people beheld his immense army, they gathered in the cathedral that evening, the Blessed Sacrament was carried in procession through the streets and all the public parts of the city. When it had been placed on the high altar, the people cried out that they were ready to live and die in the faith of the Holy Eucharist. The vicar apostolic, Dr. James White (who is the source of this narrative), says that having heard this solemn declaration, he told them: "I promised them that, on the part of God and the Apostolic See, that if they persevered in that faith and died in it they certainly would obtain eternal salvation."[346]

The hopes that the Irish had for greater religious tolerance under James I were soon dashed. He retracted all his previous promises of toleration and confirmed this in an edict of 1605. The Acts of Supremacy and Uniformity were renewed, and Catholics who absented themselves from Protestant services were to be fined or imprisoned. All priests were required, under penalty of death, to withdraw from Ireland by December 10. After this date, if anyone received a priest into his house or supported him or failed to denounce him to the tribunals, he was to be hanged at his own door.

---

[346] Cf. Concannon, *The Blessed Eucharist in Irish History*, 261–263.

The Most Holy Eucharist

From many contemporary sources we have full and vivid descriptions of a regime of raids, ruinous fines, and arbitrary imprisonment. Bands of soldiers were sent throughout the country in pursuit of priests, and all who were seized were hanged. The priests passed themselves off in many disguises — as grooms, as servants, even as fools and strolling players, but obviously the disguises failed at times. In Waterford in 1606, three Catholics were arrested merely on suspicion of being priests; they were instantly put to death by the soldiers. One of them was in fact a priest, but the other two were laymen.[347]

Perhaps we can obtain a deeper understanding of the situation by quoting from a *relatio* (report) sent by Archbishop Kearney of Cashel to Rome in 1609:

> As for us ecclesiastics, being always encompassed with dangers, we imitate the skilful seaman, who, when the tempest threatens, draws in the sails, and re-unfurls them on the return of calm. When the persecution threatens and the soldiers are in pursuit, we fly to secret recesses; when the persecution relaxes we venture out again in public. As they leave nothing undone to capture us, we are ever on the alert, and seldom can they obtain any certain information about our whereabouts. We go from one city to another dressed in secular clothes, only using the long dress at the altar, and following our Redeemer's counsel, we fly from one town to another, generally a very distant one. We do not stop long at any one place, but pass from one house to another, even in the cities

---

[347] Letter from Rev. James White, Vicar Apostolic of Waterford and Lismore, to Cardinal Baronius, May 1606; cf. Fr. Augustine, *Ireland's Loyalty to the Mass*, 74.

and towns. This journey, too, is made at dawn, or by night. Sometimes even at the third or fourth watches thereof. Though we hope to be children of light, yet we love the protecting darkness, nay we prefer the winter to the summer. It is at night that we perform all the sacred functions, that we transfer the sacred vestments from one place to another—celebrate Mass, give exhortations to the faithful, confer Holy Orders, bless the chrism, administer the sacrament of confirmation, discharge, in a word, all our ecclesiastical duties.

The heretics make diligent search to seize those who assist at Mass, and they, moreover, inflict fines on all who absent themselves from the heretical temples. They cast into prison not only those who favor the priest, but those who refuse to prosecute and deliver up the priests. They interdict the use of chapels, they prevent pious pilgrimages, and punish whom they will, and rage arbitrarily against us.

Last year when the persecution relaxed a little, I administered the sacrament of Confirmation at noon day in the open fields to at least ten thousand persons; for our Catholics so venerate this sacrament that they even come from the most distant parts of the country when there is an opportunity of receiving it.[348]

Ordinations were usually held in some big house of the Catholic gentry. Archbishop Kearney, in his letter to Rome

[348] Cardinal Patrick Moran, *History of the Catholic Archbishops of Dublin Since the Reformation* (Dublin: James Duffy, 1864), 235; Concannon, *The Blessed Eucharist in Irish History*, 277–278.

dated March 12, 1612, tells us how ordinations were carried out during the persecution:

> Those who present themselves for ordination are generally received in some suitable place, where we erect portable altars, taking care not to trust ourselves in any but those in whom we have the greatest confidence — today in one town, and tomorrow in another. When the ceremony of ordination is ended, we lose no time in going to another place, in order to avoid risk; having first appointed trusty parties to remove the portable altars and warned those ordained not to mention to anyone the place where they received Holy Orders, lest the master of the house might be brought to trouble.[349]

Sir John Burke of Brittas, County Limerick (1550–1607), a wealthy man with large estates and the father of nine children, had great devotion to the Mass and often walked long distances to assist at it. He became known for his work of harboring priests, something which was forbidden by a recent proclamation (1605). One Sunday in 1607, he sent word around the vicinity that Mass would be celebrated in his castle, about eight miles from Limerick. The event became known to the authorities, however, and the place was surrounded by a body of cavalry just as the priest was about to begin Mass. On seeing the soldiers the people who were coming from all sides dispersed, while Sir John and his chaplain, Fr. John Clancy, betook themselves with the sacred vessels to the castle tower to avoid their desecration. Although besieged for several days, both succeeded in escaping separately, but after many hardships Sir John was captured and

---

[349] Concannon, *The Blessed Eucharist in Irish History*, 293.

conveyed to Limerick, where he was put on trial, condemned to death, and executed in 1607. His remains are buried in St. John's Church in Limerick.[350]

Flight was not the only reaction in face of the soldiery, however. In Drogheda an old Franciscan was seized at the foot of the altar just as he finished saying Mass. As the prisoner was hurried through the town, the news spread and the women rushed from all sides. They pelted the soldiers with stones and missiles to great effect and rescued the Franciscan. The intense loyalty of the people to their priests was a defining characteristic of Irish Catholicism during these difficult years.

Most of the churches of the religious were taken over and desecrated by Elizabethan troops. Their monasteries were taken over by the alien law courts.

In the summer of 1611, owing to the widespread persecution, Archbishop Matthews of Dublin, having stated that all the churches in Ireland were either destroyed by the late persecution or occupied by the heretics, and that in no way could the Holy Sacrifice be offered in public but only in private houses, orchards, or caverns, asked the Holy Father to permit him the use of a privileged portable altar.[351]

Because of the failure of the Catholic members of Parliament in Dublin to attend Protestant services, in May 1614, James I issued an edict commanding all archbishops, bishops, Jesuits, and seminarians to withdraw from the kingdom of Ireland. In the very teeth of this proclamation, however, a provincial synod of the Church was held in Kilkenny for the eastern province, under the presidency of Archbishop Matthews. All the suffragan

---

[350] Cf. ibid., 251.
[351] Cf. Fr. Augustine, *Ireland's Loyalty to the Mass*, 79.

sees were at this time vacant, but the dioceses were represented by their vicars general.

The first act of the synod was to profess obedience to the Holy See and to accept all that had been ordered by the Council of Trent (1545–1563). It was also stipulated that if no consecrated place was available in which to reserve the Body of the Lord, the priest was to keep two particles of the Blessed Sacrament in his residence to provide Viaticum for the dying.

The synod further ordered that only the most becoming localities should be selected for the celebration of the Holy Sacrifice. In addition to this, the greatest care was to be taken so that no dust might mingle with the consecrated elements and no wind blow away the sacred particles. To obviate this, sheets were to be hung over and around the rude altar. When it was necessary to celebrate in the fields and bogs and on the mountainside, the utmost care was to be taken that the table of the altar should be protected and secured, above, at the back, and at each side, against the wind and rain, so that the sacred vessels should not be overturned. Special care was to be taken that the corporals and other cloths, more especially connected with the Holy Sacrifice, were to be kept spotless.

Perhaps the most moving canon was one that reflected the tender solicitude of the bishops for their persecuted flocks. Laymen were empowered, in case of necessity, to carry the Blessed Sacrament in a pyx to the dying. How many a deathbed must this permission have comforted, and how many a soul must, as a result, have been strengthened for the journey into eternity by the Bread of Everlasting life.[352]

---

[352] Moran, *Catholic Archbishops of Dublin*, 266; cf. Fr. Augustine, *Ireland's Loyalty to the Mass*, 82–84.

A History of Fidelity to the Mass

In 1616 Oliver St. John succeeded as the king's deputy or viceroy and swore that within two months all the priests would be rooted out of Ireland. He built new prisons and filled them with Catholics. By rigorous infliction of the Sunday fines he gathered into the royal treasury six hundred thousand crowns of gold.

In 1618, although the persecution intensified as never before, the number of priests increased due to the arrival of recently ordained men from the continent, where they had been educated. Still the persecution continued. Absence from the Protestant service was punished by taxes, even on the poorest. Heavy fines were imposed on all those who attended Mass. Catholics were reduced to the lowest offices in government administration and had their lands stolen from them. James I caused between four and five million acres of land to be confiscated and allotted to Protestant aliens.

James I was succeeded by his son Charles I. The fact that he had married a Catholic, Henrietta Maria, a daughter of the king of France, encouraged the belief that he would be favorable to the religion she professed. Charles was badly in need of money to finance his army, and as a gesture of goodwill, Irish Catholics offered to supply an army of five thousand foot soldiers and five hundred horse soldiers in return for toleration of their religion and the liberation from fines for not attending Protestant services, which they loathed.

The Protestant bishops reacted bitterly and violently to the suggestion that Catholics be given toleration and used repressive action against any public manifestation of the Catholic religion. Still, despite their frantic efforts, the Catholic religion was forcing itself into public life and the Mass continued to be said. In some places, even in Dublin, at the center of things, by catechizing and preaching, a great number of Protestants were won back to the public profession of the Faith.[353]

The king's necessities had now become very pressing, and in return for certain concessions known as the "Graces," the Catholics promised a voluntary subsidy of £120,000 for the support of the army in Ireland. The "Graces" were fifty-one in number, but no more than four or five were specifically framed for the relief of Catholics, and only one of them promised toleration of their Faith.

In 1629 the government issued a proclamation that prohibited religious orders from preaching or saying Mass in their chapels anymore. Nevertheless, on Christmas night the superior of the Franciscans celebrated High Mass and gave a homily to the people. News of this reached the ears of the state, and the following day a motley crowd consisting of the Protestant archbishop of Dublin, the mayor, sheriffs, and a group of musketeers arrived to apprehend the priests (which they did). In addition they took away the crucifixes, candlesticks, and altar cloths.

So stunned were the people at this sudden incursion and wholesale destruction that nobody offered any resistance. A lady called the widow Nugent, however, raised the cry of attack. She flung herself at the soldiers and was joined by the rest of the women. They struck, pummeled, and scratched the soldiers and trod underfoot whomever they could lay hands on so that the Protestant party was glad to retreat out of doors. They were met, as they fled through the streets, with a shower of stones thrown by women and boys.[354]

---

[353] Cf. Fr. Augustine, *Ireland's Loyalty to the Mass*, 90.
[354] Cf. ibid., 93–94.

A History of Fidelity to the Mass

The Confederation of Kilkenny

The Irish rebellion of 1641 was an attempt by the Catholic gentry to seize control of the English administration in Ireland and to force concessions for Catholics, but the coup failed, and the rebellion developed into a conflict between native Irish Catholics on one side, and English and Protestant settlers on the other. Thus began the conflict known as the Irish Confederate Wars. The Irish rebellion, which broke out in October 1641, was followed by several months of violent clashes before the Catholic gentry and the clergy founded the Confederation of Kilkenny in 1642. The confederation became a de facto government of most of Ireland, free from the control of the English administration. This situation continued until the country was reconquered by Oliver Cromwell in 1649.

In 1642 a fresh supply of soldiers arrived in Dublin under the command of Sir Simon Harcourt, a bitter enemy of Catholics. They broke into chapels, overturned altars, and trampled underfoot every sign of religion. Churches were closed, convents were sacked, and priests were imprisoned.

In the same year, a national synod was held in Kilkenny. Declaring that the war in which Catholics were engaged was just, the bishops appealed to their countrymen to take up arms and ordered a three-day fast, a general Communion after Confession, and special prayers that God might crown their efforts with success. The bishops asked all priests to celebrate Mass once a week for the triumph of the cause so dear to their hearts. Many of the Catholic gentry and nobility attended this historic gathering of the Irish Church.

The wars of the Confederation of Kilkenny were fought for the freedom of the Mass. It was because she realized that the

Stuarts, as far as Stuart perfidy and weakness allowed, stood for the freedom of the Mass that Ireland accepted them as kings of the kingdom of Ireland and fought for them even after James II had fled to France and left his crown behind.

Pope Innocent X (1644–1655), took a keen interest in what was happening in Ireland and, as an expression of his support, sent John Baptist Cardinal Rinuccini as his nuncio extraordinary to the confederation, armed with the highest ecclesiastical privileges and powers.

The Catholics were particularly encouraged by the victory of Owen Roe O'Neill against the English forces at Benburb in County Tyrone in 1646. A *Te Deum* and High Mass were sung in thanksgiving to God in Limerick cathedral.

Cromwell's War against the Mass

This short period of toleration, however, was followed by the darkest period in the religious history of Ireland. Oliver Cromwell, the fanatical incarnation of triumphant Protestantism, arrived from England in 1649. After a short stay in Dublin, he set out for Drogheda. Knowing what to expect, the inhabitants closed the gates, but after three attacks the Puritans stormed the walls and the Catholic garrison was slaughtered. The slaughter of the inhabitants continued for five days, and nobody was spared. Cromwell's fanatical hatred of the Mass drove him to massacre nearly a thousand people at Mass in St. Peter's Church in Drogheda.

Cromwell and his army next rode south to Wexford and massacred thousands of its citizens. Having made an example of Drogheda and Wexford, he invited other cities and towns to surrender. Nevertheless, he said that "wherever the authority of Parliament extends, the Mass shall not be tolerated."

A History of Fidelity to the Mass

Cromwell's offer was rejected out of hand—no Irish city was found willing to purchase the security of its property by the abolition of the Mass. The Mass was like a light in the darkness of a fanatical persecution that eclipsed all other terrors through which the country had passed since the unhappy dawn of the so-called Reformation.

A few years later, Cromwell devised an oath that, by act of Parliament, every Irish Catholic was bound to take. The oath, among other things, denied transubstantiation and made the presence of Jesus Christ in the Blessed Sacrament a mere fiction and the Sacrifice of the Mass a meaningless mummery. Every effort was made all over the land to compel Catholics to take this repulsive Oath of Abjuration. Threats and fines, imprisonment and banishment were employed to force the nation's conscience, to pervert the people's faith. All who refused to take the oath were to lose two-thirds of their property, and this was to be repeated every time they refused. This, it was thought, would conquer the obstinacy of the gentry, who would be reduced to penury, and of the poor, who might be shipped to Barbados.

Neither threats nor fines, neither prison or banishment, not even death, however, could overcome the extraordinary tenacity of the Irish in their loyalty to the Mass and the Blessed Eucharist. When the Mass had been outlawed from the churches, the people opened their homes to it. And when they were driven from their homes, they took it with them to the mountainsides.

The imposition of the Oath of Abjuration was a signal to priests in their hiding places to go fearlessly from house to house, exhorting rich and poor to despise temporal possessions, to think of eternal rewards, to remember that the sufferings of this life are not worthy to be compared with the glory to come.

Such words cheered the hearts of the people and roused their spirit of faith.

This spirit was displayed in many ways, such as in Cork. All Catholics of the surrounding county above fifteen years of age were commanded to come to Cork city to take the Oath of Abjuration. To show their contempt for the Mass, the heretics were accustomed to hold the assizes in the Catholic churches. Within the sanctuary, near the high altar, the magistrates took their seats and gave orders that the vast throng should be arranged in processional order so as to facilitate the work of administering the oath individually.

In the first rank was a young man whose quick step as he entered had attracted attention and seemed to betoken willingness to subscribe to whatever was required. To him, therefore, the clerk tendered the oath first. Contrary to expectation he asked that it be translated into Irish, knowing that only then would those all around him fully understand its contents (Irish was then the common language of the people). His request having been granted, a crier next read it aloud: "I ... abhor, detest and abjure the authority of the Pope.... I firmly believe and avow that no reverence is due to the Virgin Mary or to any other saint in heaven.... I assert that no reverence is due to the sacrament of the Lord's Supper, or to the elements of bread and wine after consecration, by whomsoever that consecration be made."

The words of the oath horrified the people, who were silent for a few minutes. Then the young man asked the magistrates, "What is the penalty for those who refuse the oath?" "The loss of two-thirds of their goods," replied one of the magistrates. "Well then," added the young man, "all that I possess is six pounds. Take four of them; with the two that remain and the blessing of God, my family and I will subsist. I reject your oath." The crowd, deeply impressed by the courage of the young man, shouted out, "Reject the oath, the impious oath!" The gathering of six thousand voices kept up this chorus for half an hour. The magistrates were dumb with terror, but managed to order the assembly to disperse and leave the city within an hour. The people scattered with grateful hearts. Thus in Christ Church, in the city of Cork, the faith of Christ was confessed as it never had been confessed before. The story of this event spread quickly to the whole of Munster.[355]

In 1651 Edward Ludlow, a Cromwellian general, came from England to head up the army in Ireland. Marching one day from Dundalk to Castleblaney, passing by a deep cavern, he discovered that some Irish were hidden inside. He decided that they should be smothered rather than captured. Fires were lit at the mouth of the cave, and late in the evening, feeling certain that all inside were dead, a small party of soldiers entered the mouth of the cave. Suddenly a pistol shot rang out from the cave, and one of the soldiers was wounded. Pulling him after them, the others beat a hasty retreat. After some consultation all the crevices of the cave were closed, and the following morning "another smother" was made. In the evening, some more of the soldiers cautiously entered the cave. Just inside the entrance they found the only armed man lying dead, but they did not have the gratification of seeing the others suffocated. They found a group of men and women bent down over a stream that flowed through the cave who had thus managed to keep themselves alive. These were immediately massacred by the soldiers. A crucifix, a chalice, and vestments were found,

[355] Cf. Concannon, *The Blessed Eucharist in Irish History*, 350–351.

clearly pointing to the fact that one of the little band was a priest whose Mass the others had hoped to attend.[356]

In 1653 a decree of banishment of priests was published. Even to harbor a priest was now punishable by death. In spite of this decree, many priests remained to minister to the spiritual needs of the people.

In 1654 it was decreed by Cromwell that all Catholic land-owners should be transplanted to the western province of Con-nacht, the poorest part of the country. Their lands were given to Protestants from England and officers from Cromwell's army. This operation, referred to as the Cromwellian Plantation, was carried out with the utmost cruelty. The clergy, however, or-dered a general fast for three Saturdays with Confession and Holy Communion. It was announced by the government that any Catholic who renounced "the Mass and Popery" would be exempt from transportation. Although famine and death met Catholics beyond the Shannon, strengthened by the Eucharist, they spurned the treacherous offer. There is no record of anyone proving false to the ancient Faith. Before the 1641 rebellion, two-thirds of the lands of the country were in the hands of the Catholics; after 1665, scarcely a third was left to them. But this settlement failed to make Ireland either English or Protestant. In setting up a system of alien landlords and native tenants, it established a social structure that was to last for the next 250 years.

Some thousand priests and bishops were banished, except for the old and bedridden Eugene McSweeney, bishop of Kil-more. The sixty-four flourishing convents of the Friars Minor and the Poor Clares were entirely destroyed. The priests who

[356] Cf. Fr. Augustine, *Ireland's Loyalty to the Mass*, 121.

remained had to live in the mountains and forests and in the midst of bogs to escape the cavalry of the Crown. Seventeen Catholic martyrs from this period were beatified by Pope John Paul II in 1992.

Sixty thousand were exiled to Barbados and other American islands. Whole colonies were transported as slaves to St. Kitts. A Limerick Jesuit, Fr. John Stritch, volunteered to go and look after these Irish exiles. He landed in St. Kitts and built a chapel in the French quarter. He was welcomed by the Irish as an angel from Heaven. Despite the fact that they exposed themselves to imminent danger of the lash or even death, they made their way to the priest to participate in the Mass and the sacraments. Fr. Stritch heard confessions from dawn to one o'clock in the afternoon, administered Holy Communion, and baptized their children. The exiles had a hunger for the sacraments and the Mass, so that Fr. Stritch's congregation grew week after week until it reached almost three thousand souls.[357]

The Mass after the Restoration

Charles II was restored as king of England in 1660. The restoration of the monarchy brought high hopes to Catholics, since the king was married to a Catholic, Catherine of Braganza, of the Portuguese royal family. But his first act of giving over to the Episcopalian Protestants the fine churches that belonged to the Catholics did not augur well. In fact, the persecution of the Catholic clergy was carried out almost as actively as before. To destroy the priests and to suppress the Mass was still the government's ambition. The attitude toward priests, however, was given a new emphasis—a determination to find in them

[357] Cf. ibid., 128.

evidence of intrigue, especially with the French. All priests were construed to be rebels, and any assembly of the people for Mass was considered conspiracy.

From a report sent to Sacred Congregation of Propaganda in Rome by Dr. John Brenan, bishop of Waterford and Lismore, we can glean many details about the situation in Ireland. "We live in peace," he wrote, "and the minority are to be found only in the garrisons.... Exercise of the sacred ministry is more freely permitted in the country than in the cities, and greater freedom is allowed in Dublin than in the other cities.... All the ancient churches now in the hands of the Protestants are stone buildings. The Catholic oratories are almost all houses of straw." Then he adds in a sadly illuminating sentence, "In none of the oratories is the Blessed Sacrament reserved with a lamp before it, on account of the poverty of the clergy and the danger of irreverence from our adversaries. The Holy Oils are preserved in the house of the parish priest."[358]

In 1672 Bishop Brenan wrote to Propaganda that "many of the priests have no Mass-houses, and celebrate in the mountains or in the open country, spreading some tent or covering over the altar. This is occasioned not only by the poverty of the priest, but by the fact that all the land is held by the heretics, who will not allow a Mass-house to be built. In other districts of the diocese, where Catholics hold the land in fee or lease, oratories are erected and are, for the most part, commodious and decorous."[359]

By 1676 the penal attitude had improved to such an extent that Dr. Brenan was with comparative freedom able to hold a

[358] Cf. Fr. Augustine, *Ireland's Loyalty to the Mass*, 146–147.
[359] Ibid., 151.

diocesan synod in Carrick-on-Suir. Among the decrees of the synod was one which indicated that the Blessed Sacrament was no longer to be borne in any other than a silver vessel, and the sacred vessels which were formerly committed to the care of the laity for motives of safety, were to be recovered and restored to their proper churches.

In 1679, a special proclamation was published against the secular priests and a further one ordered the suppression of "Mass-houses and meetings of popish services in the cities and suburbs."

James II, a Catholic, succeeded Charles on the English throne. The position of Catholics improved; the Mass was once more said publicly throughout the country. Despite all the efforts that had been made to exterminate them, in 1698 there were still in Ireland 892 secular clergy and 495 of the various religious orders. But after that year a special act was passed banishing all bishops. In spite of beggary and prison, in spite of banishment and death, the line of apostolic succession was never broken.[360]

Mass in Penal Times

The Treaty of Limerick (1691), by which the last Catholic stronghold was surrendered to the Williamite army, treated the vanquished nation honorably. The Irish were granted freedom of religious worship and were confirmed in their proprietorial rights and privileges. They were entitled to sit in parliament. But the anti-Catholic faction that ruled in England resolved

[360] Cf. Moran, *The Catholics of Ireland under the Penal Laws of the Eighteenth Century*, 25; cf. Fr. Augustine, *Ireland's Loyalty to the Mass*, 159.

without delay to tear to shreds the Treaty of Limerick. The Protestant bishops in Ireland prepared the ground. In the 1692 session of parliament a resolution was adopted which excluded Catholics from both houses of parliament. The legislature made rapid progress in the work of enacting penal laws against the Irish. While a number of these laws related to property and civil rights, many others concerned the Catholic Faith.

The Penal Laws, which lasted a hundred years or more, were introduced at the beginning of the eighteenth century and came into being at a time when Ireland was regarded as beaten, broken, and crushed forever. The purpose of the Penal Laws was to confirm the Protestants in their possession of the land of Ireland and to ensure that Catholics would never be able to recover the property the Protestants had stolen from them. As Lecky, the great Irish historian says, the objective of these laws was "to make the [Catholics] poor and to keep them poor, to crush in them every germ of enterprise, to degrade them into a servile caste who would never hope to rise to the level of their oppressors."[361] Society in eighteenth-century Ireland was organized on the assumption that Catholics, who formed the majority of the population, were an inferior class, unworthy of trust and unfit for civil rights.

In 1697 an act was passed that banished all popish archbishops, bishops, vicars general, Jesuits, monks, friars, and all the regular popish clergy, and made their return an offense

[361] John Brady and Patrick Corish, *The Church under the Penal Code: A History of Irish Catholicism* (Dublin: Gill and Macmillan, 1971), 2. William Lecky (1838–1903), a Protestant, was professor of history at Trinity College, Dublin, and was sympathetic to the situation of Irish Catholics.

punishable by death. The parochial clergy were left alone for a while; but as there were no bishops who could ordain new priests, there was a consoling prospect for the Protestant victors that the supply of priests would soon be exhausted, and the Catholic religion would die out. Catholics were prohibited from sending their children to the continent to be educated. Catholics were disqualified from the legal profession, and the marriage of a Protestant to a Catholic was prohibited.

In 1703 laws were passed that practically abolished Catholic landlords. Catholics were rendered incapable of purchasing lands of inheritance. These and a hundred other vexatious enactments brought ruin on Catholic proprietors. By 1778, scarcely 5 percent of Irish land was left in Catholic hands.[362] While as a result of favorable legal enactments Protestant proprietors were practically freed from supporting their own clergy, the small Catholic landowners had to suffer the injustice of paying the tithe-proctors a contribution to secure a rich maintenance for the alien ministers of an alien creed.

It gives us an idea of the mentality of the Protestant ascendancy that as late as 1760 the lord chancellor of Ireland could declare that the laws of the kingdom "did not suppose any such person to exist as an Irish Catholic."[363] So completely were the Catholic laity crushed and ignored by the government that, when about the middle of the century an address of loyalty was drawn up by Charles O'Conor and other Catholic landed gentry, the viceroy refused to pass it on.

[362] T. W. Moody and F. X. Martin, eds., *The Course of Irish History* (Cork: Mercier Press, 1984), 220.
[363] Moran, *The Catholics of Ireland under the Penal Laws of the Eighteenth Century*, 11.

The penalty for instructing children at home in the Catholic Faith was forfeiture of all legal rights, as well as all personal property. If a laborer refused to work on a Catholic holy day, he was punished by whipping. A heavy fine was imposed for burying relatives in old consecrated churchyards or for taking part in pilgrimages and other public acts of devotion. Magistrates were instructed to demolish crosses, pictures, and inscriptions related to the Faith.

No means were left untried to add to the numbers as well as to enhance the privileges of the Protestants. The legal inducements offered to Catholics to change their religion were based, not on spiritual values, but on the ambition to own and to rise in the social scale.

The conversion of Protestants to the Catholic Faith was beset with the severest penalties. The convert at once forfeited all rights and privileges. He was regarded as an enemy of the state and punished as such; and the priest who was instrumental in his conversion became subject to the same penalties. The convert forfeited his lands, goods, and chattels to the king. A Protestant who married a Catholic woman but failed to make her a Protestant within twelve months forfeited his civil rights. A Protestant woman who had personal property to the value of five hundred pounds forfeited her whole property by marrying a Catholic.

When the child of a mixed marriage was baptized by a Catholic priest, the Protestant parent became classified among the reputed Papists and had to suffer all the penalties of such offense. A Protestant man married to a Catholic woman had their infant baptized by a Catholic priest. The man was immediately thrown into prison, where he was detained for a considerable time, and then subjected to a heavy fine, but he came out of prison a Catholic, and his son, Dr. Young, became one of the most dedicated bishops during those perilous times.[364]

In 1704 an act of Parliament was passed by which only a certain number of the parochial clergy, duly registered, were to be tolerated in each county. Since this drastic legislation was not killing the Church in Ireland with sufficient speed, a new act was put on the statute book that required the registered priests to take the Oath of Abjuration. Since no priest could take this nefarious oath, the registered priests had to shut their chapels and go "on the run" with the bishops and the regular clergy.

The words in which Edmund Burke, the great parliamentarian, described the Penal Laws are memorable: "It was a complete system, well digested and well composed in all its parts. It was a machine of wise and elaborate contrivance, and as well fitted for the oppression, impoverishment, and degradation of a feeble people, and the debasement in them of human nature itself, as ever proceeded from the perverted ingenuity of man."[365]

About this time there was a priest named McKenna who ministered in County Monaghan. The "priest hunters" and the troops were always on the lookout for him, but failed to catch him, so carefully was he guarded by his own people. On one occasion, however, information was brought to the barracks at Monaghan that Mass was to be celebrated before daybreak the next morning at a particular place. A party of soldiers was despatched early in the night, and some time before dawn they observed the light of two candles. The officer, fearing to approach too near the place where the people assembled, lest some of the scouts would detect them and give the priest an opportunity

[364] Moran, *The Catholics of Ireland under the Penal Laws of the Eighteenth Century*, 18.
[365] Ibid., 2.

to escape, picked a good marksman and told him to approach within gunshot, cover one of the lights and fire when it was darkened by the priest passing before it. The soldier fired when the priest went to read the last Gospel, and the ball passed through the priest's head.[366]

Yet despite all that heartless and diabolical legislation, the spiritual life of the people was strong and their devotion to the Mass and the Eucharist laudable. In 1706, in a letter to the Holy Father in Rome, an Italian priest, John Donatus Mezzafalce, a missionary to China who was forced to stay some months in Galway because his ship was not ready to sail, commented on religious practice in Galway in glowing terms:

> They make profession of their faith in the presence even of the officials and heretical ministers, and they call themselves Roman Catholics, and indeed more frequently they use the mere title of Romans, thus the more directly to rebut the insolence of these heretics who, in their impiety, designate themselves as Apostolic Catholics.
>
> This profession of faith is not a matter of mere words, but is most unmistakably proved by the deeds, and particularly by the observance of the precepts of the Church. The aforesaid missionary [himself] has, on several occasions, seen persons of every rank, rich and poor, come on board the ship and observe abstinence when at meals with the heretics, though they were exposed to derision in consequence of doing so....
>
> In order to hear Mass, the celebration of Mass not being tolerated within the walls, they go forth, men

---

[366] Concannon, *The Blessed Eucharist in Irish History*, 391–392.

and women, outside the city walls, and they do this to assist, not only at Mass but also at Vespers, which, in the absence of the clergy, is sung by seculars.

Even within the city many families have secret chapels in which Mass is celebrated, especially on Christmas night, when the city gates being closed, they cannot go forth, and thus they run the risk of forfeiting all their goods and property should they be discovered. Nor are they at all afraid of the most bitter laws enacted in the Dublin parliament against the Catholics.... If such constancy, Most Holy Father, were found in a few individuals, amid so many hardships, it would be deserving of great praise, but when as a rule, it holds good in almost all of every class and of each sex, and of the young as well as the old, it is difficult to retain one's tears for compassion, and we are forced to recognize how justly Ireland has received the designation of *Insula Sanctorum*.[367]

One of the laws passed against Catholics was that on the death of a priest, no other was to be appointed to replace him. It was thought that, deprived of a pastor, the Mass, Communion, and the other sacraments, Catholics would become indifferent and faith an easy prey to heresy. As this was not happening, however, the fury of intolerance grew great, but no suffering, however bitter, could drive them to apostasy, coldness, or indifference.

Consequently in 1709 an act was passed compelling all priests to take an Oath of Abjuration under penalty of transportation. Even the miserable Mass-houses were now out of

---

[367] Cardinal Patrick Moran, *Spicilegium Ossorience*, II, 395–397; Fr. Augustine, *Ireland's Loyalty to the Mass*, 164–165.

bounds, and to attend Mass people had to have recourse to valleys, mountains, forests, and caves. There is scarcely a district in Ireland that does not have a place-name reflective of the people's devotion to the Mass. Because of the variety of places in which the Holy Sacrifice was offered during the years of religious persecution, the Mass has been indelibly written across the map of Ireland, carved forever into its place names: Ard an Aifrinn (the Mass Height); Cor an Aifrinn (the Rounded Hill of the Mass); Lug an Aifrinn (the Mass Hollow); Mullach an Aifrinn (the Mass Summit); Clais an Aifrinn (the Mass Trench)—place names such as these are to be found in every town in Ireland.[368]

However, the pace of persecution quickened. Informing against a priest was declared an honorable act deserving of the nation's gratitude—£50 for the discovery of a bishop, and £20 for any other ecclesiastic; these were substantial sums of money at the time. But neither bribes nor threats could separate the pastors from their flocks. With heroic courage the clergy braved every peril to say Mass for the people. Except during short intervals of comparative peace, they were obliged to travel from district to district in disguise, and they joyfully endured the privations, humiliations, and hardships to which they were exposed every day.

As late as 1743 a proclamation was issued by the Privy Council of Dublin offering £150 for the conviction of a bishop and for every priest a sum of £50; £200 was offered for those who had been concealing a priest. The priests passed from cabin to cabin dispensing blessings, instructing the young, and administering the sacraments. They lived with the peasantry and

[368] Cf. Fr. Augustine, *Ireland's Loyalty to the Mass*, 167–171.

partook of their humble fare. Professor Lecky does not fail to recognize the heroism of the clergy:

> Their conduct in many respects was very noble. The zeal with which they maintained the religious life of their flocks during the long period of persecution is beyond praise. In the very dawn of the Reformation in Ireland, Spencer has contrasted the negligence of the "idle ministers, the creatures of a corrupt patronage" with the zeal of Popish priests, who "spare not to come out of Spain, from Rome, and from Rheims, by long toil and dangerous travelling hither, where they know that peril of death awaiteth them, and no reward or riches is to be found, only to draw the people into the Church of Rome." The same fervid zeal was displayed by the Catholic priesthood, and during all the long period of the Penal Laws.[369]

To evade the new laws, priests resorted to methods of which Dr. Hugh McMahon, bishop of Clogher, gives us a graphic description in a letter to Propaganda: "Some, in order to prevent being identified by any in the congregation, celebrated Mass with veiled faces. Others again shut themselves up into a closet with the Mass server alone, and apertures were made or a small hole by means of which the people could hear the voice of the celebrant but could not recognize it."[370] In this way the people, if questioned by the army, could truthfully say that they did not know the identity of the priest. McMahon continues: "And the

---

[369] Moran, *The Catholics of Ireland under the Penal Laws of the Eighteenth Century*, 50; cf. W. Lecky, *A History of England in the Eighteenth Century*, vol. 2, 282.

[370] Moran, *Spicilegium Ossorience*, II, 473; Fr. Augustine, *Ireland's Loyalty to the Mass*, 173–174.

mercy of God was only manifested the more, for as the persecution increased, the fervor of the people increased also. Not uncommonly one would come across men and women with their hands joined in prayer—having got the signal that Mass was begun—and thus they united themselves in spirit with those who, afar off, were praying on bended knees although they could not see the priest."

In Offaly a tradition has come down telling how, some generations back, the local chapel was on one occasion surrounded and set fire to, during the celebration of holy Mass. Priest and people were trapped and burned and buried beneath the ruins. To test the truth of the tradition, during the winter of 1917 the parish priest had the place dug up, and the ghastly reality was established in the discovery of the bones and sculls of a few hundred people, with the chalice that was used at their last Mass.

Catholics at times defended their religious rights even physically. In May of 1756 the magistrates of Cork city ordered all the chapels and oratories to be closed. To ensure that the Mass would not be said there, they not only seized the keys but also published a proclamation prohibiting any meeting for divine worship. On learning this, the ire of the Catholics rose, and with righteous indignation they rushed into the streets, seized whatever weapons were at hand, and presented a bold front to the Protestants. These latter in turn mustered their forces and a pitched battle ensued. Nobody was killed, but several on both sides were wounded, and a parish priest was arrested. The Catholics, however, carried the day and won admission to their poor but beloved churches.[371]

[371] Cf. Fr. Augustine, *Ireland's Loyalty to the Mass*, 187–188, 190–191.

A History of Fidelity to the Mass

Here is the judgment of Professor William Lecky:

> They cling to their old faith with a constancy that has never been surpassed, during generations of the most galling persecution, at a time when every earthly motive urged them to abandon it, when all the attractions and influence of property and rank and professional eminence and education were arrayed against it. They voluntarily supported their priesthood with an unwearying zeal, when they themselves were sunk in the most abject poverty, when the agonies of starvation were continually before them. They had their reward. The legislator, abandoning the hopeless task of crushing a religion which was so cherished, contented himself with providing that those who held it should never rise to influence or to wealth, and the Penal Laws were at last applied almost exclusively to this end.[372]

In 1829, the year of Catholic emancipation, the Count de Montelambert published in Paris some letters (*Lettres sur le Catholicisme en Irlande*) which describe what he had seen and heard in country districts on a visit to Ireland:

> Often on a Sunday, when entering an Irish town, I have seen the streets encumbered with kneeling figures of laboring men in all directions, turning their looks always towards some low doorway, some obscure lane which led to the Catholic chapel, built behind the houses in those times of persecution, when the exercise of that worship

[372] Moran, *The Catholics of Ireland under the Penal Laws of the Eighteenth Century*, 18; cf. W. Lecky, *A History of England in the Eighteenth Century*, vol. 2, 256, 289.

was treason. The immense crowd which endeavored an entrance into the narrow and hidden interior prevented the approach of two-thirds of the faithful, but they knew that Mass was being said, and they knelt in all the surrounding streets joining themselves in spirit to the priest of the Most High. Very often I have mixed with them, and enjoyed their looks of astonishment when they saw a stranger, not poor like themselves, taking the holy water with them and bowing before the altar.

Often, too, I looked down from the gallery reserved for the women, on the nave of the Catholic chapel as the priest preached to the people during Mass. This part of the church was given up to the men. There were no seats, and the population crowded into it in floods, each tide rising higher until the first comers were pushed forward against the altar-rails, and so packed that they could not move a limb. All that could be seen of them was a moving mass of dark-haired heads, so close together that one could have walked across them without danger.

From moment to moment this mass moved and wavered. Long groans and deep sighs became audible; some dried their eyes; some beat their breasts; every gesture of the preacher was understood on the instant, and the impression produced was not concealed. A cry of love or of grief answered each of his entreaties, each of his reproaches. The spectator saw that it was a father speaking to his children, and that the children loved their father.

In another portion of the same letter he describes what he witnessed in a country district about six miles from Cork:

A History of Fidelity to the Mass

I shall never forget the first Mass which I heard in a country chapel. I rode to the foot of a hill, the lower part of which was clothed with a thick plantation of oak and fir, and alighted from my horse to ascend it. I had taken only a few steps on my way when my attention was attracted by the appearance of a man who knelt at the foot of one of the firs. Several others became visible in succession in the same attitude; and the higher I ascended the larger became the numbers of those kneeling peasants. At length on reaching the top of the hill, I saw a cruciform building, badly built of stone, without cement, and covered by thatch. Around it knelt a crowd of robust and vigorous men, all uncovered, though the rain fell in torrents and the mud quivered beneath them. Profound silence reigned everywhere. It was the Catholic chapel of Blarney and the priest was saying Mass.

I reached the door at the moment of the Elevation, and all this pious assembly had prostrated themselves with their faces on the earth. I made an effort to penetrate under the roof of the chapel thus overflowed with worshippers. There were no seats, no decorations, not even a pavement; the floor was of earth, damp, and stony, the roof dilapidated, and tallow candles burned on the altar in place of tapers. I heard the priest announce ... that on such a day he would go, in order to save his parishioners the trouble of a long journey to a certain "cabin" which should for the moment be turned into the House of God—there to administer the sacraments and receive the humble offerings with which his flock supported him.

When the Holy Sacrifice was ended, the priest mounted his horse and rode away. Then each worshipper rose from his knees and went slowly homeward; some of them, wandering harvestmen carrying their reaping hooks, turned their steps to the nearest cottage to ask the hospitality to which they were considered to have a right; others, with their wives riding behind them en croupe, went off to their distant homes. Many remained for a much longer time in prayer, kneeling in the mud in that silent enclosure chosen by the poor and faithful people in the time of ancient persecutions.[373]

Five years after Catholic emancipation had been granted, things were still in a deplorable state in the west of Ireland. At a public meeting of Catholics in the diocese of Killala on January 8, 1834, a petition to the House of Commons was adopted, setting out some things that seemed incredible. The petition testified that since "the parishes in this diocese have long been deprived of Catholic churches, the consequence is that a numerous population, destitute of every other source of instruction, are obliged to absent themselves from religions worship, or to attend it under all the inclemency of the most rigorous seasons, that in this diocese alone upwards of 30,000 souls are obliged on every Sunday to hear Mass under the canopy of heaven."[374]

Thomas Babington Macaulay, the historian, writer, and politician, in the House of Commons described how the Established Church of Ireland had been given so much yet had

[373] Moran, *The Catholics of Ireland under the Penal Laws of the Eighteenth Century*, 86, 87.

[374] Fr. Augustine, *Ireland's Loyalty to the Mass*, 197–198; Moran, *The Catholics of Ireland under the Penal Laws of the Eighteenth Century*, 85.

achieved so little. In all this time, he said, while Catholics were starving and oppressed, the prelates of the Established Church "were gorged with wealth and sunk in indolence.... Their chief business was to bow and job at the Castle."[375] On the night of April 23, 1845, speaking in the House of Commons, Macaulay declared "the Established Church of Ireland is a bad institution," and "of all the institutions now existing in the civilized world the most absurd." Surveying the course of things from 1560 to 1845, he said:

> Two hundred and eighty-five years has this church been at work. What could have been done for it in the way of authority, privileges, endowments, which has not been done? Did any other set of bishops and priests in the world ever receive so much for doing so little? Nay, did any other set of bishops and priests in the world receive half so much for doing twice as much? And what have we to show for all this lavish expenditure? What but the most zealous Roman Catholic population on the face of the earth? Where you were one hundred years ago, where you were two hundred years ago, there you are still, not victorious over the domain of the old faith, but painfully and with dubious success defending your own English Pale.... On the great solid mass of the Roman Catholic population you have made no impression whatever. There they are, as they were ages ago, ten to one against the members of your established church.[376]

---

[375] Thomas Babington Macaulay, *Miscellaneous Writings and Speeches,* quoted in Fr. Augustine, *Ireland's Loyalty to the Mass,* 176.

[376] Fr. Augustine, *Ireland's Loyalty to the Mass,* 689, 693.

The Most Holy Eucharist

The English politician goes on to say that "the quality as well as the quantity of Irish Romanism" deserves to be considered:

> Is there any other country inhabited by a mixed population of Catholics and Protestants, any other country in which Protestant doctrines have long been freely promulgated from the press and from the pulpit, where the Roman Catholic spirit is so strong as in Ireland? I believe not. The Belgians are generally considered as very stubborn and zealous Roman Catholics. But I do not believe that in stubbornness or in zeal they equal the Irish. And this is the fruit of three centuries of Protestant archbishops, bishops, archdeacons, deans and rectors.[377]

As the ferocity of the persecution gradually eased off, priests and people surfaced from caves to wooden boxes, from wooden boxes to new chapels, and from new chapels to more decent buildings.

But around this time a sad event occurred that deeply impressed the Irish nation. It happened in the parish of Gweedore in County Donegal. It is a particularly wild and beautiful spot, where from the beginning of penal times, the faithful came to hear Mass, protected by the seclusion of this narrow glen. Ever since the beginning of the eighteenth century it was here that Catholics from the surrounding hills assembled for the Holy Sacrifice.

A mountain stream that flowed through the valley became a rushing torrent in midwinter. Lookouts for priest hunters were posted on the cliffs above, and a ledge down below served as an altar. When the Penal Laws were somewhat relaxed the

---

[377] Fr. Augustine, *Ireland's Loyalty to the Mass*, 694.

lookouts were dispensed with. The rock altar was replaced by a wooden altar covered by a hut and facing downstream. At last it was decided to build something permanent, but not one of the Protestant landlords in the neighborhood would give a site for the church. So they decided to build a temporary church in the valley, over the stream, where they had long worshipped. This continued as a parochial church until Easter 1854, when it was accidentally burned down. However, a roomy and well-built church was consecrated by Bishop McGettigan, who as a young boy often acted as a lookout during Mass for priest hunters.

On August 15, 1880, during holy Mass, a terrific thunderstorm broke. This was accompanied by torrential rain that caused the stream to rise rapidly and flood the church. Practically all survived—only five lives were lost. But as Cardinal Patrick Moran commented: this disaster "served to fix the attention of the civilized world on the fact that even in the last quarter of the nineteenth century, there were districts in Ireland where a site would not be granted for a Catholic church, and where it was only in the hills and the ravines that the faithful could kneel around the altar of God and worship in the faith of their fathers."[378]

It Is the Mass that Matters

One of the ways in which the British government recognized the failure of centuries of persecution to anglicize the Irish race was its decision to de-establish the Protestant Church in Ireland in 1869. On the other hand, in the second half of the nineteenth century a great program of church building was

[378] Canon Maguire, *History of the Diocese of Raphoe*, vol. 2 (Dublin: Browne and Nolan, 1920), 263, 264.

promoted by the Catholic Church all over Ireland. These were in the main of neo-Gothic design and were in general of high quality in relation to the meager resources of the faithful.

When Pope John Paul II visited Ireland in 1979, his homily in the Phoenix Park, in Dublin, focused on the Mass and the Eucharist. In his homily he recalled:

> How many and how varied the places where the Mass was offered — stately mediaeval and in splendid modern cathedrals, in early monastic and in modern churches; at Mass rocks in the glens and in forests by "hunted priests" and in poor thatch-covered chapels, for a people poor in worldly goods but rich in the things of the spirit; in "wake-houses" or "station houses" or at great hostings of the faithful on the top of Croagh Patrick and at Laugh Derg. Small matter where the Mass was offered. For the Irish, it was always the Mass that mattered. How many have found in it the spiritual strength to live, even through times of greatest hardship and poverty, through days of persecution and vexations.[379]

"It is the Mass that matters." We have to go back to the end of the nineteenth century to find the origin of this striking phrase. Augustine Birrell, the son of a nonconformist minister, who was Chief Secretary of Ireland (1907–1916), wrote in an English journal an article that showed a particular insight into the religious history of Ireland.

Our children, he wrote, if not ourselves, will make up their minds about what happened at the Reformation,

[379] *The Pope in Ireland: Addresses and Homilies* (Dublin: Veritas, 1979), 8–9.

and my suggestion is that they will do so in a majority of cases ... by concentrating their attention upon what will seem to them most important. And especially will they bend their minds upon the Mass.

It is doubtful whether any poor sinful child of Adam ever witnessed, even ignorantly ... the Communion Service according to the Roman Catholic ritual without emotion.

It is the Mass that matters, it is the Mass that makes the difference: so hard to define, so subtle it is, yet so perceptible between a Catholic country and a Protestant one, between Dublin and Edinburgh.[380]

Irish Catholics were ignorant because they were cruelly deprived of the benefits of education; they were poor because they were brutally robbed of the goods of this world. Though uneducated, their minds were enlightened by the light of God. They had hope that one day God would remove the dark cloud that hung like a pall of death over the land of Ireland. They had faith that although driven from their cathedrals and churches and mud hovels, God would be with them still in the mountains and the bogs and the caves until better days would dawn.

Conclusion

Ireland's sacred history tells us of a time when no altar or church was allowed. And even when the latter was permitted, no church could have the simplest steeple to beautify it, or the smallest bell to call the faithful to divine worship. It recalls a

[380] Augustine Birrell, in the journal *Nineteenth Century* (April 1896), quoted in Fr. Augustine, *Ireland's Loyalty to the Mass*, 210.

time when the priest was hunted like a wild beast, and when the same price was put on his head as that of a wolf. It speaks of an age when the Mass was proscribed as an idolatrous rite, and when to celebrate, or even assist at it, was punished by imprisonment or banishment, confiscation or death.

However, the Irish met all this with unshaken resolve, and all the many devices of devilish ingenuity could not eradicate from their hearts the love for the Mass and the desire to be present at it. The laments heard during the penal days are for our instruction and are designed to teach us a powerful lesson — that of patient endurance for conscience's sake. The day may come when we need this lesson — perhaps we may need it even now.

Even men and women of advanced age often set out at night and traveled long distances in frost and snow to be present at a dawn Mass the following morning. Irish Catholics would shelter a priest in spite of every penalty and never betrayed him for the most tempting reward. They clung tenaciously to their religion. They fought valiantly for the Mass.

In 1932 Dublin hosted the International Eucharistic Congress. Over one million people attended the pontifical High Mass in the Phoenix Park, in a spirit of gratitude to God for the wonder of the Mass and the Eucharist, but above all in a deep sense of gratitude for the fidelity of those generations of Irish men and women who fought so bravely over a period of nearly three hundred years to be loyal to this same Mass in the midst of brutal persecution and the deprivation of the most basic human rights.

It is not then to be wondered at that the most perfect objects that Irish artistry ever fashioned are two beautiful chalices — the Ardagh and the Derrynaflan chalices — both dating from the ninth century.

A History of Fidelity to the Mass

The Eucharistic Congress of 1932 was celebrated with great faith during the week-long ceremonies. The winter of humiliation was past; the rain of persecution was over and done with. This was why the joy of the Eucharistic Congress filled Irish hearts in a way that would be difficult for other nations to understand fully. In all humility they knew they were the descendants of recusants and saints.[381]

In the early centuries, the people organized "Masses and Adoration" when they met for the great assemblies such as the Aonach Tailtean. Medieval fairs usually coincided with some saint's day and began with Mass. The greatest victories in Irish History—the battle of the Yellow Ford, the battle of the Curlew Mountains, the battle of Benburb—were won by soldiers who had assisted at holy Mass and received the Blessed Eucharist before they went into battle.

At the opening of the Congress in the Pro-cathedral, Dublin, the papal legate read a letter from the Holy Father, Pope Pius XI, in which he said: "Exhort them to be faithful followers of their forefathers.... Arouse their spirits so that, never

[381] G. K. Chesterton attended the Eucharistic Congress and was a guest of the nation staying at the Vice-Regal Lodge. He was moved by many of the things he heard and saw during that week. He was particularly taken by the comment of a poor woman in a tram, discussing with her neighbor whether the rain would hold off for the Pontifical High Mass in the Phoenix Park. "Well," the other replied, "if it rains now He'll have brought it on Himself." This remark caused him to do an excursus of fifteen pages on the Incarnation! Conscious of Ireland's history, he said, "she was too poor and too oppressed to shelter the Divine Humanity under the roof of mighty cathedrals, or even to print his coloured shadow upon frescoes or palace walls" (G. K. Chesterton, *Christendom in Dublin* [London: Sheed and Ward, 1932], 59, 68).

forgetful of the 'Mass-Rocks,' they shall faithfully cherish devotion to the Holy Eucharist, as the standard of their faith, and as a defense against errors."[382]

The religious persecution of Irish Catholics endured for over 250 years. It is doubtful if ever any other persecution of Catholics was so long and so intense. Recalling these events is not a question of evoking bitter memories or of living off the spiritual capital of the past. Rather its purpose is to allow ourselves to be inspired by the love and fidelity which our forefathers had for the Eucharist so that we grow in appreciation of this great sacrament.

These men and women of past generations are linked with us in the great Communion of Saints and are interceding for us in the presence of God. We do well to ask their help to ensure that the great love for the Mass which they sowed with faithful lives, and at times with their blood, will not be diluted by modern secularism or a loss of faith. It is surely in the shadow of the sanctuary lamp, burning before the tabernacle, that the spirits of our forefathers are most likely to speak to us about the significance of the Holy Sacrifice of the Mass, about regular Holy Communion, and about love for the Real Presence of Christ in the Eucharist.

[382] Fr. Augustine, *Ireland's Loyalty to the Mass*, 222.

Epilogue

In a World Youth Day homily in 2000, John Paul II spoke to a crowd of two million young people about the Eucharist:

> To celebrate the Eucharist, "to eat his flesh and drink his blood," means to accept the wisdom of the Cross and the path of service. It means that we signal our willingness to sacrifice ourselves for others, as Christ has done.
>
> I entrust to you, dear friends, this greatest of God's gifts to us who are pilgrims on the paths of time, but who bear in our hearts a thirst for eternity. May every community always have a priest to celebrate the Eucharist! I ask the Lord therefore to raise up from among you many holy vocations to the priesthood. Today as always, the Church needs those who celebrate the Eucharistic sacrifice with a pure heart. The world must not be deprived of the gentle and liberating presence of Christ living in the Eucharist.

If our devotion to the Eucharist is authentic, we also will feel the call to make our lives one of service to others.

The Most Holy Eucharist

God Lives in Our Midst

In many passages of the Old Testament it is announced that God "will dwell in the midst of the people" (cf. Jer. 7:3; Ezek. 43:9; Sir. 24:8). These signs of God's presence, first in the pilgrim Tent of the Ark in the desert and then in the Temple of Jerusalem, are followed by the most amazing form of God's presence among us — Jesus Christ, perfect God and perfect man, in whom the ancient promise is fulfilled in a way that far exceeded man's greatest expectations. Also the promise made through Isaiah about the "Emmanuel" or "God-with-us" (Isa. 7:14; cf. Matt. 1:23) is completely fulfilled through the dwelling of the Incarnate Son of God among us.[383]

Jesus is present in the tabernacle, and he invites us to bring to him there our concerns and petitions. It is there we can have recourse to find new strength, to tell Jesus that we love him, to tell him that we need him very much. At the tabernacle we learn how to love and draw the strength necessary to be faithful. Jesus waits for us and he rejoices when we come to greet him. He comforts us with the warmth of his understanding and love. We also find time for expressions of reparation and sorrow.

St. Thomas's antiphon for the Office of Corpus Christi, *O Sacra Convivium*, offers a summary of eucharistic doctrine, referring to the past, the present, and the future:

> *O sacred banquet*
> *In which Christ is received,*
> *The memory of the Passion recalled,*
> *The mind filled with grace,*
> *And a pledge of future glory given us, alleluia.*

[383] Cf. Francis Fernandez, *In Conversation with God*, vol. 4, 262.

Epilogue

The Eucharist, by recalling our Lord's death and renewal of the work of redemption, reminds us of the deep sense of gratitude we owe to God. The Eucharist fills our mind with grace in the present through receiving Jesus Christ in Communion every day. With the devotion of spiritual communions we can have a continuous eucharistic presence in our souls. The Eucharist is a promise of future glory, a promise given us by Christ himself (cf. John 6:54). This is the consummation of our eucharistic life on earth.

Eucharistic Congress in Rome

The opening of the Eucharistic Congress in Rome to mark the Jubilee Year 2000 took place with solemn vespers at which John Paul II presided. In his homily he focused on the words of St. Paul, about the Church being one body.

He continued:

> *Ave verum Corpus, natum de Maria Virgine*—Hail the true Body of Christ born of a virgin. Born when time had fully come, born of a woman, born under the law (cf. Gal 4:4). In the heart of the great Jubilee and at the beginning of this week dedicated to the Eucharistic Congress, we return to the historic event which marked the fulfillment of our salvation. Let us kneel as the shepherds did before the manger in Bethlehem; like the Magi who came from the East, let us adore Christ the Savior of the world.

Having traced the path of Christ's life to the Upper Room, John Paul II prays: "We adore you, true Body of Christ, present in the sacrament of the new and eternal covenant, living memorial of the redeeming sacrifice. You, Lord, are the living bread come down from heaven, who gives life to man! On the Cross you gave your flesh for the life of the world (cf. Jn 6:51)."

The Holy Father goes on to emphasize the unity which is created by the Eucharist, referring to the classic text in St. Paul (1 Cor. 10:16–17): "With heartfelt gratitude let us thank God, who made the Eucharist the sacrament of our full communion with him and with our brothers and sisters."

At the end of his homily, the Holy Father prayed to Christ to unify all the members of his Body and "transform them in your love, so that the Church may shine with that supernatural beauty which is resplendent in the saints of every era and nation, in the martyrs, in the confessors, in the virgins and in the countless witnesses of the gospel."[384]

We can make this prayer our own as we reach the end of our reflections on the Holy Eucharist as sacrament and sacrifice. Our love for the Eucharist should not be just a personal experience. If we really appreciate this great gift from God, as Catholics we will feel the need to share it with others, to encourage them to enter into this great mystery so that their hearts will be filled with a joy and a peace that nothing else on this earth can provide.

[384] Bl. John Paul II, Homily, June 18, 2000, for the opening of the Eucharistic Congress in Rome in the Jubilee Year.

Bibliography

DOCUMENTS OF THE MAGISTERIUM

Council of Trent

Decree on the Sacrament of the Eucharist, session 13.

Decree on the Sacrifice of the Mass, session 22.

Vatican II

Apostolicam actuositatem (Decree on the Apostolate of the Laity). November 18, 1965.

Gaudium et spes (Pastoral Constitution on the Church in the Modern World). December 7, 1965.

Lumen gentium (Dogmatic Constitution on the Church). November 21, 1964.

Presbyterorum ordinis (Decree on the Ministry and Life of Priests). December 7, 1965.

Sacrosanctum concilium (Constitution on the Liturgy). December 4, 1963.

Papal Documents

Benedict XVI, *Deus Caritas Est* (Encyclical Letter). December 25, 2005.

———. *Sacramentum caritatis* (Apostolic Exhortation). February 22, 2007. Pius X. *Sancta Tridentina synodus*. December 20, 1905.

John Paul II. Bull of Indiction of the Great Jubilee of the Year 2000. November 29, 1998.

———. *Christifideles laici* (Apostolic Exhortation). December 30, 1988.

———. *Dies Domini* (Apostolic Letter). May 31, 1998.

———. *Dominicae Cenae* (Letter). February 24, 1980.

———. *Ecclesia de Eucharistia* (Encyclical Letter). April 17, 2003.

———. *Ecclesia in Europa* (Apostolic Exhortation). June 28, 2003.

———. *Familiaris consortio* (Apostolic Exhortation). November 22, 1981.

———. Holy Thursday Letter to Priests, 1988.

———. Holy Thursday Letter to Priests, 1999.

———. Letter to Bishop of Liège on the 750th anniversary of the first celebration of the feast of Corpus Christi. May 28, 1996.

Bibliography

———. *Letter to Families*. February 2, 1994.

———. *Mane nobiscum Domine* (Apostolic Letter). October 7, 2004.

———. *Novo millennio ineunte* (Apostolic Letter). January 6, 2001.

———. *Ordinatio sacerdotalis* (Apostolic Letter). May 22, 1994.

———. *Redemptor hominis* (Encyclical Letter). March 4, 1979.

———. *Rosarium Virginis Mariae* (Apostolic Letter). October 16, 2002.

———. *Vicesimus quintus annus* (Apostolic Letter). December 4, 1988.

Paul VI. *The Creed of the People of God*. June 30, 1968.

———. *Mysterium fidei* (Encyclical Letter). September 3, 1965.

Pius XII. *Mediator Dei* (Encyclical Letter). November 20, 1947.

Other Documents of the Magisterium

Catechism of St. Pius V.

Catechism of the Catholic Church.

Catholic Bishops' Conferences of England and Wales. Ireland and Scotland, *One Bread, One Body*. Dublin, 1998.

Code of Canon Law, 1983.

Congregation for the Doctrine of the Faith. *Sacerdotium ministerial* (Letter). August 6, 1983.

General Instruction of the Roman Missal. Rev. ed. July 28, 2000.

Pontifical Committee for International Eucharistic Congresses. *The Eucharist and Freedom.* November 16, 1996.

Roman Missal.

Sacred Congregation for Divine Worship and the Discipline of the Sacraments. *Instruction Eucharisticum Mysterium.* May 25, 1967.

———. Instruction *Inaestimabile Donum* on Certain Norms Concerning Worship of the Eucharistic Mystery. April 17, 1980.

———. Instruction *Redemptoris Sacramentum.* March 25, 2004.

Other Works

Augustine, Fr., O.F.M. Cap., *Ireland's Loyalty to the Mass.* Dublin: Sands and Co., 1933.

Augustine. *Confessions.*

Aquinas, Thomas. *Summa Theologica.*

———. *Commentary on St. John's Gospel.*

———. Roman Missal, *Prayers before Mass.*

———. *Commentary on Book IV of the Sentences.*

Belmonte, Charles. *Understanding the Mass.* Manila: Sinag-Tala, 1989.

Bernadot, P. *Our Lady in My Life.* London: Sands, 1926.

Brady, John, and Patrick Corish. *The Church under the Penal Code: A History of Irish Catholicism.* Dublin: Gill and Macmillan, 1971.

Bibliography

Caldecott, Stratford, ed. *Beyond the Prosaic: Renewing the Liturgical Movement*. Edinburgh: T & T Clark, 1988.

Chesterton, G. K. *Christendom in Dublin*. London: Sheed and Ward, 1932.

Chevrot, Georges. *Our Mass*. London: Burns and Oates, 1958.

Chrysostom, John. *On Priesthood: A Treatise*. Westminster, Maryland: Newman Press, 1943.

John Paul II. *Gift and Mystery: On the Fiftieth Anniversary of My Priestly Ordination*. London: Image Books, 1996.

———. *The Pope in Ireland: Addresses and Homilies*. Dublin: Veritas, 1979.

Ratzinger, Joseph (Pope Benedict XVI). *God and the World: A Conversation with Peter Seewald*. San Francisco: Ignatius Press, 2000.

———. *God Is Near Us: The Eucharist the Heart of Life*. San Francisco: Ignatius Press, 2003.

———. *In the Beginning: A Catholic Understanding of the Creation and the Fall*. Grand Rapids: Wm. B. Eerdmans Publishing Company, 1995.

———. *Jesus of Nazareth, Part Two*. San Francisco: Ignatius Press, 2011.

———. *Milestones: Memoirs 1927–1977*. San Francisco: Ignatius Press, 1998.

———. *A New Song for the Lord*, New York: The Crossroad Publishing Company, 1997.

———. *The Spirit of the Liturgy*. San Francisco: Ignatius Press, 2000.

Elliott, Peter J. *Ceremonies of the Modern Roman Rite*. San Francisco: Ignatius Press, 1994.

Escrivá, Josemaría. *Christ Is Passing By*. Dublin: Scepter, 1985.

———. *In Love with the Church*. London: Scepter, 1989.

———. *Conversations with Msgr. Josemaría Escrivá de Balaguer*. Manila: Sinag-Tala, 1987.

———. *The Way*. Dublin: Scepter, 1968.

———. *The Forge*. London: Scepter, 1988.

Fernandez, Francis. *In Conversation with God*. Vols. 1–6. London: Scepter, 1988–1991.

Gorevan, Patrick. "*O Sacrum Convivium*—St. Thomas on the Eucharist," in *New Blackfriars* 90 (2009): 659–664.

Guardini, Romano. *The Spirit of the Liturgy*. London: Sheed and Ward, 1937.

Knox, Ronald. *Heaven and Charing Cross*. London: Burns and Oates, 1935.

———. *Pastoral Sermons*. London: Burns and Oates, 1960.

———. *The Window in the Wall*. New York: Sheed and Ward, 1956.

Lecky, W. *A History of England in the Eighteenth Century*. Vol. 2. London: Longmans, Green, 1878.

Bibliography

Liguori, Alphonsus. *The Practice of the Love of Christ.*

———. *Reflections on the Passion.*

McGovern, Thomas J. *Generations of Priests.* Dublin: Open Air, 2010.

———. *Priestly Identity: A Study in the Theology of Priesthood.* Dublin: Wipf and Stock Publishers, 2002.

Maguire, Canon. *History of the Diocese of Raphoe.* Dublin: Browne and Nolan, 1920.

Moran, Cardinal Patrick. *The Catholics of Ireland under the Penal Laws of the Eighteenth Century.* London: Catholic Truth Society, 1899.

———. *History of the Catholic Archbishops of Dublin since the Reformation.* Dublin: James Duffy, 1864.

———. *Spicilegium Ossorience*, II. Dublin: Brown and Nolan, 1884.

Moody, T. W. and F. X. Martin, eds. *The Course of Irish History.* Cork: Mercier Press, 1984.

Murphy, Joseph. *Christ Our Joy: The Theological Vision of Pope Benedict XVI.* San Francisco: Ignatius Press, 2006.

The Navarre Bible: St. Mark's Gospel. Dublin: Four Courts Press, 1986.

The Navarre Bible: St. John's Gospel. Dublin: Four Courts Press, 1987.

The Navarre Bible: St. Luke's Gospel. Dublin: Four Courts Press, 1987.

The Navarre Bible: St. Matthew's Gospel. Dublin: Four Courts Press, 1991.

The Navarre Bible: Romans and Galatians. Dublin: Four Courts Press, 1990.

The Navarre Bible: Hebrews. Dublin: Four Courts Press, 1991.

The Navarre Bible: Corinthians. Dublin: Four Courts Press, 1991.

Nichols, Aidan, O.P., *The Holy Eucharist.* Dublin: Veritas, 1991.

————. *Looking at the Liturgy.* San Francisco: Ignatius Press, 1996.

————. *The Service of Glory.* Edinburgh: T. and T. Clark Publishers, Ltd., 1997.

O'Connor, James T. *The Hidden Manna.* San Francisco: Ignatius Press, 1988.

O'Rourke, John. *The Battle of the Faith in Ireland.* Dublin: J. Duffy, 1887.

Pickstock, Catherine. *After Writing: On the Liturgical Consummation of Philosophy.* Malden, Massachusetts: Blackwell, 1998.

Pieper, Josef. *In Search of the Sacred.* San Francisco: Ignatius Press, 1991.

Portillo, Alvaro del. *On Priesthood.* Chicago: Scepter, 1974.

Quasten, Johannes. *Patrology.* Vols. 1–4. Westminster, Maryland: Christian Classics, 1986.

Bibliography

Ronan, Myles V. *Reformation in Ireland under Elizabeth*. London: Longmans, 1930.

Rutler, George. *The Curé d'Ars Today*. San Francisco: Ignatius Press, 1988.

Schroeder, J. *The Canons and Decrees of the Council of Trent*. Rockford, Illinois: TAN Books, 1978.

Sales, Francis de. *Introduction to the Devout Life*.

Scheeben, Matthias Josef. *The Mysteries of Christianity*. St. Louis: B. Herder Book Co. 1946.

Smith, G. D. ed. *The Teaching of the Catholic Church*. London: Burns and Oates, 1960.

Sokolowski, Robert. *Eucharistic Presence: A Study in the Theology of Disclosure*. Washington DC: Catholic University of America Press, 1994.

Suarez, Federico. *The Sacrifice of the Altar*. London: Scepter, 1990.

Theological-Historical Commission for the Great Jubilee Year 2000. *The Eucharist: Gift of Divine Life*.

Tolkien, J.R.R. *Letters*. Edited by H. Carpenter. London: G. Allen and Unwin, 1981.

Teresa of Avila. *The Way of Perfection*.

Vianney, John. *The Eucharistic Meditations of the Curé of Ars*. Dublin: Carmelite Publications, 1961.

Vonier, Anscar, O.S.B. *A Key to the Doctrine of the Eucharist*. London: Burns and Oates, 1952.

About the Author

Rev. Thomas J. McGovern is a priest of the Opus Dei prela-
ture who works in Dublin. He was ordained to the priesthood
by His Holiness Pope John Paul II in Rome in June 1982. He
holds a doctorate in theology from the University of Navarre,
Pamplona, Spain.

He is the author of three books on the priesthood: *Priestly
Celibacy Today* (1998); *Priestly Identity: A Study in the Theology
of Priesthood* (2002); and *Generations of Priests* (2010).

He has also published a number of articles in various jour-
nals: *Irish Theological Quarterly*; *Homiletic and Pastoral Review*;
Josephinum Journal of Theology; *Scripta Theologica*; *The National
Catholic Bioethics Quarterly*; and *Annales Theologici*.

An Invitation

Reader, the book that you hold in your hands was published by Sophia Institute Press.

Sophia Institute seeks to restore man's knowledge of eternal truth, including man's knowledge of his own nature, his relation to other persons, and his relation to God.

Our press fulfills this mission by offering translations, reprints, and new publications. We offer scholarly as well as popular publications; there are works of fiction along with books that draw from all the arts and sciences of our civilization. These books afford readers a rich source of the enduring wisdom of mankind.

Sophia Institute Press also serves as the publisher for the Thomas More College of Liberal Arts and Holy Spirit College. Both colleges are dedicated to providing university-level education in the Western tradition under the guiding light of Catholic teaching.

If you know a young person who might be interested in the ideas found in this book, share it. If you know a young person seeking a college that takes seriously the adventure of learning and the quest for truth, bring our institutions to his attention.

www.SophiaInstitute.com
www.ThomasMoreCollege.edu
www.HolySpiritCollege.org

SOPHIA INSTITUTE PRESS

THE PUBLISHING DIVISION OF